CZESLAW

Milosz's ABC's

TRANSLATED

FROM

THE

POLISH

BY

MADELINE G. LEVINE

FARRAR, STRAUS AND GIROUX / NEW YORK

Farrar, Straus and Giroux
19 Union Square West, New York 10003

This edition composed of portions from Abecadło Miłosza, *published in 1997 by*
Wydawnictwo Literackie, Poland, and Inne Abecadło, *published in 1998*
by Wydawnictwo Literackie, Poland

Grateful acknowledgment is made to Henry Holt and Company, LLC, for the use of
"The Most of It" from The Poetry of Robert Frost, *edited by Edward Connery*
Lathem, © 1969 by Henry Holt and Co., copyright 1942 by Robert Frost, © 1970 by
Lesley Frost Ballantine. Reprinted by permission of Henry Holt and Company,
LLC.

Library of Congress Cataloging-in-Publication Data
Milosz, Czeslaw.
    [Abecadło Miłosza. English. Selections]
    Milosz's ABC's / Czeslaw Milosz ; translated by Madeline G. Levine.—
1st ed.
        p. cm.
    Translation of selections from the author's Abecadło Miłosza and
Inne abecadło.
    Includes bibliographical references and index.
    ISBN 0-374-52795-4 (pbk.)
    Milosz, Czeslaw—Translations into English. I. Levine, Madeline G.
II. Milosz, Czeslaw. Inne abecadło. English. Selections. III. Title.
PG7158.M553   A66213   2001
891.8'587307—dc21   00-042176

Designed by Abby Kagan

www.fsgbooks.com

1 3 5 7 9 10 8 6 4 2

MILOSZ'S ABC'S

•

CZESLAW MILOSZ

Czeslaw Milosz is the winner of the 1978 Neustadt International Prize in Literature and the 1980 Nobel Prize in Literature. He is the author, most recently, of *Road-side Dog* (FSG, 1998). He lives in Berkeley, California, and Cracow, Poland.

OTHER WORKS IN ENGLISH BY CZESLAW MILOSZ

·

Beginning with My Streets

Bells in Winter

A Book of Luminous Things:
An International Anthology of Poetry

The Captive Mind

Collected Poems

Conversations with Czeslaw Milosz
(by Ewa Czarnecka and Aleksander Fiut)

Emperor of the Earth

Facing the River

The History of Polish Literature

The Issa Valley

The Land of Ulro

Native Realm

Nobel Lecture

Postwar Polish Poetry: An Anthology

Provinces

Road-side Dog

The Seizure of Power

The Separate Notebooks

Striving Towards Being:
The Letters of Thomas Merton and Czeslaw Milosz

Talking to My Body: Poems by Anna Swir
(translated by Czeslaw Milosz and Leonard Nathan)

Unattainable Earth

Visions from San Francisco Bay

With the Skin: The Poems of Aleksander Wat
(introduction by Czeslaw Milosz)

The Witness of Poetry

A Year of the Hunter

MILOSZ'S ABC'S

MILOSZ'S ABC'S

[A]

ABRAMOWICZ, Ludwik. Wilno always was a city verging on a fairy tale, although when I lived there I never noticed that aspect of it. Of course, there were those secret societies in the past (we knew about the Scoundrels' Society, the Masonic lodges, the Philomaths), but during my student years I didn't think of the then present time as equally picturesque, and it was only later that I reconstructed it, after learning various details.

Prior to World War I and well into the thirties, Ludwik Abramowicz published *The Wilno Review* at his own expense. This was a slender journal, far more significant than its modest appearance and circulation would indicate. He voiced the opinions of a select group of knowledgeable people, something like the élite circles of the Enlightenment. He was a Mason by conviction, which meant that he was faithful to those customs of our city which, in the twentieth century, too, favored the formation of exclusive groups in the name of noble slogans.

In 1822, when the Masonic lodges in the Grand Duchy of Lithuania were ordered to disband, Wilno had ten such lodges, not counting the secret youth societies. Still, certain families preserved the Masonic traditions—the Romers, Puttkamers, Wereszczaks, Chreptowiczes. It was only in 1900, however, that the Societas Szubraviensis (the Scoundrels' Society) was resurrected and held its weekly meetings in the House Under the Sign of the Dogcatcher, in a building, that is, with a view of the statue of Muravyov the Hangman. This was not a lodge; at most, it was a discussion group, organized by Attorney Tadeusz Wróblewski, who was a legendary figure in Wilno and the founder of the Wróblewski Library.

I have no firsthand knowledge of these resurgent lodges, but I have heard and read about them. Circa 1905, the Lithuania and Tomasz Zan lodges were formed (Wróblewski was active in the former), and it seems the Zealous Lithuanian lodge, too, was reborn. The lodges (many university professors belonged to them) were active in the interwar period, as I learned from my former professor, Stanisław Swianiewicz, who, even though he was a fervent Catholic, was on very friendly terms with the Masons. Without that particular milieu, in which social ties were almost indistinguishable from organizational ties, Wilno's soul would have been much poorer.

Ludwik Abramowicz was the spokesman for an ideology in which democratic thinking, multinationalism, and "localism" were united. Before World War I, not only Poles but also Lithuanians, and Belorussians, too, belonged to the Lithuania lodge. After the war, it split along ethnic lines; at the same time, the adherents of "localism" opposed the National Democrats (Endecja) and condemned discrimination against other languages. The best-known "localist" Masons (these concepts virtually overlapped) were Michał Romer, Attorney Bronisław Krzyżanowski, and Jan Piłsudski (the Marshal's brother), but the localist orientation also had adherents in other semisecret groupings such as the Senior Vagabonds' Club. *The Wilno Review* was a publication of Polish-speaking Wilno, but it took a stand against the incorporation of Wilno into Poland and in favor of restoring the multiethnic Grand Duchy, with Wilno as its capital, and criticized Józef Piłsudski for renouncing the federal idea.

This was a completely utopian program, rejected alike by the majority of Poles and by Lithuanians and Belorussians. Abramowicz's close collaborator, Michał Romer, who had joined the Polish Legions in Krakow in 1914, cut the Gordian knot in his own way, breaking with Piłsudski on the issue of Wilno. He moved to Kaunas, where he taught law at the university, and was twice elected rector of Kaunas University. He left a multivolume diary, written in Polish.

I used to read *The Wilno Review*, and I think it had an influence on me. I cannot stop myself from imagining Abramowicz as the high priest Sarastro in Mozart's *Magic Flute*—a noble and somewhat naive reformer who believes in mankind's reasonableness.

ABRASZA. I first met Abrasza in Paris, when I was living in the Latin Quarter after breaking with the Warsaw government, so it would have been 1952. He was a Polish Jew; his surname was Zemsz. He was studying at the Sorbonne; to be more precise, he was an eternal student, or rather, he was one of those people who cling to a student's existence as an alibi, to avoid bearing the burden of a career, a salary, etc. He told me a few things about his past. He had served with the Polish armed forces in England where, according to him, he was tormented by anti-Semites. Then he fought against the English in Palestine. In Paris, he was very poor; he lived in a garret somewhere, and Jeanne Hersch and I made several attempts at helping him, but here my memory has gaps. I met him again in 1970, I think, after the student revolt of 1968. He had played a very active role in that uprising. Asked why, he responded: "For no reason; for the sake of a row."

The year 1968 was different in Berkeley than in Paris, with different causes and a different course. True, the Berkeley students tried to burn books, but they didn't destroy trees like the French students, who cut down the plane trees on Boulevard Saint-Michel in order to build barricades. Seeing the demagogues who were the leaders in Berkeley, I felt not the slightest temptation to join them; at the same time, I can understand Kot Jeleński, who approved of the Paris revolt, a more radically liberating universal revolution, and universal copulation. Unfortunately, one's assessment of those events depended on one's age, it seems. I was fifty-seven at the time, and I suspected that, at best, I envied the students.

Abrasza committed suicide, but I know neither the date nor the circumstances.

ACADEMY of Arts and Letters, American. It is modeled on the Académie Française, which also functioned as a codifier, heatedly condemning words considered too regional or specific to a profession (agriculture, fishing, hunting), standing guard, as it were, in defense of a unified "classical" French language. When Poland achieved independence in 1918 there were endless debates about a Polish Academy of Letters until finally it was called into existence, but not without some wild clashes. It established a Youth Prize, and when Stanisław Piętak was awarded it in 1938, Bolesław Miciński, who was in France at the time, wrote to his mother in the mock Russian he used when he wanted to be funny, "It vood hev bin bedder hed Miłosz gut prize."

I myself would become an academician. America has two academies. The first, in Cambridge, is the Academy of Arts and Sciences, which mixes scientists from various fields with scholars of literature, music, and the fine arts. I was elected to it—as a professor, it seems. The other, in New York, led a dual existence for a long time as the Institute of Arts and Letters and as the Academy of Arts and Letters. I was elected a member of the Institute in 1982, and several years later we voted to merge into a single Academy. All the most famous creative people in the fields of literature, music, architecture, sculpture, and painting in America belong. Generous prizes from bequests by private individuals are distributed annually. The Academy has its own beautiful building in which parties and dinners are held so the élite can celebrate each other's honors. Living on the West Coast, I was able to participate in these celebrations only once or twice. Over many drinks in the garden, in the bright light of a May afternoon, I conversed with Dwight Macdonald for the last time; he died soon afterward. The old goat was fascinated by my companion, who really did have on a beautiful dress, and who looked beautiful, too.

The Academy is not made up solely of distinguished old men, and there are definitely names on its membership list which will last. Nonetheless, election to it is determined by fame as measured by the rumors and gossip of the New York establishment, which means that enduring value and momentary fame reside in the same house. One can see that in the roster of foreign honorary members of the Academy. The seven stars of our Eastern constellation were Bella Akhmadulina, Václav

Havel, Zbigniew Herbert, Milan Kundera, Alexander Solzhenitsyn, Andrei Voznesensky, and Evgeny Evtushenko. When the last was elected, Joseph Brodsky resigned from the Academy in protest.

ADAM AND EVE. The greatest virtue of the biblical tale about our first parents is that it is incomprehensible; perhaps that is why it speaks to us more powerfully than any rational explanation. This is why Lev Shestov says it is hard to imagine illiterate shepherds, on their own, dreaming up that mysterious myth which philosophers have been wracking their brains over for several thousand years.

Paradise, where there is neither sickness nor death, and a man and a woman experience complete happiness. In the eating of the forbidden fruit from the tree of the knowledge of good and evil, the popular imagination eagerly discerned sexual gratification, but John Milton follows a different tradition in *Paradise Lost* and very persuasively describes Adam and Eve's love as part of their paradisiacal condition:

> *So spake our general Mother, and with eyes*
> *Of conjugal attraction unreprov'd,*
> *And meek surrender, half imbracing lean'd*
> *On our first Father; half her swelling Breast*
> *Naked met his under the flowing Gold*
> *Of her loose tresses hid....*

What, then, does the tree of the knowledge of good and evil signify? There are multiple interpretations. Some Jewish biblical scholars find a hidden meaning in the Hebrew letters. Observers of our civilization and the blind alleys into which human reason has rushed see the temptation of rationalism in the voice of the Serpent. Others assert the opposite: that the eating of the forbidden fruit initiates the history of humankind, because before it was consumed Adam and Eve lived an unconscious life, an animal existence, so that the Serpent-Satan was correct when he said that their eyes would be opened. The Creator was also right, for he had warned them that if they tasted that fruit, they would die. Most often, however, commentators have emphasized the perfect, friendly confidence they manifested in God before they broke the prohibition. Catastrophe ensued when they dragged him down to the level of created beings and accused him of jealousy. Original sin, in this view, was in essence an act of hubris.

Why is it that after breaking the prohibition they realized that they were naked, and why were they ashamed? Their shame at their nakedness is apparently important, but why this is so is not at all clear. One could ponder this endlessly. They entered upon the road of history, of civilization; but is nakedness its negation? Is that why God had to sew them clothing out of animal skins? And why did that single moment provoke such terrible results—not only their own death, but an entire transformation of nature, because nature, too, was immortal in Paradise? And not only that; there is also original sin, which weighs upon every man and every woman for generations without end. Fortunately, Catholic theology counts original sin as one of the mysteries of faith and does not attempt to explain why it is that we inherit it.

In our deepest convictions, reaching into the very depths of our being, we deserve to live forever. We experience our transitoriness and mortality as an act of violence perpetrated against us. Only Paradise is authentic; the world is inauthentic, and only temporary. That is why the story of the Fall speaks to us so emotionally, as if summoning an old truth from our slumbering memory.

ADAMIC, Louis. I am certain that none of my Polish contemporaries has taken an interest in this man; they have probably not even heard of him. My twentieth century, however, is not just Polish, it is also American, and since that is the case, Adamic must not be ignored. He was one of the best-known American writers of the Roosevelt era. He was from Slovenia and came to America at age thirteen; his English language and his enthusiasm for democracy he owed to his schooling. At a young age, he emerged as a writer of prose on the boundary between reportage and fiction. It was mostly reportage, because he greedily observed and took notes. In the American melting pot he noticed something that other writers, unfamiliar with the languages of Europe, had failed to see: the contribution of the masses of immigrants from the Slavic countries, the Slovenians, Slovaks, Poles, Czechs, Croats, Serbs, Ukrainians. The fates of these immigrants, very difficult in the main, supply the themes for Adamic's books; as author, he is able to be both defender and introducer of his heroes. This is proletarian America, of course, openly and secretly discriminated against (the laws passed in the 1920s limiting the number of visas for inferior countries, that is, for the countries of Eastern and Southern Europe, is proof of that). Many decades later, prose and verse about the milieus of various ethnic groups—Blacks, Jews, Chinese, Japanese—would enter American literature. Adamic was the first in this arena, but he has had almost no successors. Considering the high percentage of Slavic newcomers, their scant participation in higher culture is shocking. The main reason for this, most likely, was the generally low social position of the families; also, the children were sent out early to earn money, and if they were sent to college, they avoided the humanities. Furthermore, these white Negroes benefited from the color of their skin and frequently changed their names to make them sound Anglo-Saxon, so that it is difficult to determine their origins.

Adamic remains an important voice of the progressive and liberal New Deal. An invitation to attend a White House conference with Roosevelt and Churchill toward the end of the war bears witness to his fame. His sudden death in 1948 was widely discussed in the press: Was it suicide or political murder? He never lost interest in his native land and proclaimed his support for Tito's Yugoslavia, which earned him a great many enemies among the Yugoslav immigrants, divided into ethnic groups who hated each other.

Today, Adamic is so thoroughly forgotten that this must mean something, or in any case be proof that a new America came into being at the end of the war. When I came to America for the first time, right after the war, I encountered Adamic's books immediately and learned a great deal from them; they also shaped my American experience with empathy and pangs of conscience.

I was not fated to experience any discrimination in America; on the contrary, I was instantly a member of the white élite. First, with my diplomat's documents, and the second time round as a full-fledged citizen of an American campus. This accorded with my fate as a man born to class privilege, but always conscious of my advantages. Perhaps the Polish scholarship students in Paris in the thirties did not think about the crowds of unemployed Polish workers, but I did. It was the same later on, when I was well aware that I needed to temper my assessment of

America, for I was never one of those immigrants who had nothing to sell but the strength of his muscles.

When the workers in Detroit learned that a Pole had won the Nobel Prize, they said something that summarizes their bitter knowledge: "That means he is twice as good as they are," because they knew from their own experience with factory foremen that only a double investment of skill and labor could compensate for the defect of their origins.

Postwar America, with its mass youth movements against racism and war, was, in a sense, less populist and proletarian than Adamic's America. Students from wealthy, educated families had little sympathy for working stiffs and their old-world values. "Political correctness," the residue of those movements, did not embrace so-called ethnics, or rather, it did not condemn disdain for specific ethnic groups.

Ethnics—that is to say, those people whom Adamic wrote about, and also Greeks, Italians, Portuguese—are not sufficiently organized to be a pressure group. The Ethnic Millions Political Action Committee (EMPAC), as envisioned by its founder, Michael Novak, was supposed to substitute coordinated action for the activities of individual ethnic groups. I think I joined that organization mainly because I remembered Adamic.

ADAMITES. Everyone should walk around naked—in my childhood, that was my vague erotic dream. But such dreams are almost universal and are the impulse for those sects of Adamites who appear, disappear, and reappear throughout the ages. Reading about the Hussites in the Czech lands, I learned that they had a great deal of trouble with Adamites who lured away followers from the fringes of their movement. The return to Paradise, to original nakedness and innocence, must really have been difficult in that northern climate. I am curious about how they coped. That was at the start of the fifteenth century, but there must have been something in the air because somewhat later Hieronymus Bosch, borrowing from local, if heretical, sources in Holland, painted his *Garden of Earthly Delights*, a highly sensual dream of a land of universal nakedness, although, to be sure, we do not know if he painted it in praise or as a warning.

Stanisław Jerzy Lec writes somewhere about how tormenting it is to be in the company of naked women who are clothed up to their necks. At dinners in wartime Warsaw, when the drinking had gone on past the curfew hour, I was astonished to discover among the female half of the company the need to remove everything—perhaps an ever-present need, but only liberated by alcohol.

ADMIRATION. I have admired many people. I have always considered myself a crooked tree, so straight trees earned my respect. Indeed, we should remember what happens to us before Christmas when we set out to buy a Christmas tree. Rows of lovely trees, and all of them look terrific from a distance, but close up, none of them really meets our desire for an ideal tree. One is too thin, another crooked, the third too short, and so on. It's the same with people; no doubt some of them seemed so imposing to me because I did not know them better, while I knew my own defects only too well.

Not only my own, but also those of my circle of poets and painters. The link between art and a genetic flaw, a disability, deviance, or illness is almost axiomatic. The biographies of writers and artists reveal this link, and looking around, I could find confirmation in the life histories of my friends and acquaintances. One may suspect this supposed connection derives from an error in perspective, however. If one were to subject the most ordinary mortals to just as serious an examination, it might turn out that "normality" is as rare among them as among individuals who are famous in the fields of literature and art. The lives of famous people are simply more often on display.

That is how I comforted myself, but my thinking did not interfere with my search for individuals who were superior to me because they were not deformed. In the final analysis, whether I was mistaken or not, I must record my capacity for admiration as a plus, not a minus.

AFTER ALL, I've done quite a lot of traveling. Partly of my own volition, but mainly as a result of circumstances which carried me about the world. Already as a high school student in Wilno I was trying to make order out of images of war and revolution in Russia; beyond that, everything was the future and a pledge that would never be redeemed. How many emotions I must have experienced, both good and bad, to have been, one after the other, in France, Italy, Switzerland, Belgium, Holland, Denmark, Sweden—I can't even count them, and then there's North and Central America. So I fulfilled, and then some, my adventurer father's dreams, although despite my romantic desires I never succeeded in assuming the role of a collector of places and countries, because life made too many demands on me. In any event, what at the beginning of the century might have seemed exotic was transformed with the passage of time into something universally familiar, in accord with an era of increasing motion.

My ancestors only rarely crossed the borders of their native

Kiejdany district to visit one of our cities, either Wilno or Riga, but my father, even before Krasnoyarsk, had brought back from a journey through the Baltic region something of Europe in 1910, and leafing through the album about Holland, I would study the Amsterdam canals. Just as I studied his photograph, from 1913, taken on the deck of Fridtjof Nansen's steamship at the mouth of the Yenisei River.

There weren't many photographs in my childhood, and my imaginings about foreign countries were fed by a drawing or a woodcut—for example, the illustrations to Jules Verne's and Mayne Reid's books. But cinema had already come into play.

Many cities, many countries, and no habits of the cosmopolite; on the contrary, the timidity of a provincial. Once I had settled down in a city, I didn't like to venture beyond my own district and had to have the same view in front of my eyes every day. What this expressed was my fear of being broken down into my constituent parts, fear of losing my center, my spiritual home. But I would define this somewhat differently. We construct our private mythologies throughout our lives and those from the earliest years last the longest. The farther afield I was carried (and California, I'd say, is quite far), the more I sought a link with my former self, the one from Szetejnie and Wilno. That is how I explain my bond with the Polish language. That option seems lovely, patriotic, but in truth I was locking myself inside my own fortress and raising the drawbridges: let those others rage outside. My need for recognition—and who doesn't need it?—was not strong enough to lure me out of there and incline me to write in English. I felt called to something else.

My return after more than half a century to my birthplace and to Wilno was like a closing of the circle. I could appreciate the good fortune that had brought me such a rare encounter with my past, although the power and complexity of that experience were beyond my linguistic abilities. Perhaps I simply fell mute from an excess of emotion, and that is why I went back to expressing myself indirectly; that is, instead of speaking about myself, I started assembling a registry, as it were, of biographical sketches and events.

ALCHEMY. During my lifetime I have had occasion to be a witness to the changing social position of this word. At first, everyone knew that alchemy was just prescientific chemistry, a field that properly belongs to a time when the boundary between magic and science was blurred. Later, researchers who studied intensively the century of alchemy, the seventeenth century, posed the question: "What exactly did the hope of finding the philosopher's stone and of extracting gold mean at that time?" These researchers discovered the spiritual dimension of alchemical operations and their connection with the Hermetic tradition. There followed an era of respect for symbols and archetypes to which Carl Jung and Mircea Eliade, as well as many others, contributed so much. The alchemist's workshop ceased to be merely a place where there were strange-looking retorts, alembics, and fire-sustaining bellows, because *transmutation* (a favorite word signifying the transformation of one element into another) of the highest order happened there. Ultimately, the concept of spiritual alchemy, well-known in the seventeenth-century circles of the Hermetics, was vindicated.

My life experience can be understood thus: Green, provincial, poorly educated, without deserving it, I gained the right to enter the alchemist's workshop and for many long years sat there in a corner, hunched over, observing and thinking. And when I went out from there into the wide world, it turned out that I had learned a great deal.

ALCHIMOWICZ, Czesław. We were in the same class in the King Sigismund August First State Gymnasium for Boys in Wilno, for all eight years, if I'm not mistaken. At some point I came to hate him. Those hatreds of mine (for the twin brothers, the Kampfs, for instance) must have been caused by some kind of envy; for example, Alchimowicz, with his long legs, swarthy good looks, and skill at basketball probably irritated me—a chubby boy. In any event, it got to the point where we duked it out inside a circle of kibbitzers. We passed our *gymnasium* graduation exam together and then I lost track of him. I believe he studied at the Central School for Commerce in Warsaw and then worked in a bank in Wilno. Then the Home Army and imprisonment in Russia. After his return he worked in an office in Warsaw and was one of the Sigismund August alumni who signed an annual greeting card on the anniversary of our graduation exam, sent to their friends in California, that is, to Staś Kownacki and me. He died a long time ago, and Staś is also gone.

ALCOHOL. "So after supper we would drink most diligently at Mr. Rudomina's place, and after each deeply felt 'vivat' the French horns would blare and the girls sing merrily in a chorus:

> *He drank it all, he drank it all, and didn't leave a drop!*
> *Hu! ha! he didn't leave a drop!*
> *God must have placed His blessing on him—*
> *Hu! ha! He's blessed!"*

(Ignacy Chodźko, *Lithuanian Sketches*, Wilno, 1843)

That past weighs on me. I come from a people who are afflicted by centuries of drunkenness. It didn't start early for me. My first drinking bout was at our high school graduation banquet in the Zacisze Restaurant, but during my years as a university student I didn't belong to any "brotherhood," I never wore a fraternity cap; in fact, our Vagabonds' Club didn't even drink beer. If some spare change turned up, though, I would go (usually with Draugas) to one of those little Jewish restaurants in the narrow side streets near German Street to have some cold vodka and Jewish delicacies.

My real drinking began in earnest in occupied Warsaw with my future wife Janka and Jerzy Andrzejewski. In him, it gradually developed into alcoholism and he contracted cirrhosis of the liver, which ended up killing him. It is a rather pathetic triumph to have lived to old age with a healthy liver, especially since it's not my accomplishment, but that of my genes. I drank a lot, but I always took care to separate time for work from time for letting go. Vodka; in France, wine; in America, bourbon.

The worst thing about alcohol is that it turns us into fools. Yet a sober eye inside us observes and later sets before us images that destroy our good opinion of ourselves. The shame that one feels then can have a pedagogical import, reminding us that whatever our achievements may be, they are undermined by the stupidity that resides within us, so there is no reason for us to put on airs. Shame, and also fear after the fact, for example, when one recalls one's senseless drunken provocation of Germans.

Revulsion at drunks because of their slovenliness is well founded. Among writers, I was able to observe closely Władysław Broniewski and Marek Hłasko; also, Oscar Milosz used to tell me about Esenin's drunken exhibitions in Paris. These examples should have sufficed to incline me toward abstinence, but alas, too many generations of my ancestors drank for me to have been free of the urge for the bottle. I cannot conceive of a drunken Gombrowicz. He would not have allowed himself to appear without his armor.

Perhaps (this is only a hypothesis) Polish men dislike themselves so intensely, in their heart of hearts, because they remember themselves in their drunken states?

ALIK PROTASEWICZ. My first encounter with God's cruelty, or my discovery that the Highest Order may be concerned about many things, but not about the principle of sympathy as we understand it. Aleksandr, or Alik, a Russian, was my schoolmate. There were only a few Russians, left over from tsarist times, in Wilno. Later, his sister and I studied law together at the university. There was no talk in our class about Alik's being an outsider because he was Russian. He participated in all our affairs, and also in our outings (I remember a hike to Troki). When we were exhausted he would say that it was time to take a "collapse," and we would collapse into a ditch for a rest.

Alik fell ill when he was about fifteen years old and never returned to school. He became paralyzed; it was probably polio, but it wasn't called that then. I was fond of him and used to visit him. Years of being crippled. Slowly, he learned to take a couple of trembling steps with crutches. Later, I knew various people who, through sheer willpower, learned to live normally despite being crippled, but Alik, vigorous and sturdily built, bore his helplessness badly, was profoundly depressed, and in his room one could almost hear the question "Why me?"

AMALRIK, Andrei. Perhaps the most incomprehensible event of the twentieth century was the fall of the state that called itself the USSR, but was referred to by others as the Soviet Union or L'Union Sovietique. The astronomical sums expended on the largest political police force in the world allowed it to grow into a mighty organization with millions of informers at its disposal and a network of forced labor camps across the breadth of Eurasia. Its propaganda and espionage activities were also generously financed to ensure that foreigners would not know the truth about the system. The costly terror machine itself and its masking with humanitarian slogans seemed to guarantee the permanence of the imperium. Its victories on the battlefields of World War II and participation in the partition of Europe suggested its internal efficiency and predisposed the populations of the newly conquered countries to a fatalistic acceptance. True, as time passed, cracks appeared in the monolith; however, optimists who observed the signs of disintegration exposed themselves to the rebuke that they were mistaking their desires for reality.

I was one of the moderate optimists; that is to say, I expected changes, and an enduring domination of Moscow over our countries did not seem likely to me. Changes would surely occur, but not in my lifetime. It seemed to me that Jerzy Giedroyc was much more certain, since he would make references to the end of the British and French empires, but he, too, did not predict when it would happen. I knew only two people who insisted that the imperium would fall, and not just at some time in the future, but right away, in ten, or perhaps fifteen, years at the most.

One of them was Andrei Amalrik, who was born in Moscow in 1932, the son of a historian. A Russian, an inhabitant of the Soviet Union, but conscious of his family's French ancestry. He liked making reference to his Visigoth family name, Amalric, which had belonged to two kings who participated in the crusades in the twelfth century, and also to a papal legate who was famous for crying out, after the conquest of the city of Béziers in the crusade against the Albigensians: "Kill them all, and God will sort them out." A medieval Amalric de Bène was a heretic and a martyr for his faith. A forebear of the Russian Amalrik came to Russia from Avignon in the nineteenth century. Interested in the past, Andrei studied history and wrote his master's thesis on Kievan Rus. However, when he was ordered to change its contents to fit the official thesis about the original rulers being Slavs, not Scandinavians, he refused and remained without a diploma. He crafted his own way of life, working at odd jobs, just so long as he could preserve his internal freedom. He neither fought against nor recognized the state. He did not read the press because it lied, and what he wrote was unprintable, including five satirical theater pieces in the spirit of the theater of the absurd. His tactics of programmatic withdrawal remind me of Joseph Brodsky's tactics. Also similar was the charge leveled against him after his arrest in 1965: parasitism (referring to his assisting well-known painters in sending their pictures abroad). The sentence was two and a half years of exile to Siberia to work on a kolkhoz. He wrote a book about this, *Involuntary Journey to Siberia*, which he sent abroad in manuscript. It was published in New York in 1970. I read it, and its detailed observations of daily life in the Russian countryside helped me to understand better Amalrik's essay, *Will the Soviet Union Survive Until 1984?* In accordance with his strategy of expanding freedom, but not illegally, he spoke out openly, under his own name, giving his address. That slim book, really just an essay, appeared in Amsterdam in 1969, then in various other languages, including Polish, in a Paris *Kultura* edition.

Amalrik was allowed to return from exile in 1966 but, arrested again in 1970, he was sentenced to three years in a strict regime camp and served out his sentence in Kolyma. He survived, but then he was given an additional three years. An international protest, organized by Andrei Sakharov, caused a transfer from camp to internal exile, from which he returned to Moscow in 1975, and in 1976 he left for the West. The University of Utrecht in Holland, Harvard University, and the Hoover Institution hosted him in turn.

Amalrik's prediction came true. He erred by only a few years. Naturally, we have a different understanding of his prediction today than in those days when the author could reasonably be suspected of irresponsible raving. As an exception among his contemporaries, he has been compared to Piotr Chaadaev, whom Tsar Nicholas I ordered declared a madman. Amalrik's judgments, as it turned out, though extreme, were perfectly sober.

As a historian, he had written about the origins of Kievan Rus, and now, as he said, he was writing about the end of that same imperium. Unlike the Sovietologists, who were concerned most of all with Marxism, which had been imported from the West, he argues that the imperium had extended its rule thanks to Marxism, just as Rome, accepting Christianity, prolonged its existence by several centuries. He does not prove this thesis, but in conformity with it he directs his study toward the peculiar characteristics of his own country, and in this he has many predecessors, beginning with Chaadaev. He compares the state of the tsars and their successors to fermenting dough, which rises and swells through inertia. He detects signs of imminent collapse and the loss of territorial gains (the two Germanies will unite, the countries of Eastern Europe gain their independence) in the mental sclerosis of the "middle class" or bureaucracy, which is no longer capable of intelligent and bold decision making. He predicts that many of their decisions will be made only on the basis of their fear of losing power. In general, reading Amalrik, we recognize the complex of causes of the fall of the Soviet Union, which people are now discussing endlessly, after the fact, whereas he discerned them beforehand. He includes among these causes the mentality of a people for whom individual rights and dignity are alien concepts, freedom is identical with anarchy, and justice means that my neighbor should fare as badly as I do, and if he fares better, that's unjust. Linked to this is the contrast between scientific progress and ingrained habits. "Soviet rockets have reached Venus, while in the village where I live potatoes are still dug by hand. This should not be regarded as a comical comparison; it is a gap which may deepen into an abyss. The crux of the matter is not the way in which potatoes are dug but the fact that the level of thinking of most people is no higher than this manual level of potato-digging."*

Amalrik deserves to be admired as a free man despite the conditions in which he lived, but I am not making a prophet out of him. He foresaw a war between Russia and China, seeing in it one of the causes of catastrophe (the war in Afghanistan substituted for it). He also had an apocalyptic presentiment of the end as an eruption of the murderous appetites pent up in the masses, but that did not occur. I believe that his experience of the Siberian kolkhoz lurks behind his attempts at rationalizing his insights, a feeling of horror at a way of life which was so miserable, so brutalized, that it cried out for some kind of historical vengeance. Nevertheless, the causes he enumerates appear to be insufficient, and the event appears to us in all its improbability.

*Andrei Amalrik, *Will the Soviet Union Survive Until 1984?* (Harmondsworth, England: Penguin Books, 1980), p. 62.

I met Amalrik in Palo Alto. I also met his beautiful wife Gyuzel, a painter whom he married in Siberia. From Gyuzel, who was a Tatar, I learned that she was born in Moscow and was the daughter of an apartment house janitor, a trade dominated there by Tatars: "Long ago, we ruled over ancient Rus, so they took revenge by making us into watchmen."

Gyuzel shared Andrei's fate in Siberia and after he was released, and therefore she could not be admitted to the Union of Artists, and therefore could not exhibit her work. I did not see her paintings in America and do not know what kind of painter she was. I was captivated by her beauty and charm.

Amalrik did not live to see the fulfillment of his prophecy. He died in 1980 in an automobile accident, en route to some convention in Spain. Since then, I have often tried to imagine what Gyuzel did for the remainder of her life after she lost him.

Another person who insisted that the Soviet Union was on the verge of collapse was the Lithuanian political scientist Aleksandras Sztromas, a recent émigré from Lithuania who taught at an American university. To be sure, our mutual friend Tomas Venclova, who had been aware of the system's chaos and corruption ever since he did his military service in the Soviet army, also did not predict a long future for that regime, but Sztromas insisted it would last only a few years more, not decades.

AMBITION. It makes itself known when it is wounded, and because there are sufficient causes to wound it, we must always cope with it somehow. The entire theater of social encounters rests on it; it is the power pulling the strings of our tragi-farce.

About myself, I can say that I have been both on top and on the bottom. On top, ambition becomes a little more relaxed, which is one virtue of success. On the bottom, it turns out that, for lack of some better alternative, it is capable of being consoled by small successes. More than one unsuccessful artist has been buoyed by praise from the lips of some Kasia or Jolanta; more than one petty functionary in some provincial town takes pride in his collection of postage stamps.

Ambition, after all, is Schopenhauer's Will, a force equal to biological terrors and drives. The will, however, cannot do everything, even in sports, where tenacious daily training means so much. Laying oneself open, letting oneself go, a certain comfort with passivity, allows the body to work in harmony. This is even more true in poetry; straining comes to nothing, for we receive the gift whether we are deserving of it or not. There is a contradiction between striving for recognition and fame on the one hand, and creating something that may bring one fame on the other.

On the bottom for years on end, a professor in an obscure department of unknown foreign languages, I think with amusement of the small joys which soothed my ambition's lament.

AMERICA. What splendor! What poverty! What humanity! What inhumanity! What mutual goodwill! What individual isolation! What loyalty to the ideal! What hypocrisy! What a triumph of conscience! What perversity! The America of contradictions can, not must, reveal itself to immigrants who have made it here. Those who have not made it will see only its brutality. I made it, but I have always tried to remember that I owe it to my lucky star, not to myself, and that right next door are entire neighborhoods of unfortunates. I will say even more: the thought of their grueling labor and unfulfilled hope, of the gigantic prison system in which the unneeded are kept, taught me to look skeptically at its decorations—those well-kept houses amidst the suburbs' greenery.

During my school years America rose to meet me as a loaf of white bread and a mug of cocoa from Hoover's postwar relief effort, as blue-striped shirts, and then as films with Mary Pickford and Charlie Chaplin. When a few years later I adored the actress Sylvia Sidney, how astonished I would have been had someone told me that some day my photograph and hers would be neighbors in the pages of *American Biography*. The movies meant that America was already beginning its expansion, but a number of streets signaled this, too—German Street in Wilno, or the one in Drohobycz that Bruno Schulz depicted as the Street of Crocodiles. As I was able to confirm later on in my life, the poorer streets on Manhattan's East Side were just like them.

During the course of this century "the beast emerging from the sea" overwhelmed, one after the other, its enemies and rivals. The most important of these rivals was Soviet Russia, because this clash was not only about military might, but about a model for man as well. The attempt to create a "new man" according to utopian principles was an enormous undertaking, and those who dismiss it after the fact apparently do not understand what were the stakes in this game. The "old man" won, and with the help of mass media is imposing its model on the entire planet. Looking at it from a distance, one should seek the causes of the Soviet defeat in the cultural sphere. Russia, expending astronomical sums of money on propaganda, was unable to persuade anyone to adopt its model, even in the conquered countries of Europe which accepted its efforts with derision, seeing in them the unattractive self-adornment of barbarians.

The Cold War, that conflict between democratic America and

gloomy Eastern totalism, deprived many people of their freedom of judgment and even of clear-sightedness, since a lack of enthusiasm for America could be perceived as an inclination toward the Communist side.

The twentieth century brought America into a new dimension which she had previously not known. At the beginning of the century, artists and writers fled to the old cultural centers of Paris and London from a country known to be dull, materialistic, concerned only with making money. At the end of the century, artists and writers from all kinds of countries journey to America as to a land of opportunities. By now, New York, not Paris, is the world capital of painting. Poetry, reduced to something akin to coin collecting in Western Europe, has found an audience in America on university campuses, and also entire departments, institutes, and prizes. I realize that had I remained in France I would not have received the Neustadt Prize in 1978 (which is referred to as the Little Nobel and is usually a first step toward the Nobel), or the Nobel Prize after that.

Today it is difficult to imagine how distant America was from Europe at the beginning of the century. An ocean separated the two continents, and voyages were accompanied by images of shipwrecks, which appear in illustrated magazines throughout the nineteenth century. My first voyage to America from England in the winter of 1945–46 took some twelve days. The little vessel climbed earnestly up the watery mountain only to find itself in a trough and to clamber up again. Then transatlantic flights became commonplace, and once I even flew on the French *Concorde*: dinner accompanied by wine had barely progressed to the cheese plate, and we were already in Paris.

People traveled to America, but they rarely came back. It did happen on occasion, though. In the wealthy and beautifully laid-out village of Peiksva, not far from the manor where I was born, "the American's house" stood out. Then something took place that provides, in brief, a glimpse of what happened to Lithuania under Soviet rule: collectivization. The village, bordering on great forests, had given aid to the "forest brotherhood." The family from "the American's house" were murdered, the house was burned down, the villagers were deported to the Siberian taiga, and the village itself was leveled.

Janka's father also was one who returned from America. Before World War I Ludwik Dłuski worked for several years in various metallurgical plants on the East Coast. I thought of him when I looked at the rusted skeletons of abandoned factories in the Hudson River Valley north of New York City. In those old-fashioned factories Mr. Dłuski shared the fate of the disinherited of the earth who labor from dawn to dusk, without the rights and privileges won later on by labor unions. In the Warsaw he returned to, life may have been difficult, but without that exhausting labor (he became a court bailiff), and, at least, not as lonely.

AMERICAN POETRY. First, there was America's poetry, but in prose, not verse. Fenimore Cooper, in abridged versions for young readers, so that his entire cycle of novels about the Pathfinder fit into a single volume (which improved it), Mayne Reid, Karl May. Edgar Allan Poe's poem "The Bells" in a reference book about styles as an example of onomatopoeia. Much later, I learned that American poets consider these imitations of sounds to be hideous, and that English does not tolerate such rhythmical jangling. But Poe was a great poet for the French and the Russians, for whom poetry is chiefly the "magic of sound." I am prepared to forgive him a great deal for one poem of truly magical incantation, "Ulalume," although it is easier to translate that work into Russian, with its iambic beat, than into Polish.

Were I a Hungarian, Czech, Serbian, or Croatian poet, my dependencies and borrowings would have been formed more or less in the same way, because, I am ashamed to confess, our countries mostly imitate the West. Their modernism was French and partially German. For a brief period before World War I Walt Whitman's renown spread throughout Europe but met with fanatical admirers only in one country, and with dreadful results. The young revolutionaries in Belgrade read him politically as a singer of democracy, of the crowd *en masse*, the enemy of monarchs. One of them, Gavrilo Princip, shot Archduke Ferdinand, and that is how an American poet was responsible for the outbreak of World War I.

Some of Whitman was translated in Poland; a couple of his poems in Alfred Tom's translation made a lasting impression on me. But in general, American poetry was unknown before the war. In Warsaw, it became fashionable to study English only in the late 1930s. The last play that I saw in Warsaw in 1939 was Thornton Wilder's *Our Town*, a piece of poetical theater, American to its roots. Later, in America, I became friendly with Wilder.

In the spring of 1945 I edited an anthology of English and American poetry in Krakow, collecting scattered translations by various authors. Of course, like all of the Polish intelligentsia, I was a snob about Western culture, and my leftist leanings did not change my pro-Westernism. Add to that a sober calculation: if I succeeded in publishing the anthology, it would serve as an antidote to Soviet grayness. Government policy soon became less liberal, however, and the anthology could not be published.

Next, I translated a large number of American poets, also not without some thought of administering an antidote. After 1956 everything changed; it became acceptable to translate Western poets. Gradually, American poetry was discovered until there was a virtual flood of translations. So there was no need for me to do what others could do, especially since I do not consider myself to be as gifted a translator as Stanisław Barańczak.

Of all American poets, I will always have the greatest affinity with Walt Whitman. He fulfills the condition of greatness which Oscar Milosz spoke of when he demanded that a work should be like a river, bearing rich silt and broken pieces of trees, not just nuggets of gold. That is why longueurs and repetitions, entire catalogs of objects, should not be irritating. Whitman is the opposite of "pure poetry." But at the same time, one's experience of him is like one's experience of large canvases by master painters, on which one can discern, through attentive observation, many minute and fascinating details.

I reacted distrustfully toward Americans who were my contemporaries. Undoubtedly, I borrowed the idea for *Treatise on Poetry* from the young Karl Shapiro's poem *Essay on Rime*; both works are lengthy poems. However, I remained astonishingly independent because of my immersion in Polish verbal culture and my deliberately cultivated stance of "provincialness."

The wonders of the place of American poetry. After all, it arose from wounds and protest (we should not be misled by the seeming democratic impulse of Whitman), from the escape to Europe (Pound, Eliot, Frost), from the anarchism of the beatniks, who spat on Moloch (Ginsberg), and all of this was to be consumed by Moloch and employed by him on other continents in praise of himself.

AMERICAN VISA. Why, since you were able to stay in America, did you go back to Europe and leave your family behind? Janka loved America; she wanted me to stay, but she was afraid that I would hold it against her. I placed one limit on my recklessness in the dangerous year of 1950: if something should happen, the people in Warsaw should not be able to get at my family. Could I really have stayed? Polonia—the Polish-American community—would have set their dogs on me. After all, I was guilty of a great crime, because it was I and not they who created the first endowed chair of Polish literature in America, placing Professor Manfred Kridl in it, with money from Warsaw—"Bolshevik money," as it were. Perhaps I might have survived despite Polonia, but I wanted to try sticking it out in the Paris embassy until better times. The attempt did not succeed and I wound up in France without money and without work.

We see ourselves differently from the way other people see us. It makes no sense to go on fuming about it; they see us as they want to see us, and that's that. Ryszard Wraga (Niezbrzycki), who reported on me to the American Embassy in Paris, was an idiot in my opinion, because as the former chief of Polish intelligence in the East he should have been smart enough not to suspect that I was a Soviet mole, but he honestly believed I was. For American Polonia I was "the poet Miłoś, the bard of Bierut's Poland," and I could hardly reproach them for not having heard of my prewar book of poetry, *Three Winters*, nor of the literary journals *Pion* and *Ateneum*, and so on, and they knew nothing about Manfred Kridl's stature as a scholar of Polish literature. The opinion that everything possible should be done to prevent a dangerous person from entering America was expressed in the large number of letters and notes that successfully scuttled my hopes of getting a visa. Janka's interventions with the State Department, which went on for a couple of years, were destined to be fruitless, and her outburst must have been absolutely incomprehensible for the bureaucrats there, when she screamed at them, "You'll regret it, because he's going to win the Nobel Prize." At best, they considered that outburst proof that she lost all balanced judgment when it was a matter of her husband.

Even much later, after a lengthy stay in France and when I had long since given up on emigrating to America, the news that I had been granted a visa in 1960 following my invitation to lecture at the University of California angered a lot of people. I found out about this from the correspondence of Andrzej Bobkowski, the author of *Pen Sketches* (1960). By then I had already published *The Captive Mind* and that book, in Bobkowski's opinion, proved that I would impart nonsense to the students because I had invented some sort of "ketman" and similar fictions in it. That was written by Bobkowski, a man whose *Pen Sketches* I admired, and he was only expressing his deepest convictions. True, he was also convinced that the election of John F. Kennedy as president was a disaster for Americans because he was a Democrat. When I was hired as a professor, Zygmunt Hertz wrote to me that a certain well-known man in Paris said, "I will never believe that."

More than twenty years passed, and I was sitting in the White House, invited by President Reagan to receive from his hands a medal for my service to American culture. Beside me was the famous architect, Mario Pei, who designed the Louvre pyramid in Paris, and the best-selling author James Michener. My immediate neighbor at the dinner table was Frank Sinatra, Reagan's personal friend. Should I have spoken of my difficulties in getting a visa? That they had not wanted to let me in? It all seemed to me as far in the past as the Paleolithic period. I could only smile to myself, thinking about the scarcely imaginable tricks of fate.

ANCEWICZ, Franciszek, or Ancevičius Pranas. From Samogitia. An atheist, Marxist, socialist, anti-Communist, internationalist. Large, with a hemplike mane of hair, wearing horn-rimmed glasses. Assistant Professor Ejnik's pro-seminar on the philosophy of law 1929–1939. Professor Lande, an adherent of Petrażycki's theories, had just left the university and Miss Ejnik was the sole lecturer on the faculty who continued his line of thinking. Pranas appeared at the pro-seminar and spoke up, but he only stammered, red in the face, because he could barely speak Polish. He had come from Vienna, from the Karl Marx Houses, where Austrian Marxists took good care of him. Since 1926, when he participated in the socialist putsch, he was a marked man in Kaunas, so he had been leading the life of an émigré. My long friendship with him was part of my nonprovincial upbringing.

Draugas finished law school in Wilno and got his doctorate, after which he participated in the Sovietology seminar at the Institute for the Study of Eastern Europe. There he became friendly with Teodor Bujnicki, who was the secretary of the Institute, and also with Stanisław Baczyński, the father of the poet Krzysztof, who came to give lectures. When the governor Bociański carried out his anti-Lithuanian and anti-Belorussian campaign at the end of the thirties, Baczyński suggested that Pranas should move to Warsaw and got a position for him, as a librarian, I think. The year 1939, war, Pranas's return to Wilno and his departure for Germany as a newspaper correspondent for neutral Lithuania. He was there when the Soviets occupied Wilno. We met in the fall of 1940 in Warsaw; he had come from Berlin to liquidate his apartment. He tried to talk me into visiting him in Berlin. When I asked how I could do that, he responded, "It's a cinch. Our consulate may be closed, but it has all the necessary stamps. I'll send you a safe conduct pass." I asked my chief in the socialist "Freedom" organization, Zbigniew Mitzner, if I should accept it. He said, "Take it, because someone has to go to Berlin to carry those microfilms." That is how I came to possess a Lithuanian travel document which might have protected me in a roundup, but not necessarily, because it wasn't registered with the Germans. In the meantime, the socialists' "post office box" at the Swedish Embassy in Berlin was discovered by the Gestapo.

After Lithuania was occupied by the Germans Pranas returned and became a lawyer in Szawle. Immediately afterward, his exodus with his wife and children across burning Prussia to the West. A couple of years later, emigration to Canada where, although they both had doctorates, they became factory workers. Well liked and valued as a trade union activist, Pranas was a candidate for Parliament, but he lost. He had a large library of books on politics and political science in his house.

I would be searching for explanations of his suicide if I didn't remember his lengthy periods of depression, so overwhelming that they felled him like a physical illness, from the time when we lived together in the dormitory in Wilno. Strong as an ox, he suffered throughout his life from a periodically recurring sickness of the soul.

ANGELIC SEXUALITY. When does the one and only woman make her appearance? Dante's Beatrice was neither his wife nor his betrothed, merely a young maiden glimpsed occasionally from a distance, but she meets him in *The Divine Comedy* and takes over as guide when Virgil leads the poet to the highest circle of Purgatory. This medieval ideal of distant, worshipped femininity is also a constant in the troubador poetry of Languedoc. The elevation of woman to the status of a person who initiates one into *amore sacro* is a reflection of the cult of Mary.

Later, Christian culture succumbs to the influence of pagan Latin poetry, which is not open to ecstatic love, although the beauty of women is sung in countless poems. The eighteenth century, the Age of Reason, was characterized by looseness in sexual customs, in which Italy led the way, so that Casanova's diaries seem to reflect not only his own adventures. The one and only, predestined woman belongs to Romanticism, and Werther, who was unable to win her, definitely had to commit suicide. Such a reason for suicide would have been completely incomprehensible to the Stoics and Epicureans, and to the poets who embraced classical philosophy.

People at the end of the eighteenth and the beginning of the nineteenth centuries, however, including the Polish Romantics, were raised on an entirely different set of readings, from which they could learn something about the marriage of two souls. As an example: the works of Swedenborg, which fed Słowacki's imagination (and Balzac's) when these writers were still children. It is worth noting parenthetically that Słowacki's *The Hour of Thought* and Balzac's two "Swedenborgian" novels,

Séraphita and *Louis Lambert*, were written at more or less the same time, in the early 1830s. Słowacki's Ludwika Śniadecka is an imaginary love, whereas a real Mrs. Hańska inhabits the life of the highly emotional fat man, and *Séraphita* was written with more than a little thought to overcoming the Catholic scruples of his beloved and of finally uniting in marriage with the lady from Wierzchownia.

No theosophical system assigns as central a place to the love of two people as does Swedenborg's imagined edifice. Since the sensual world and the spiritual world are linked there by threads of "correspondence," what takes place on earth is continued in heaven. In his system, love here on earth does not acquire the forms of medieval asceticism nor Platonic idealization. For him, love is fulfilled in marriage; it is of the flesh, but strictly monogamous. And so is his view of heaven, because in heaven all the angels were formerly human beings, and they preserve the strength and beauty of their youth, along with their gender—masculine or feminine. They also retain the sexual drive and preserve high sexual potency. Happy earthly married couples meet again, restored to youth. Those who were single find a partner in heaven.

The angelic sexuality we find in Swedenborg, then, is not a divestiture of the body, an escape into ethereal regions, constant yearning and dreaming. It is physical, earthly in its superterrestrialness, and differs from sinful love only in that desire is directed toward one person only. The perfect harmony of two souls and bodies is the goal of earthly beings, and if they do not achieve it, then of heavenly beings, who, in addition, never experience boredom or weariness with each other.

Balzac's *Séraphita* introduces the motif of the androgyne, a union of the masculine and feminine soul such that together they form a dual-sex unity, perhaps because in Swedenborg the thoughts of a married couple in heaven are completely united and the couple is not referred to as two angels, but as one. As it turns out, neither *Séraphita*—nor the letters in which Balzac attempted to persuade Mrs. Hańska to accept Swedenborg's teachings—changed their addressee's views; at most, the critique of Christian beliefs contained in them added a dose of Voltaireanism to her Catholicism.

How do I know this? I am not a Balzac specialist, but my knowledge of French allows me to come across commentaries and studies which abound in France. Concealed behind *The Human Comedy* is a complicated philosophical scaffolding, underestimated as a rule by those who saw in Balzac only a realist. The novel *Louis Lambert*, which was reworked more than once, and whose main character is a brilliant thinker, explores two interwoven strands: the "scientific" and the mystical. Swedenborg occupies a great deal of space in the latter, even if, just as in Słowacki's case, it is based on secondhand knowledge.

The images of the (many) heavens and (many) hells in Swedenborg fascinated writers, most likely because the traditional Christian image of hell and eternal damnation did not accord with the concept of a kind God. It is easier to imagine a sort of natural attraction of like to like, who ascend to the heavens only to fall into hells by the power of this mutual affinity, rather than by any sentence. Poets also borrowed from Swedenborg by the handful when, like Baudelaire, they took from him the correspondences between the physical and the spiritual world and gave them the name "symbols."

ANONYMOUS LETTERS. "People don't like you, Mr. Miłosz." The anonymous author appended these words when he sent me a copy of a rather disgusting article about me from the Polish émigré press. And it was true, because with the exception of a small group of people, I was never liked. There is no reason for us to be too certain that we are right. My enemies, who often wrote anonymous letters or shot arrows at me from under cover, believed that they were right. First, my various flaws made it difficult to raise me onto a pedestal despite the obvious social need. Second, my innate bloodthirstiness often erupted in contemptuous remarks about individuals, which I now consider to be simple rudeness. Third, from the beginning of my career accusations of arrogance were raised by people I had offended and by those I had rejected, whose presence was a moral problem for me. Let us consider what a huge number of people enter the fray through writing, painting, sculpting. A sense of hierarchy forbids us to praise results which, in our opinion, are not worthy of being praised, but it can be painful to think about a poet, for example, who sends me his new poem, who is proud of it, and expects me to praise it. I had a choice: I could write to tell him that the poem is bad, or I could not respond. This is not a made-up example; that is how I wounded Aleksander Janta, and it was the end of our friendship.

ANTHOLOGIES. Gombrowicz made fun of me in Vence: "Can you picture Nietzsche putting together anthologies?" But I assembled them assiduously, and one can see in that activity the fervor of an individual who was too unsure of himself, or else too proud, to place only himself on a pedestal. My first, *Anthology of Contemporary Poetry* (Wilno, 1933), co-edited with Zbigniew Folejewski, was the result of my revolutionary mania; the second was the underground *Independent Song* (Warsaw, 1942); the third, a compilation of English and American poetry (Kraków,

1945), was never published; the fourth was *Postwar Polish Poetry* (New York, 1968); the fifth, *Excerpts from Useful Books* (Kraków, 1994); the sixth, an English-language version of the fifth, came out under the title *A Book of Luminous Things* (New York, 1996). Something will always remain from such sowing of seeds into the wind.

The anthology may be viewed as a separate literary genre, like excerpts from the thoughts of various authors, which are called books of quotations. In the midst of ever-increasing quantity, anthologies enable individual voices to be heard above the collective noise.

ANUS MUNDI. The cloaca of the world. A certain German wrote down that definition of Poland in 1942. I spent the war years there and afterward, for years, I attempted to understand what it means to bear such an experience inside oneself. As is well known, the philosopher Adorno said that it would be an abomination to write lyric poetry after Auschwitz, and the philosopher Emmanuel Levinas gave the year 1941 as the date when God "abandoned" us. Whereas I wrote idyllic verses, "The World" and a number of others, in the very center of what was taking place in the *anus mundi*, and not by any means out of ignorance. Do I deserve to be condemned for this? Possibly, it would be just as good to write either a bill of accusation or a defense.

Horror is the law of the world of living creatures, and civilization is concerned with masking that truth. Literature and art refine and beautify, and if they were to depict reality naked, just as everyone suspects it is (although we defend ourselves against that knowledge), no one would be able to stand it. Western Europe can be accused of the deceit of civilization. During the industrial revolution it sacrificed human beings to the Baal of progress; then it engaged in trench warfare. A long time ago, I read a manuscript by one Mr. Ulrich, who fought at Verdun as a German infantry soldier. Those people were captured like the prisoners in Auschwitz, but the waters of oblivion have closed over their torment and death. The habits of civilization have a certain enduring quality and the Germans in occupied Western Europe were obviously embarrassed and concealed their aims, while in Poland they acted completely openly.

It is entirely human and understandable to be stunned by blatant criminality and to cry out, "That's impossible!" and yet, it was possible. But those who proclaim that God "abandoned us in 1941" are acting like conservators of an anodyne civilization. And what about the history of humankind, with its millennia of mutual murder? To say nothing of natural catastrophes, or of the plague, which depopulated Europe in the fourteenth century. Nor of those aspects of human life which do not need a grand public arena to display their subservience to the laws of earth.

Life does not like death. The body, as long as it is able to, sets in opposition to death the heart's contractions and the warmth of circulating blood. Gentle verses written in the midst of horror declare themselves for life; they are the body's rebellion against its destruction. They are *carmina*, or incantations deployed in order that the horror should disappear for a moment and harmony emerge—the harmony of civilization or, what amounts to the same thing, of childish peace. They comfort us, giving us to understand that what takes place in *anus mundi* is transitory, and that harmony is enduring—which is not at all a certainty.

AOSTA. Blessed be the monarchs for having loved to hunt. On the southern slopes of the Alps they chose the Aosta Valley as their royal hunting grounds; they banned woodcutting and denied everyone the right to flush game. Thanks to this, the Aosta Valley is a national park today. Rare species of animals have survived there—for example, the mountain goat (which should not be confused with the mountain goat found in the North American Rockies). When we lived in France in the 1950s we were unable to visit Aosta on our own because we were too poor to own an automobile. Mac Goodman took us there in his big American car. The road was quite difficult, with hairpin turns on steep slopes, but then there was an enchanting mountain village and the intensity of the green in the alpine meadows, with a large number of clear streams and rivulets disappearing into the greensward.

ARCATA. A small northern California town on the Pacific coast, close to the Oregon border. Always a gray sky and ocean fog. I have been there a number of times and never saw the sun. Should one live there? Perhaps as punishment. Yet people do live in Arcata, because they have to. For the most part, they work as loggers in the redwood, or sequoia, forests that have been protected until now, but they are always threatened by periods of unemployment and of course they hate the ecologists who want to deprive them of their livelihood. Against sentimental tree huggers they eagerly repeat the famous line of the governor of California and later president, Ronald Reagan: "If you've seen one redwood, you've seen them all."

Redwood forests are exceptionally gloomy. Because they require constant moisture, they grow in a zone of perpetual fog. There are those gigantic columns, which may be over a thousand years old, and among them are bands of fog, and down below is complete darkness and the total absence of undergrowth.

When one of these giants falls, shoots emerge from its body immediately and reach for the sky. One such tree supplies a great deal of excellent building material, which accounts for those wars between the timber-cutting interests and the ecologists.

ARON, Pirmas. A fictional character created as a joke by Teodor Bujnicki and me. Bujnicki remembered Kozma Prutkov, the fictional poet dreamed up by a couple of Russian writers. "Pirmas" means "first" in Lithuanian, so his name means Aron the First. Aron Pirmas published poems in *Żagary*. I recognized his poem, "My Journey Through the Czech Lands," as a creation of my pen, although it appears in a collection of Bujnicki's poetry. Pirmas describes himself in this poem as "an amalgam of Jew and Lithuanian." Other people also wrote under that name. Later (when?) Pirmas changed his name from Aron to Ariel, and it seems several people published their creations under that pseudonym in *The Wilno Courier*.

ASZKENAZY, Janina. She was the only daughter of Professor Stefan Aszkenazy, the famous historian. In Jerzy Stempowski's writings we can read about his conversation with Aszkenazy around the year 1930. It is quite horrifying. The professor had a clear awareness of disaster inevitably approaching the Polish state from both sides. Fortunately for him, he died before the war.

His daughter was like a hothouse flower from a narrow intellectual stratum. Completely defenseless. Rather large, unattractive, dark-haired, timid, psychologically troubled, with a hefty dose of schizophrenia, a reader of poetry and philosophy. During the German occupation, she belonged to our "Freedom" organization. This organization of Zbigniew Mitzner's (he was forced out of it in the end by Wacław Zagórski) brought together journalists, writers, and actors, including many Jews who were living outside of the Ghetto. Miss Aszkenazy wandered about the city with a bag stuffed with underground papers. She would visit us on what was then the end of Independence Avenue in Warsaw. She struck us as a not wholly oriented person. According to what she told us, she would occasionally lose all sense of place and time. Once, she rode the tram in a circle, completing the entire route there and back, until she finally attracted the attention of the "blue [Polish] police." She was arrested, but she managed to get rid of the contents of her bag in the toilet and somehow or other she was let go—who knows, perhaps she confessed that she was the daughter of a famous professor, or the police did not want to bother with a disturbed person. It seems she was all alone in occupied Warsaw. Certainly, no one looked after her. I have no knowledge of how she died.

Another pessimist professor comes to mind: Marian Zdziechowski, who shortly before the outbreak of the war published a book titled *In the Face of the End* and, like Aszkenazy and fortunately for himself, did not live to see the fulfillment of his prediction. But thoughts about his completely defenseless son are as painful to me as my memories of Miss Aszkenazy. He was swept up in the great deportations from Wilno in June 1941 and went to a Soviet labor camp where people such as he were among the first to die.

That crater, pit, abyss of the suffering of innocent beings—so many of them mentally ill or on the border of illness, with their awareness of terror magnified by their illness. It keeps coming back.

ATILA. He was a thirteen-year-old Hungarian youth who fought in the Hungarian Revolution of 1956 and escaped to Austria after its defeat. Mac and Sheba Goodman, who were living in Paris at the time, looked after him out of the goodness of their hearts, sent him to America, and paid for his education. Atila remains a difficult moral problem for me. When America intervened in Vietnam, Atila naturally volunteered to go, because it was obvious to him that one must beat the Communists, wherever they might be. Since he knew us as friends of the Goodmans, he visited us in Berkeley on his way to the Far East. At the time, the mood in Berkeley was strongly antimilitary. But aside from that, what could I say—to him, who sought my moral support? After all, in France I had followed the defeat of the French in Vietnam; why did the American generals think they would win? How could I explain to Atila that the Vietnamese were waging a patriotic war against foreigners, and that foreigners could not win such a war? Should I have infused him with pessimism? Weakened him, when he had already made his decision? I felt awful. The only thing I could do was to mumble that American opinion wasn't unified and that the question of a struggle between the two blocs was not as simple as he thought it was. Poor, diligent, uncomplicated Atila! He didn't die in the war, however. He served in the air force and came home as a highly qualified electrician.

AUTHENTICITY. My great fear: that I am pretending to be someone who I am not. I have been aware of the fact that I am pretending. But let us think about this: What else could I have done? My ego was unhappy. Had I been preoccupied only with myself, I would have created a literature of accusations and groans. Instead, I kept my distance from the substance I extruded (comparable, perhaps, to a silkworm's thread, which turns into a cocoon, or to the calcareous matter from which a mollusk builds its shell) and this helped me artistically.

I have been tempted to reveal myself and to confess that nothing really matters to me but my own toothache. I was never confident enough, however, that my toothache was authentic, that I had not talked myself into thinking I had one, which is always a problem when we focus our attention on ourself.

My readers have thought that my Form is close to my self. Even an exceptionally perceptive reader thought so—Konstanty Jeleński, for whom my life and my poetry formed an astonishing unity. He might have been led to believe that by my Dionysian ecstasy, which was truly part of me, except that I employed it consciously as the most effective means to hide my pain.

Authenticity in literature requires that we do the least possible writing with one or another audience in mind. We do not live in the wilderness, however, and language itself, along with its traditions, rules us and is accompanied by the pressure of expectations from other speakers of that language. I have experienced writing for my Marxist colleagues in my youth; I have experienced writing for patriotic Warsaw under the German occupation. It may be that going into emigration was my salvation, because during my many years in France and America I did not write *for* a Western audience, but *against* it. And in fact, I treasure my success because it happened to someone who had his hackles raised, who was constantly pointing out that he was not one of them. In contrast, until I broke with the Warsaw government, I was already beginning to write under the demands of socialist realism.

I cannot react favorably to those Polish writers who, after 1989, began to write for the Western publishing market. Nor to those young poets who ape American poetry, while I and the whole "Polish school" did our own thing, conscious of our historical experience.

We are dependent on the language we use. I could cite for example those poets whom Form allowed to do nothing of their own because they were unable to break through their language to more daring ideas.

AUTOMOBILE. Surely, the automobile was invented in order to make a mockery of those pessimists who predicted that the number of horses would grow exponentially and that cities would choke to death from the stench of horse excrement. From Kiejdany county, in which there was a single automobile (Count Zabiełło's), I was catapulted into California, where the automobile is just the same as electricity and bathrooms. I am not nostalgic for the good old days. I lived amidst filth and stench without being aware of it. And I belonged to the so-called upper social strata. The Wilno of my school years had cobblestone streets and only a couple of neighborhoods had sewers. One can imagine the mountains of garbage and excrement in Wilno during the Romantic era. It would be worthwhile to describe the female readers of *La Nouvelle Héloïse* not from above, but from below: from the perspective of their chamber pots (where were they emptied?), their underpants (they didn't wear any), and their gymnastic contortions while washing.

True, our apartment had a tin bathtub, but heating water for it was a major operation since we burned wood. Today, I cannot imagine a morning without a shower, but I must humbly admit to myself that I am that same person who used to bathe once a week at most, and usually in one of the city bathhouses. And I accepted that as normal. Not long ago, Ignacy Święcicki reminded me that in his parents' apartment on Makowa Street (we used to shoot at crows with an old fowling piece there) water was brought in buckets from the courtyard well. I was unaware of it at the time, so it must have been part of normal life.

It is surprising that in the midst of such backwardness I succumbed early to conservative and, what was more or less the same thing (though the word was unknown then), ecological impulses. My herbaria, ornithological atlases, aquariums, birdcages, and *The Polish Hunter*, which my father subscribed to, were responsible for that. And also Zofia Rodziewiczówna's *The Forest People's Summer*, which I read at that time. It was enough that when I was about thirteen years old I was deeply concerned about protecting nature and I would draw maps of my ideal country in which there were no fields or roads, and the only permissible means of communication were boats on the rivers and canals.

I saw the automobile as a threat, because of its noise. It is difficult to understand this today, but cars in those days filled the landscape with the loud roar of their motors, meaning that they ruined the silence of nature with a human presence. Even later, when our Vagabonds' Club used to go hiking, we did not look sympathetically on the automobile, and I remember a particular car which flew past us, roaring, and then suddenly came to a stop, and Robespierre and I started chanting, "Oh, the proud auto got all choked up."

My ideal country had a constitution which closed its borders to most mortals; they were open only to nature lovers. That is, to those adults who still preserved enthusiasm. I used to promise myself that I would be one of them, that I would become a naturalist. But it turned out otherwise.

Transformed from a man outside an automobile to one

seated behind the wheel, I ought to write a song of thanksgiving to the car, because thanks to it I have toured the West Coast of America from the Mexican border to the Canadian Rockies, slept in a tent beside lakes in the Sierras, and baked in the heat of the desert known as Death Valley.

[B]

BAAL. In the summer of 1862 Dostoevsky traveled to France and England, and this trip supplied the contents of his short *Winter Notes on Summer Impressions*. Chapter Five, which is about London, is titled "Baal" because it seemed as if humans were being sacrificed to that god of Syria and Canaan, whose name means simply "Lord". No one, not even Dickens in his blackest pages, has said such terrible things as Dostoevsky did about the then capital city of capitalism. Certainly, as a Russian he had reason to dislike the West, but his moral outrage is so powerful and his descriptions so realistic that it is difficult not to believe him. Poverty, stupefaction caused by heavy labor, drunkenness, hordes of prostitutes, many of them underage, proved that the upper classes in England had truly sacrificed these victims to the Baal of money. It is not surprising that Karl Marx's prophecy, conceived in that same London, contained such vengeful power. Because it ought to be beneath human dignity to submit to the law of Nature, which is "eat or be eaten." My strong socialist leanings derived from thinking about those millions of human lives trampled into the mud. True, one may question whether those who were trampled upon would have derived any pleasure from knowing about those other millions who were to die in the Gulag.

Another Russian, Maxim Gorky, visited New York at the very beginning of the twentieth century and reported his impressions under the title *City of the Yellow Devil* (the dollar, that is). When I read it, I thought he had exaggerated, but not by much, because that is what those cities were like for those on the bottom, and many of their features have been preserved into the present. Later, Gorky went to Solovki and politely pretended that he had not noticed he was visiting a death camp.

BACZYŃSKI, Krzysztof. When I met the well-known critic Stanisław Baczyński in Wilno in the thirties, I did not know that some day I would meet his son, and that that son would become famous as a poet. Stanisław Baczyński had come from Warsaw to lecture at the Institute for the Study of Eastern Europe. He was handsome, with a straight back, a very military bearing, which conformed with what people said about his service as an uhlan in the Polish Legion and his wartime exploits during the Silesian uprising. Politically, he was located among the Piłsudskiist left, which had developed out of the Polish Socialist Party. He was a Marxist, as could be inferred from his articles. He intrigues me with that blend of characteristics; I, at least, had never met anyone like that.

I visited Krzysztof Baczyński in their (his and his mother's, because the father had died already) Warsaw apartment during the German occupation. He gave me some poems for my anthology. I remember him in a reclining position, because he was always suffering from asthma. His delicate appearance and pallor brought to mind an image of Marcel Proust in his cork-lined room. He was not aligned with either the "Art and the Nation" group among his generation nor with their opposite, Tadeusz

Borowski; he edited his own little journal, *The Road*. At the time, I was not aware of the evolution he had undergone during his high school years. For a while, he considered himself a Trotskyist. Konstanty Jeleński was his classmate at the Stefan Batory Gymnasium; he described a fight that started over the class's mockery of Rysiek Bychowski, a Jew. "Only five classmates, including Krzysztof Baczyński, fought on our side, against thirty-odd on theirs." Bychowski, it should be noted, served as an airman in England. He wrote a letter to his father in New York about the incurable anti-Semitism of Poles and his decision not to return to Poland should he survive the war. Shortly afterward, he died, shot down over Cologne.

Baczyński's transformation from an asthmatic coddled by his mother into a soldier is a stunning triumph of willpower: "My beloved is called the will." Probably the family tradition of a Legionnaire father who fought in the battles of Stochód contributed to his willpower. Critics have written about that transformation, paying tribute to the heroic soldier-poet. Another conflict with which his will had to contend is passed over in silence. His mother, née Zieleńczyk, was from a well-known assimilated Jewish family. Jadwiga Zieleńczykówna, apparently one of Krzysztof's cousins, and also my colleague when I studied law in Wilno, achieved some renown by winning a competition in rhetoric. Krzysztof, then, was Jewish on his mother's side, and it appears that his father's family name, too (though here I lack specifics), was assumed. One way or another, he must have been perfectly aware that his place was in the ghetto, which created an insoluble problem of solidarity. He must also have been aware that behind the fraternity of arms with his contemporaries in the Home Army was concealed that same proportion that had existed in his high school fight: five against thirty-odd, and among those five only a couple of non-Jews.

This heir of Polish romantic poetry, especially of Słowacki, consciously sacrificed his life for his country, even though he knew that his country did not want him. Moreover, he believed that his people, to whom he was connected not only by blood but by the history of several millennia, were the Jewish people in the ghetto. Several of his poems clearly bear witness to this, although considering his existential complications, the poetry could have been even more revealing. The romantic tone concealed traces of clearer self-knowledge, like a dark veneer.

BALLADS AND ROMANCES. The unchanging magic of Mickiewicz—an incomprehensible magic. Of course, there is magic that can be more or less understood. But here we are dealing with content that is not particularly refined (except for "Tukaj") and with borrowed form. Other writers, after all, also wrote ballads on similar themes and in verse, as was expected then. I have attempted to rationalize their seductiveness somehow. Mickiewicz was tempered by classicism, whose features included, among other things, a light, witty presentation of spirits both male and female (for example, the sylphs in Alexander Pope's *The Rape of the Lock*). The ballads are written by a classicist, which means that the author does not necessarily have to believe in apparitions and ghosts. Even when Karusia claims in "Romanticism" that she sees her dead beloved, Jasieńko, we are given to understand that it is the creative power of her heart, and not her belief, that leads her to think Jasieńko has really appeared. Thus, there is in Mickiewicz's ballads a playing with the world of "as if," on the border of belief in the existence of uncanny phenomena. The humorous note is actually the stronger one, and when an author is having fun it helps a great deal. This is somewhat like Ovid in the *Metamorphoses*. He believed in the mythological transformations which he described, at least in the maiden who was changed into a nightingale—or did he? Yes, to an extent, although the theme itself forced him to suspend judgment. This is all very well, but Mickiewicz, the backwater provincial, was inclined to take folk legends seriously, and was superstitious himself, as one can tell from reading his *Forefathers' Eve*.

And did I not myself, like the pot calling the kettle black, believe every single word of the story about the priest's housekeeper in Świętobrość and that after her death the uproar she caused was finally ended by digging up her grave (which to this day is still in that cemetery) and impaling her body with a stake of aspen wood?

Rational explanations are not particularly helpful. The seductive charm of the *Ballads* is like that of magical spells: they are *carmina*. The word *carmen* originally referred to charms, the incantations of a sorcerer, or, as we would say today, of a shaman. Later, the verb *carminare* came to signify the composition of verses. A required formula in a ritual or a prophecy has to be pithy and easy to pronounce:

"Look, Maryla, where the groves come to an end."

Or: "Whoever you may be in the environs of Nowogródek."

Or: " 'Krysiu, Krysiu,' he calls, / And 'Krysiu,' replies the echo."

Or: "I am dying, I do not weep, / But you should seek to lessen your pain."

I agree; in order to cast *carmina* into the space of some sacred

cave or a modern bookstore, it is good to be tempered by classicism. Mickiewicz was. Today's poets would do well to consider
how helpful it would be to arrange syllables in metered verse.

Always grateful to Mickiewicz, I understand little of his life
and I do not know whence he derived his poetic power. But to be
grateful, one need not understand.

BALZAC, Honoré de. Read mainly during the German occupation of Warsaw by our threesome—Janka, Andrzejewski, and me.
A brutal writer, and a good one, especially for what was happening
at that time. May that threesome be with me in these pages, as we
were then, and not later on, when our fates diverged. Balzac came
shortly after we produced in Dynasy, the neighborhood where
Janka and I were living, the first book of poetry to be printed (in
about fifty copies) in the occupied city. It was my chapbook, issued
under the pseudonym Jan Syruć, my great-grandfather's family
name. Antoni Bohdziewicz supplied the paper and the duplicating
machine, Janka sewed the books, and Jerzy helped out. Right after
that, a passion for reading Balzac. Against Conrad. That was when
Jerzy was editing a literary news-letter for circles of readers, and I
was his chief co-author, and when his short stories, which he published in it, kept returning, with high dramatic intensity, to ultimate questions. Janka was very sober-minded and inclined to
irony, and she did not care for the Conradian lyricism (Conrad
translated by Aniela Zagórska) she saw in Jerzy's work, as she
would tell him frankly during our vodka-drinking sessions at the
Under the Rooster bar. There is not a trace of romantic lyricism in
Balzac's prose, and in her opinion that author (in Boy's translations) supported her arguments.

My dearest shades, I cannot invite you to converse with me,

for behind us, as only we three know, lies our tragic life. Our conversation would develop into a lament in three voices.

BAROQUE. Their life was difficult and monotonous. They walked behind the plow, sowed seeds, wielded sickles and scythes, over and over, from morning until nightfall. Only on Sundays, when they went to church, did everything abruptly change. From out of the grayness they stole into a realm of white and gold, on the sinuous capitals of the columns, on the frames of the icons, in the ciborium at the center of the altar. And even more gold and white above, under the cupola, merging with the light and azure of heaven. They looked around, and meanwhile the organ music lifted them up.

The baroque of palaces and church spires is not as influential as the baroque of church interiors. What a splendid discovery, and one should not be surprised that the Jesuit baroque spread eastward in Europe as far as Polotsk and Vitebsk, that it conquered Central and South America. Sinuousness instead of straight lines; the indulgent, lavish robing of statues; the flying, chubby angels—all demanded gold, demanded the most richly gilded splendor. In this way, the interior of the church building transported the faithful into another dimension, the opposite of their daily existence amidst grinding labor and scarcity.

Perhaps the Baroque developed in order to compete with the golden box or hive that is the interior of many Orthodox churches, in which singing, the smell of incense, and the words of the liturgy take the place of theology and the proclamation of the Christian good news? I know nothing about this except that in the tenth century, when the Kievan knights entered Hagia Sophia, Byzantium's largest church, they did not know if they were still on earth or already in heaven, and according to legend, this influenced the prince's decision to choose the Christian religion for Rus. In any event, Baroque Catholicism competed successfully with Orthodoxy and held back the progress of the Reformation, perhaps because the bare walls of the Protestant church could not represent the promise of Heaven.

BAUDELAIRE, Charles. An unhappy life, a great intellect, an important poet. It may be that poets of such great talent existed in other countries, but Baudelaire was a Frenchman when Paris was considered the cultural capital of the world. And Paris, as a symbol of the great city during the ongoing industrial-technological revolution, a hellish city, *la cité infernale*, is the subject of his poetry and his superb essays on painting.

He is very interesting from a theological point of view, because he is on the boundary between belief and nonbelief, and in that way different from his atheistic heirs, Stéphane Mallarmé and Paul Valéry. Entirely within the atmosphere of Roman Catholicism, with a strong Manichaean stamp and exquisite sensitivity to the power of Hells—those in this earthly (or urban) vale, and those beyond death. He contributed to the mythological images of the great city no less than did Balzac. In this respect, T. S. Eliot in *The Waste Land* and James Joyce in *Ulysses* are his heirs.

Faithful in his versification to the principles of French meter, Aleksander Wat once showed me one of Baudelaire's poems and a sonnet from the sixteenth century, without telling me who were the authors or from what era. It was difficult to guess. That lengthy tradition of versification explains the revolt of the avant-garde in France, which was determined in the first instance by a desire to be liberated from the tyranny of the alexandrine. That, at least, is how St. John Perse explained it to me in conversation, commenting vituperatively on the imitators of modernity in other languages who are totally unaware of what motivated the French.

Baudelaire translates poorly into Polish. Why? If someone were to write an article about this, it would have to begin with a word by word comparison between the Polish versions and the originals, and then reach a conclusion about the unequal development of the two languages. In 1936 I worked for a long time on Baudelaire's poem "The Balcony." I consider it one of my most successful translations.

The acuity of his essays on painting, including "Salon 1846" and others, has not diminished. The most important of them, in my opinion, is *Constantin Güys: Le Peintre de la vie moderne.* That "painter of modern life" was actually a reporter who used a sketchbook and pencil instead of a camera. My reading of this treatise, which is usually published as a separate little book, was of critical importance to me in Warsaw. When? Just before the war. That is when I came to understand civilization as artificiality, as make-believe and theater, with woman as the painted, mysterious priestess of eroticism. I liked the book so much that I translated it into Polish. But the manuscript was lost in the ruins of my Warsaw apartment. Later, the text was translated by Joanna Guze.

BEAUVOIR, Simone de. I never met her, but my antipathy for her has not lessened even now, after her death, when she is rapidly slipping away into the land of small-print footnotes to the history of her epoch. Let us say that my feeling of antipathy was inevitable in a man from a provincial backwater in response to a lady from the grand monde, and that it was heightened by anger at my timidity in the face of refined civilization. Locked up in her cocoon of Frenchness, she could not even imagine how someone from outside that cocoon might judge her. Of the three classmates named Simone in the École Normale Supérieure—she, Simone Weil, Simone Petrément—this Simone, she was convinced, was the most liberated, the one who best represented the "discreet charm of the bourgeoisie" French style. I could not forgive her and Sartre their baseness in their joint attack on Camus. A situation from a morality tale: an honorable, noble, truth-speaking man and a great writer, spat upon by a couple of so-called intellectuals in the name of political correctness. What doctrinaire blindness, to the point that she had to write an entire novel about it, *Les Mandarins*, in her effort to slander Camus, linking his opinions with gossip about his private life.

Her voice is the most audible voice of feminists, which reflects badly on them. I respect and even idolize those women who defend women out of empathy with their fate. In Beauvoir, everything was adoption of the next intellectual fashion. A nasty hag.

BEND. Enormous pine trees, an azure sky, pure water flowing down from the mountains, somewhere high above the snows of the Cascade Range—this always comes to mind when I think about that little town in the Oregon forest, more accurately, on the edge of a forest which stretches all the way to the ocean, while to the east begins an enormous dry expanse, in places downright desert-like.

Bend is always on the road north to Washington State and the Canadian Rockies. Also to closer destinations, like the Indian reservation near Warm Springs. There are really hot springs there. The white man, as always, left the Indians a barren expanse of low hills, where only mesquite bushes grow. It turned out, however, that a doctor from a nearby hamlet counseled the Indians on how to profit from the hot springs on their land. They built a hotel, put in swimming pools, planted trees; lo, a beautiful oasis in the middle of a desert, with paid employment for the whole tribe.

Bend and the Indian center, Kah-Nee-Ta, also bring to my mind thoughts of happy moments, which we do not treasure enough because some worry or other is always lurking in the background. Then, later, we finger the strung beads of the good and bad moments we have lived through in our lives, trying to tell the one from the other.

BERKELEY. When I was in San Francisco in 1948 I did not know that on the other side of the Bay was the city which was fated to be my longest place of residence, so that even the Wilno of my high school and university years cannot compete with it. I was enchanted with the journey to San Francisco, but it was like going to another planet, not to a place where one might live. Despite that visit, I pictured Berkeley in a false light when in 1960 I accepted an invitation to assume the post of lecturer. I thought it was situated on the Bay. Nothing of the sort: concrete on top of landfills, land reclaimed from the sea, empty wetlands, beside them industrial and warehouse districts, then the black ghetto, and only then, higher up, the city of white people. I thought there would be beaches and swimming. Ha! Not a grain of sand, and the water too dirty and too cold, because a cold current flows past these Pacific coasts. The view of the Bay, the islands, and the skyscraper city seen from the Berkeley hills is spectacular, but lunar. Like the quintessence of American spaces and the alienation of man. I came here to endure, but not to like it. I had received two offers at the same time—from Berkeley and from Indiana University in Bloomington. Had I chosen Indiana, perhaps I would have found it easier to feel at one with nature there. Nonetheless, whether I wanted this to happen or not, the landscapes of California have merged with the landscapes of Lithuania.

BIOGRAPHIES. Obviously, all biographies are false, not excluding my own, which the reader may be inclined to posit from this ABC book. They are false because their individual chapters are linked according to a predetermined scheme, whereas in fact they were connected differently, only no one knows how. In fact, the same falseness affects autobiographies because whoever writes about his own life would have to share God's viewpoint to understand those interconnections.

Biographies are like seashells; not much can be learned from them about the mollusk that once lived inside them. Even in connection with my biography based on my literary work, I feel as if I have left an empty shell behind.

The value of biographies, then, is solely that they allow one to more or less re-create the era in which a given life was lived.

BIOLOGY. The most demonic of the sciences, because it undermines our faith in the higher calling of man. The Manichaeans, who believed that the world was created by an evil demiurge, ought to have invented this science, but it developed much later. It is concerned with life, as its name indicates, and therefore, in the first place, with the feeding of organisms, each of which uses another as its food. Nature is composed of eaters and the eaten, *natura devorans* and *natura devorata*. The basic assumption is conflict, and the survival of the strong, the extinction of the weak. The most diabolical aspect of biological discoveries is not that on the basis of scientific data even philosophy can only arrive at pessimistic conclusions. The most diabolical aspect is this placing of might on a pedestal.

The survival of the fittest is called natural selection and is supposed to explain the appearance and extinction of species. In this way, the abyss of time is revealed—the past of the earth, delineated in the Bible as almost six thousand years, extends back into time for the millions and millions of years that living organisms have existed. They are born and die without the consciousness which is our glory. But our species is also enmeshed in the evolutionary chain, and human consciousness differs by only a degree from the intelligence of the mammals which are our closest relatives.

The religious dimension was not unknown to Darwin, who studied theology at Oxford in his youth. When he published *On the Origin of Species* in 1859, he announced with regret that his work proclaimed the devil's theology. This can mean only one thing: that he had succumbed to his own observations, and they pointed to a structure of life that was no less repellent to him than to the churches which fought against his theories.

It was he who destroyed the barrier between man and beast. Man, blessed with an immortal soul, had always dominated every living creature. The Creator says in Genesis, "Let us make man in our image, after our likeness: and let him have dominion over the fish of the sea, and over the fowl of the air, and over the cattle, and over all the earth, and over every creeping thing that creepeth upon the earth." This regal privilege was placed in doubt at the moment the boundary between us and other species of living beings was torn down, the moment when, in the course of evolution, consciousness emerged from unconsciousness, became indefinable. From then on, to believe in an immortal soul became, as it were, an act of usurpation.

No other science reaches as deep into our perception of the world as does biology. It achieved complete power, however, only in the twentieth century, albeit through popular simplifications and vulgarizations. According to Jerzy Nowosielski, whose (Orthodox) thinking is not hampered by habits of mind more common to Catholics, in this century the Germans, a nation of philosophers, took upon themselves quite a task: to prove in practice that our image of the human being as an animal subject to relationships of force must have consequences. They did this by building Auschwitz.

BLASPHEMY. It is the public desecration of what is generally regarded as sacred. It ought to be called *sacrilegium*, but Polish does not have a word like "sacrilege"; it has only *bluźnierstwo*. *Świętokradztwo*, a possible synonym, is too closely connected with theft etymologically, and after all, one can desecrate holy objects without stealing church utensils.

Using the worst profanity against God has earned the public's approval and some people even consider this a new way to show respect. I, however, have had to deal with another sort of profanity, and have had occasion to blaspheme in the political sense.

In the twentieth century masses of people have shown their susceptibility to slogans which did not seem to them to be propaganda, but obvious truths, and only a madman would cast doubt on these. A German who questioned the providential role of the Führer must have been a madman. Not just the authorities, apparently, but the voice of public opinion, put a Russian dissident into an insane asylum.

In Poland I experienced the strength of collective convictions, all the more firmly grounded because they were not the subject of discussion, just as we do not discuss the air that we breathe. The Polish People's Republic managed to create a particular blend of certitudes appropriate to local conditions. In the first rank was the thesis about the geopolitically determined permanence of the existing state of affairs. It followed from this that the true center of power is and always will be in Moscow. A powerful dose of patriotism was added: industrialization, protection from German forays in the west, the state as the promoter of national culture. The privileged company of writers and artists, to which I belonged, nurtured its own variant of this ideology, priding itself on regaining freedoms and using them for the good of the nation.

Daily participation in the community, a certain collective warmth, helped to keep up one's proclaimed faith. Living abroad, I was able to observe these customs from the outside and discovered something different in them from what they saw from their position in the crucible. Even so, when I broke with Warsaw and wrote *The Captive Mind*, I had a strong feeling that I was committing an indecent act, that I was breaking the rules of the game as they were accepted by everyone, and even more, that I was trampling on something sacred, and blaspheming. My Warsaw colleagues' pens that were aimed at me expressed not only their fear, as in the case of Słonimski and Iwaszkiewicz, but also, in some instances, their authors' sincere indignation.

"I swear by my mother and Warsaw, that it still causes me pain," wrote Gałczyński in his "Poem for a Traitor," and Kazimierz Brandys, in his story "Before He Is Forgotten," created a morally flawed character, because only such a person could have broken with "the camp of progress."

Because all of intellectual Paris believed in the imminent victory of the so-called socialist system and the genius of Stalin, the voice of such a loner as I could only be the voice of a man working against his own good, and no one in his right mind would do that. Alas, I had no sense of moral superiority to defend myself with, since a blasphemer does not enjoy his exclusion from the community.

Later in Berkeley I became sufficiently acquainted with the herd thinking of leftists and its fruit in the form of political correctness. But in Warsaw, too, in 1990, to say that Russian Communism was just as criminal a system as Nazism caused such a furious response that one had to suspect entire layers of unconscious attachment to the idol.

BOCCA DI MAGRA. Literally, the mouth of the Magra River. South of Carrara. Summer; 1955, I believe. Nicola Chiaromonte and I are sitting on the terrace of the only restaurant in that town, drinking wine and talking about the theater. Mary McCarthy arrives with Jorge Semprun, the Spanish writer, living as an émigré in France. My son Tony is running around with Semprun's sons. Miriam, Nicola's wife, is there, too, and also an English girl whose name I don't remember, and my wife, Janka. From time to time, this whole company clambers aboard a motorboat in the fishing port and sails to a small bay which is inaccessible by land, ringed as it is by white marble cliffs. The smooth, greenish, transparent water, with the reflected whiteness of the cliffs shining up from the depths, and the sheer pleasure of swimming, lying about on the marble slabs, and going for a swim again. My reflection on this now: during my stay there, I had a feeling that time should always be like those moments of happiness in the marble inlet, but at the same time I experienced sorrow that that is not how it is, because my familiar pangs of conscience gnaw at me from inside. Without a doubt, were I a novelist, all those personalities, including me, would have supplied me with interesting material to write about. But enough of that. Peace be with them. And with me.

BOGOMILS. A Manichaean sect in medieval Bulgaria, situated there because when the heretical religion of the prophet Mani began to spread throughout Byzantium's eastern Asiatic provinces, the empire had attempted to rid itself of Mani's followers by exiling them to the northern borderlands. There, the monasteries became the Bogomils' refuge. The tendency of Russian sects to represent the world of matter as the domain of the devil, if not as directly created by the devil, may have been part of their Bulgarian heritage, as is the Church Slavic language. The Bogomils also migrated westward from Bulgaria, creating centers in Bosnia, traveling up the Adriatic coast to northern Italy and from there to Provence, where they emerged as the religion of Cathars or Albigensians. I exploited their wanderings as a pretext for giving a course on Manichaeism under the aegis of the Department of Slavic Languages and Literatures at Berkeley—as if claiming a Slavic pedigree for it. Of course, historians have been interested in the Cathars because the Inquisition, which was so important in the history of the Church, was established to fight them first of all, and the condemnation of the Cathars was not an insignificant contribution to the creation of hell on earth by human beings.

Simone Weil turned the twentieth century's attention to the Albigensians and to Manichaeans in general as a religious problem. Not in order to make it possible for the Manichaean faith to be resurrected, but because their refusal to accept the Jehovah of the Old Testament as anything other than a minor demiurge who was responsible for the evil world finds a response among many people today. The blurring of the boundary between animals and man as a result of the theory of evolution has contributed to this response through increased sensitivity to the suffering of all living creatures, not only of man. God, who created this world, is responsible for universal pain. The myth of the Fall—that is, of good Creation defiled by Adam's sin—has been rejected. On the contrary, it is argued, man is driven by the same instincts as animals are, and is subject to the same law of the struggle for existence.

Simone Weil remains a controversial figure. Condemned by Jews for her presumed anti-Semitism (the Catharian rejection of the Old Testament), an adherent of strict determinism in nature (and in man), she considered Christianity to be otherworldly and interpreted the words of the prayer, "Thy kingdom come," as a plea for the end of the world.

For Cathars, the created world is irremediably evil and even procreation is evil, because it prolongs the world's existence. Despite all her longing for nonexistence, Simone Weil admired the created world for its beauty (including its mathematical beauty) and her reason forced her to admit the contradiction between praise of existence and rebellion, a contradiction which the Cathars managed to ignore.

BOŁBOT, Jan. In the lower grades we were divided into a crowd of little kids and a few older athletes who had been held back in their studies, because it was right after the war. One of them was Jan Bołbot. It was clear that he didn't get anywhere with his studies, because I didn't notice him in the higher grades. Many years later I read somewhere about the armed resistance to the Soviet invasion of 1939 by units of the Border Defense Corps and about the heroic lieutenant who gave his life there, Jan Bołbot.

BOREJSZA, Jerzy. A picturesque surname, but an assumed one. He also styled himself in life as a provincial squire's son, but that was only a mask. He was the most international of the Polish Communists. Perhaps he modeled himself to a degree on Willi Münzenberg, who built a press empire in Weimar Germany and then, after his escape from Hitler's Germany, a center for Communist propaganda in Paris. Starting from nothing in 1945, Borejsza, assisted by a slender blonde, our Henryk Dembiński's widow (her sister was a nun), built his own publishing empire of books and the press. Czytelnik and other publishing houses, newspapers, weeklies—everything depended on him: positions, acceptance of books for publication, honoraria. I was in his stable; we all were. He invented the movement in defense of peace, if not by himself alone, then, I think, it at least began in his head. The 1948 Congress in Wrocław to which he managed to attract Picasso was his creation, and it was also the beginning of his fall, because the Russians were dissatisfied with something there. Right afterward came a mysterious auto accident. I have read about the fame and fall of Münzenberg, and so I cannot help putting these two careers together now. Münzenberg orchestrated the international anti-Fascist action during the war in Spain, but he incurred Stalin's anger and then refused to go to Moscow when summoned (to his certain death). From then on, he lived in constant danger in Paris, and his death during his escape to the south when the Germans were moving toward Paris had the appearance of an execution (he was found hanged in a forest). Perhaps it was not quite that dramatic in Borejsza's case, but considering his service to the state, the lengthy silence in the Party press after his death struck me as odd. He was an extraordinary individual who deserves to be written about.

BOROWIK, Anielka. The daughter of a wealthy Warsaw citizen, Aleksander Geppner, who could have gone abroad in 1939 but chose to remain out of his fundamental sense of solidarity, and then perished in the ghetto. Before the war, Anielka was a student at the Academy of Fine Arts. Her friendship with Janka, dating from that time, continued after the war, and the Borowiks' home in Manhattan was always our hospitable base. Anielka's husband, Lucjan, ran an import-export business and invested successfully in real estate. That middle-class Warsaw milieu (doctors, lawyers, merchants), transplanted to New York right before the war or during its first few months, quickly became assimilated. Liberal, tolerant, it maintained the best traditions of the prewar *Literary News*. It was the only Polish-speaking milieu that never applied the adjective "traitor" to me for my work in the Warsaw regime's embassy. I remain grateful to that circle and to the Borowiks. Thanks to Anielka, I made the acquaintance of Dr. Berlstein, a charming bookworm employed in the New York Public Library as curator of the Slavic collection. It was he who, one day when I was sitting in the library reading some journal or other, came over to me and asked me in a whisper if I knew the gentleman who was seated next to me. It was Kerensky, the prime minister of the first post-tsarist Russian government.

Dr. Berlstein, the Borowiks, the sociologist Aleksander Hertz,

Józef Wittlin, Aleksander Janta-Połczyński—these were, more or less, my New York during the period 1946–1950.

BOROWSKI, Edward. My contemporary and classmate from the "B" class (the "A" class studied French, while "B" studied German). He remains an important figure for me to this day, because he was so different from me and from the circles to which I belonged. From a wealthy gentry family, he remained loyal to his family's traditions and practiced the snobbery of good breeding as well as the snobbery of conservative and provocatively reactionary opinions. He was friendly with another classmate, Janek Meysztowicz, who was equally concerned about maintaining an élite outlook, and was the nephew, if I'm not mistaken (or the half-brother?) of Father Walerian Meysztowicz, who was first an uhlan, then a professor of theology and a Vatican diplomat, and was very well known in our city.

I ask myself why I, a scion of the gentry, did not feel comfortable in my own skin. That shame about my origins may simply have predetermined my various intellectual adventures. Where did those democratic and socialist tendencies come from? After all, I could have told myself: I am a young master to the manor born and I ought to have the appropriate political views. All the more so since the conservatism of the Wilno "bison" (the large landowners), particularly their patriarchal outlook (it was they, after all, who financed Stanisław Mackiewicz's daily, *The Word*) did not carry the connotation Pole = Catholic, as it did among the nationalists, so that it was not a matter of using religion to promote nationalist interests. Class interests, to be sure, as the guarantor of social harmony, and not without a certain Voltairean flavor.

I try to imagine myself in the role of a young conservative. My life would have followed a different course. Although, I have to admit, there was no room for someone like that in literary circles and I would have had to display enormous erudition and a gift for polemics to defend my position. True, Ksawery Pruszyński (who was married to Janek Meysztowicz's sister) declared himself a conservative. But he was certainly not an intellectual.

Apparently, that's the way it had to be, that I had to live with the consequences of my mistakes, obsessions, follies, and rages, but in exchange I saw things that they were never able to see.

BROCÉLIANDE, Forêt de la. I wanted to experience this forest and insisted upon this during Janka's and my lengthy vacation in Brittany in the late sixties. Our vacation was interrupted by a telegram from Artur Mandel in Berkeley about our son Tony's car accident. I managed to drive through the forest, but without any impressions that would fix the trip in my mind; that is, there were no places in which I could picture the nymph Vivian and her lover, the magician Merlin. In fact, it is not at all certain that the forest of Brocéliande was located in Brittany; there is more persuasive evidence that it was on the other side of the Channel. But Merlin, Vivian, King Arthur, and the Knights of the Round Table—everything, alas, that happened around 500 A.D.—suffer from a lack of written sources and the legend changes shape like clouds in the sky above Wilno. The name Brocéliande seems to be French, apparently from the Celtic *bro*, land, earth, and *llan*, sacred place—land of the sacred place.

BRONOWSKI, Wacław. In school, we often sat on the same bench. During our first year of studying law we rented a room together on Embankment Street, with a view of the power plant on the other bank of the Wilia River. Intellectually, we had absolutely nothing in common, and now I think that all those rooms that I shared with classmates who were essentially strangers to me bear witness to something, for example, to the ease of living together superficially while hiding one's truly private side. This should not be taken to mean that it becomes easy when real mutual understanding is required.

Wacław amused me with his pedantry and manias. We were both smokers. In those days one bought tobacco and cigarette paper and rolled one's cigarettes at home. The boxes of cigarette papers came in various colors and patterns. Wacław collected these boxes and derived pleasure from placing them in stacks. *Nota bene*, cigarette paper was a rather short-lived technology; it disappeared after the war. In those days, well-cured home-grown tobacco was sold in Warsaw, on the streets; usually, the goods were displayed on the sidewalk. One purchased the paper separately, and one could become quite adept at rolling those "bankrupts" (as they were called in Lithuania). As far as I can recall, the cigarettes that the Kronskis manufactured for sale did not use the kind of wrappers which were divided into a paper mouthpiece and smokable section.

Wacław's pedantry had something to do with his lack of youthfulness. A raw-boned, sharp-featured blond, he seemed to move ceremoniously and systematically, which made him look immediately older. He had a great sense of humor, however. An only child, the son of a woman estate owner. In fact, most of my schoolmates at Sigismund August Gymnasium were from similar backgrounds, which is the subject of my musings now about the dividing line between the gentry and the people in our region.

That I studied law instead of the humanities was not a wise choice. But the law agreed perfectly with Wacław and his cast of mind. He took pleasure in the logic of proof and the formulas of Roman law, which we had to memorize. Soon afterward, I lost track of him, but I believe that after he received his diploma he served an apprenticeship, but not as a defense attorney. In 1939 he must have already become an assistant prosecutor or a judge, which would have made him an ideal candidate for deportation. People from the Wilno area were deported mainly to the Gulag complex in Vorkuta. All I know is that he was deported and died in a camp, most likely there.

BUDDHISM. Today, I would probably endorse Oscar Milosz's advice to deepen our knowledge of our own Mediterranean tradition, as well as an admonition of Carl Jung, who remained skeptical about the possibility of the Western mind understanding the religions of the East. The presence of Buddhism now, in comparison with the beginning of the century, however, is much more impressive in the countries of the West, since it is already a faith that coexists with Christianity, Judaism, and Islam. My attraction to the teachings of the Buddha is obvious, since what has troubled me throughout my life—the suffering of living creatures—is at the center of the all-embracing empathy of Prince Siddhartha. Buddhism is charitable, bringing experience of the sacral to many people who are unable to reconcile themselves to the contradictions of the biblical religions, to a personal God. Buddhism, neither theistic nor atheistic, simply does not speak about the beginning of the world and a first cause, and therefore it need not wrestle with the question of how the Creator can be at one and the same time both good and evil.

In America I was not particularly interested in the Buddhism of immigrants from Japan, China, and Vietnam, which is part of their cultural heritage; they have their temples in all the large cities. On the other hand, I was acutely responsive to the presence of a purely American Buddhism, without temples, but with meditation centers. Not antagonistic to other faiths, it does not exclude belonging at the same time to Catholicism, Protestantism, or Judaism, and it bears ecumenical fruit in theological dialogue, particularly between Buddhists and Christians.

BULSIEWICZ, Tadeusz. Lucky Bulsiewicz, the most handsome member of Irena Byrska's Theater Studio in Wilno. Your beauty, very masculine, derived from the harmony of your muscular body. Not very tall, you gave the impression of equally distributed strength and dexterity. You suffered greatly when they deported you to the Gulag, but your strong organism helped you, and you survived. Later, the euphoria of the departure from the prison house across the Caspian Sea, the colorful bazaars of the Orient, uniforms and weapons, soldiers' tents. You knew how to value the taste of an adventure such as is granted to few, which one only reads about, but at one time you, after all, had learned by heart fragments from *Verses for the Polish Legions*. And then there you were in Italy, in the army, the legions, and in battles that were always victorious. And during one of them, on the slope of a mountain, in an offensive action, when the lungs suck in air deeply before a leap forward, and the heart beats in praise of youth, a bullet reached you. You have your plot on Monte Cassino, and you were spared the exile wanderings of your colleagues across Argentina and Canada.*

*After the 1997 publication in Poland of *Abecadło Miłosza*, the first volume of his *ABC's*, the author learned that the circumstances of Bulsiewicz's death were probably not what he had believed them to be for half a century (see the entry "Inaccuracy").

BYRSKI, Tadeusz and Irena. Magnificent. Wise, decent, noble. I idolized them; they were my closest friends, and I consider their friendship a great privilege. My radio period in Wilno is the Byrskis. We were driven out of there together. It is interesting that after experiencing culturally vibrant Wilno, Byrski thought of Warsaw, his native city, as a quiet provincial town.

During the war we used to visit them in Bielany. They were famous among their neighbors there for their five-year-old son Krzyś's adventure. He had been playing with the other children, playing at war, of course, and for a helmet was wearing an old chamber pot he had found in a junk heap. An "enemy" hit him on the head with a stick and drove the chamber pot down around his neck. They had to wrap his head in newspaper and transport the poor kid by tram. He would become Poland's ambassador to India and a professor of Indian studies in Warsaw.

For a couple of weeks when he had to disappear, Tadeusz lived with us on Independence Boulevard, but that was not a safe apartment because of the concierge who was always sniffing out whether anyone was helping Jews, and black-haired Tadeusz looked like a Jew.

Tadeusz visited us in France during one of his trips to the West. Then, after my Nobel Prize, in the summer of 1981, the two of us drove around Warsaw in a convertible.

[C]

CALAVERAS. What once seemed most authentic, spontaneous, natural, usually turns out to be an imitation of some cultural construct. Folk costumes that derive their patterns from hussar uniforms, paintings on glass that imitate church Baroque, so-called folk ballads whose derivation is literary, like the one sung in the Kiejdany district in my childhood, about a cemetery ghost who abducts his beloved at night on horseback.

It's the same with places, which may be just geographical, but sometimes an idea from the literary imagination attaches to them. Bigfoot, a kind of yeti, an ape-man with gigantic feet, whose footprints are said to be seen now and then on Mount Shasta in California and in the Trinity range, may have been born during the talk around Gold Rush campfires, but I suspect this legend is connected with the interests of journalists from the surrounding towns, which have nothing to offer tourists other than the thrill of a wild man's proximity.

Every year in May a frog-jumping contest takes place in Calaveras. No one would have heard of Calaveras County had Mark Twain not made it famous with his story "The Celebrated Jumping Frog of Calaveras County." The contest takes place in a field near the little town of Angels Camp, southeast of Sacramento, in the foothills of the Sierra Nevada. When Mark Twain wrote his story, there were only gold mining camps there; he turned an anecdote he had heard into a short story. Nowadays, there is a local festival which is not too widely known, although the newspapers do report on it when a frog breaks a record. There are a great many automobiles and parked light planes, because the frog raisers (mainly school-age boys) and fans come in even from the neighboring states of Arizona and Oregon. How can a frog be persuaded to jump? You have to frighten it by stamping your foot. I had not known that frogs are so gifted. A good competitor can jump nineteen feet; differences among the best of them are measured in inches. We brought Dr. Wikta Winnicka, Józef Wittlin's half-sister, to this competition, so it must have been in the mid-sixties. She had a grand time. Later, trips in our Volvo had to cease due to illness. We traveled throughout northern California, and also took more northerly trips, through Oregon, Washington state, to Canada, including camping in the Canadian Rockies.

Literature and place. For some inhabitants of Warsaw, Bolesław Prus's novel *The Doll* (1890) was so vividly realistic that during the interwar years a plaque was placed on one of the apartment buildings on Krakowskie Przedmieście: "Here lived the hero of *The Doll*, Stanisław Wokulski."

CAMUS, Albert. I followed what was done to him in Paris when he published his book, *L'Homme révolté*, or *The Rebel*. He wrote like a free man, but it turned out that that was not permitted, because the "anti-imperialist" (i.e., anti-American and pro-Soviet) line was obligatory. That ugly campaign in Sartre's *Les Temps modernes*, in which the chief attackers were Sartre and Francis Jeanson, joined immediately by Simone de Beauvoir, coincided with my break with Warsaw in 1951. That was when

Sartre wrote this about Camus: "If you like neither communism nor capitalism, then I see only one place for you—the Galápagos Islands."

Camus gave me the gift of his friendship and it was important to have such an ally in the Gallimard publishing firm where he worked. Camus liked the typescript of *The Issa Valley* in Jeanne Hersch's French translation. My novel reminded him, he told me, of Tolstoy's writings about his childhood.

My relations with Gallimard were not good. As a result of the Prix Littéraire Européen they published *The Seizure of Power* and immediately following that, *The Captive Mind*, but the latter book was never in the bookstores and there was no lack of reasons to suspect that the people in charge of book distribution were boycotting it for political reasons. They published *The Issa Valley* on Camus's recommendation, but according to their accounting department it did not sell at all—while at the same time someone brought me a copy of the fourth edition from Africa. After Camus's death I no longer had an advocate in the firm. In accordance with an option in my contract with them, I offered them the typescript of *Native Realm* in Sédir's translation, but then Dionys Mascolo, a Communist in charge of their foreign division, asked Jerzy Lisowski (a Polish Communist Party member who was then in Paris) to evaluate the manuscript in the hope that he would kill the book, just as in the nineteenth century the tsarist embassy was asked to evaluate political émigrés. Lisowski wrote a flattering review. They published the book. After that, I preferred to have nothing to do with Gallimard.

I remember one conversation with Camus. He asked me if, in my opinion, it was appropriate that he, an atheist, should send his children to first communion. This conversation took place shortly after my visit with Karl Jaspers in Basel, whom I had asked about raising my children as Catholics. Jaspers had responded that as a Protestant he was not favorably inclined toward Catholicism, but that children must be raised in their own faith, if only to give them access to the biblical tradition, and that later they could make their own choice. I responded to Camus's question in more or less the same vein.

CAPITALISM, The End of. Of course I believed in it. In the 1930s the world was becoming too absurd to bear without seeking an explanation. We had to convince ourselves that irrationality was somehow an exception, and that reason would prevail when the system changed. After all, millions of the unemployed in the most industrialized countries were standing in soup lines, dictators were roaring from their grandstands and seizing power, an arms race was the only means to give people jobs, to "prime the pump," there was no letup in warfare—in China, in Africa, and in Spain. The intellectuals in Western Europe were busy ridiculing democracy, and Poland, with its dusty roads through country fields, was vegetating on the brink of poverty. So, the system had to be responsible for all this; reason, uncontaminated by the surrounding stupidity, awaited its hour. Such was my mental state, and that is how, as a friend of reason, I treated the Polish nationalist ideology of the time.

CARMEL.

If you should look for this place after a handful of lifetimes;
Perhaps of my planted forest a few
May stand yet.

(Robinson Jeffers, "Tor House")

The trees didn't survive very well because land right beside the ocean is too expensive for his heirs to have resisted the temptation to sell lots for development, but the tower that he erected with his own hands is still standing and also the house, which he called Tor House. It is even the seat of the Tor House Foundation.

I was a defender of Jeffers's poetry, justifying with some difficulty what today goes by an abbreviated name: inhumanism. It is simply that Jeffers deliberately turned against modernism at a time when no one was even thinking of postmodernism. For his rejection of that compression of verse which begins in the symbolism of Mallarmé, and his decision to express his philosophical views by speaking directly, are nothing but postmodernism. It was a very big bet. Carmel makes me melancholy—because of those trees that he planted, and the transience of fame. After all, in the 1920s Jeffers was the greatest American poet and Dwight Macdonald, for one, placed him much higher than T. S. Eliot, while today, although he has his admirers who know his work well, he is like "an amateur woman"—an ugly woman, that is, who, in Marek Hłasko's clever formulation, is only for amateurs.

It is too soon for a final pronouncement on his work; it will still be weighed on the scales many times, although it will probably be difficult from the point of view of language to defend his long tragedies in verse. But even in the defeat of this man, who wrote against everything, there is nobility.

He had at least one faithful disciple: William Everson, who was for some time a lay Dominican brother in Oakland, writing under the pen name Brother Antoninus. I visited him in the monastery on Chabot Road and translated a couple of his poems into Polish. He is the author of several volumes of verse and a monograph on the philosophy of Jeffers, in which he probably pulls him too much to his side. Which means that two components of Jeffers's philosophy are eclipsed—his "scientific world view" and Nietzsche—while his pantheistic religiosity is pushed into the foreground.

CENTER and periphery. Did everything that informs our civilization—the Bible, Homer, Plato, Aristotle—arise in the centers of power? Not always. There were more powerful capitals than Jerusalem, and little Athens can hardly be compared with Egypt. True, Imperial Rome gave us Virgil, Horace, and Ovid; the French monarchy gave us classical tragedy and the English kingdom, Shakespeare. In China, masterpieces of poetry arose in the period named after the emperors of the Tang dynasty. But the peninsula of western Europe, divided into many states and statelets, should also be recognized as a center. Dante, Cervantes, the music of the Baroque, Dutch painting.

The wandering of the creative impulse from country to country is extremely mysterious, and for want of clear causes we are taught to say, "the *Zeitgeist.*" This matter gains in forcefulness when we test it on our own skin, because the division of Europe into the creative West and the imitative East (which replicates Western patterns) is a well-known fact. Architectural monuments in Poland repeat imported styles; indeed, they are usually the work of builders from Flanders, Germany, Italy. Church painting is generally of Italian derivation. A Parisian may well pose the question, Why should I look at a couple of Polish impressionists when I know the paintings that they imitated?

Let us complicate the matter somewhat. An Anglo-Irish traveler, describing Moscow in the year 1813, noted that educated

Russians used French for reading and writing, which was understandable, because no body of writings could develop in a barbarous language and a barbarous alphabet. The same traveler, riding through Nowogródek en route to Warsaw, asserted that that monotonous, ugly, inhospitable district would never give rise to geniuses like Sterne or Burke. (And yet he might have encountered the teenage Mickiewicz in the street.)

The Russian upper classes not only learned to write in their own language soon afterward, but created a great literature in it, beginning with imitations of French writers. To be sure, this instance supports those who connect intellectual activity with centers of power—Russian literature was born in Petersburg, the capital of the empire.

Creative ability has been explained in different ways—by landscape, race, an indescribable national spirit, social structure, etc., and on the whole, without success. In any event, the stereotype of the cultural center and the periphery is deeply codified in the minds of the inhabitants of Western Europe, and it is not morally neutral, nor innocent. Convinced of the cultural inferiority of the Slavs, the Germans murdered them en masse as "subhumans," while contempt for primitive cowboys is concealed in the anti-Americanism of the French. Yet today, it is hard to avoid making one's peace with the fact that the center of science and art has moved from Europe to America.

This is an area of lingering, and at the same time, disintegrating stereotypes. One point must be acknowledged: the youth and age of cultures, that is, their longer or shorter cultivation of language, for example. Since I work with language I am aware that stages of development cannot be skipped, and that wishing to participate in world literature, I am limited by what my predecessors introduced into Polish, even though I myself have been able to add to it a bit.

CHIAROMONTE, Nicola. This name has always been linked in my mind with thoughts about greatness. I have known many famous people, but have carefully distinguished between fame and greatness. Nicola was not famous, and his name meant a lot only within his circle of friends, because even his reportage and articles, scattered among various journals, were at most his enigmatic way of thinking. His thought, shaped by Greek thinkers, always remained in the public sphere and attempted to define the obligations of a humanist toward the *polis*. His life is an example of engagement with political movements that repeatedly devolved into ideological servitude in our chaotic twentieth century. Chiaromonte had a heightened sense of historicity and history, but he rejected all ideologies. An opponent of Italian Fascism, he emigrated from Italy. He participated in the war in Spain on the Republican side, as a pilot in Malraux's squadron, but he did not side with the Communists. During his American years, hailed as a master and teacher by the non-Communist left of Dwight Macdonald's and Mary McCarthy's group, he published in *The Partisan Review* and in *Politics*. After his return to France and, finally, in 1953, to Italy, he and Ignazio Silone edited the journal *Tempo Presente*, which meant shouldering the obligation of opposing public opinion, dominated as it was by the Communists and their sympathizers.

Ignazio Silone, who had been at one time a Communist and a delegate to the Comintern, elevated by the political "elevator" to the height of fame for his novel *Fontamara*, broke with Communism on moral grounds and in complete awareness of what that would mean: his name, absent in Fascist Italy, ceased to exist in the anti-Fascist press and later, after the fall of Fascism, while he and Chiaromonte edited *Tempo Presente*, it did not exist for a wider public. Nicola and Silone represented for me uncompromising rightness of motives. They were the greatest Italians I ever met.

CHURCHES. People go to church because they are divided beings. They wish, for a moment at least, to find themselves in a reality other than the one that surrounds them and claims to be the only true reality. This daily reality is unyielding, brutal, cruel, and hard to bear. The human "I" is soft in the center and feels every moment that its adaptation to the world is doubtful.

The Catholic religion teaches that the world which surrounds us is temporary and its laws were negated by the Son of God's act of submission to them. The Prince of This World triumphed, and as a result he lost. Participating in the Mass we once again deny a world without meaning and without mercy; we enter into a dimension where what matters are goodness, love, and forgiveness.

If to participate in the Mass it were necessary to have a strong faith and a consciousness that we act in life as our religion requires us to, all the churchgoing faithful would deserve to be called hypocrites and Pharisees. In truth, however, strong faith is a rare gift, and as for acts, the liturgy reminds us that we are all sinners. Attending church is not, therefore, for the elect.

The needs of the individual determine church attendance, and knowledge of the catechism or even familiarity with the so-called truths of the faith are not the most important matters, although they are advisable.

CITY. I have thought a great deal about the phenomenon of the city, but not at all about the silly slogan "*Miasto, masa,* *maszyna"* ("metropolis, masses, machine"—a slogan of the Polish avant-garde). I have had occasion to live in very large metropolises, in Paris and New York, but my first city was a provincial capital, barely different, but yet different, from a village, and it was that city which supplied the data for my imagination. I could imagine Wilno in its various stages, which I could hardly do elsewhere. Take, for example, Wilno of the Enlightenment or Romanticism. Those stinking piles of garbage, the sewage streaming down the center of the roadways, the dust or mud that one had to wade through. But the upper-class men and women (am I the last living person who heard the words "Your Honor" used in ordinary daily speech?) didn't move to town to live out their old age, but settled in the manor houses in Antokol (Antakalnis), because they felt at home there, and didn't have far to go to attend daily mass. The bells of forty churches pealed while the women who lived in the numerous brothels received officers and students—in other words, everything took place all together, the high and the low, not as in memoirs which beautify the past. Certainly, after the French soldiers encamped on Cathedral Square, that crowd of men dressed in the strangest clothing—in anything, just to get some protection from the frost, in copes and chasubles; after the epidemics, the field hospitals, the thousands of buried corpses, some sort of harmony returned, and the professors would go to the Romers' house on Bakszta Street, the seat of the Masonic lodge, and started publishing the *News of the Street*. In the immediate vicinity of the tower of St. John's the narrow lanes of the Jewish quarter had their own affairs: the great Gaon's struggle against the disrespect for the letter of the law evinced by the Hasidim, who had moved up from the south; preserving the memory of Walentyn Potocki, a righteous man, who had converted to Judaism in Amsterdam and was burned at the stake in Wilno; and also talk about Officer Gradé, who had been hidden in a pious Jewish household, about how he had already recovered from his wounds and decided to become a Jew, had himself circumcised, and intended to marry the daughter of the house. This was the man whose descendant would be a poet in the Yiddish language, Chaim Grade, a member of the Yung Vilne group, which was on friendly terms with our Żagary.

The city is alive for me, then—there's nothing to be done about it—simultaneously today, yesterday, and the day before yesterday. Also in the year 1655, and that is because of the discovery in the sub-basements of the Church of the Dominicans of a large number of skeletons dressed in *kontusze* (the outer robes worn by nobles in old Poland) and silk robes, evidence of a massacre by the Russian forces who occupied Wilno briefly at that time. As it also exists in the year 1992, when I found myself there after fifty-two years of absence, and wrote a poem about walking through a city of spirits.

Like the cities of Silesia, Wilno wavered during its history between two cultures. First it was a settlement of merchants from old Rus, perhaps from Novgorod, with a large number of wooden Orthodox churches, which have all vanished; most likely, they burned down. Wilna (with an "a") was its old name, derived from the small Wilna River, which in my youth was called the Wilenka. When Giedyminas transferred his capital here from Troki, the city, because the Grand Duchy's population was predominantly East Slavic and Orthodox, looked toward the East—especially since Old Belorussian was the language of official documents and the *Statuty litewskie* (Lithuanian Statutes) were written in it. But after Lithuania's rulers were baptized, the city grew more and more Roman Catholic and its churches were built first in the Gothic and then in the Baroque style. That indicated a Polish influence. The Polonization of Wilno and the surrounding area continued through the eighteenth century, and in the nineteenth it came into conflict with Russianization. The population of the villages on the outskirts of Wilno gradually changed from speaking Lithuanian to speaking Polish, but had Lithuania remained a Soviet republic, most likely they would have adopted Russian. I ought not conceal my fear of the East, which in my mind has the shape of a bottomless crater or a boggy maelstrom. In this regard, I am probably a typical specimen of a Pole from that region. Tsarist historians worked feverishly to publish documents demonstrating the Eastern Slavic nature, if not the absolute Russianness, of the city, but the rebirth of Lithuanian sentiment and Lithuanian nationalism spoiled their plans. Similarly, the local dialect, referred to as "simple talk," succumbs, like Belorussian and Polish, to Russification, because they are all Slavic languages; Lithuanian, as a non-Slavic language, can put up a successful resistance.

CONGRÈS pour la Liberté de la Culture. I could write an entire book about it, but I have no desire to. After all, there are already books about the "liberal conspiracy," as it was called. An important episode in the Cold War. The thing is, New York was very Marxist before the war and the Trotskyists and Stalinists there were eating each other alive. With the outbreak of the war, the American intelligence agency (the Office of Strategic Services, or OSS) hired a large number of New York leftists of the so-called NCL, or non-Communist left. They understood the importance of ideology, especially in Europe. Immediately after the war no one else was concerned about Communism's subjugation of European minds. Then the employees of the OSS found themselves in the CIA, the new name of the institution, and had the means to act. But the initiative for organizing a convention of anti-Communists in West Berlin in 1950 came from Arthur Koestler, who had been a Communist functionary in the 1930s in the famous Willi Münzenberg stable. Koestler had worked for Münzenberg's center. In Paris now, after breaking with the Party, he floated the idea of creating a similar center of liberal ideology. Melvin Lasky and other New Yorkers supported him. After the convention in Berlin it was decided that Paris should be the center's headquarters and a French name was chosen. Thus, "le Congrès" was the work of minds which had passed through Marxism, revisionism, Trotskyism; only such minds, it turned out, understood the danger of the Stalinist system because they were the only ones in the West who had the desire to follow what was going on there. In short, it was mainly Jewish intellectuals from New York who founded the Congress. Józef Czapski and Jerzy Giedroyc participated in the founding convention in Berlin, which explains my early familiarity with the Congress.

No one then knew who was financing the Congress. People talked about some big businessmen and they actually did attend, but then in 1966, when the truth came out about the CIA, it turned out that these firms were acting as fronts. The way the Congress was administered in Paris, however, was such that you could smell big money from a mile away, and the French, who in any case were stewing in their anti-Americanism, boycotted it totally.

Today, looking back with hindsight, I have to say that the "liberal conspiracy" was necessary and justified. It was the sole counterweight to the propaganda on which the Soviets expended astronomical sums. The Congress published high-quality journals in the major European languages: *Preuves* in Paris, under the editorial direction of the Swiss, François Bondy; *Encounter* in London and *Quadrant* in Australia; *Tempo Presente* under the editorship of Ignazio Silone and Nicola Chiaromonte in Rome; *Der Monat* in German; *Quadernos* in Spanish. They wanted to draw *Kultura* into this net, but Giedroyc refused, although this would have relieved him of financial worries.

I was too besieged, pained, and suspicious, and above all, too poor, to feel good in that company. Poverty sees right through the fatty tissue in which the rich encase themselves, and in those days Americans with good salaries were rich men in Paris. Perhaps today I can be more fair toward Michael Josselson, on whom everything depended. I didn't like his self-assurance and his cigars. Those people were oblivious to their own mistakes. One such mistake was setting up their posh offices in the most expensive district of Paris, on Avenue Montaigne. To further clarify my only casual relations with the Congress, I should add that I was an individual who had been denied an American visa. The Congress was not responsible for that, but nonetheless . . .

There are no grounds for assuming that Josselson did not possess strong convictions; on the contrary, he devoted his life to his work as the Congress's chief administrator. He was no primitive. Born in Tallinn, the son of a Russian-speaking timber merchant, after World War I he and his family found themselves in Germany, which was a great center of the Russian emigration, and he attended university there. Then he was a successful businessman in Paris for several years, after which he emigrated to America, became a citizen, and served in the army during the war. He spoke four languages fluently; I believe he also knew Polish, but did not admit that he did. As I found out later, he suffered greatly at having to pretend that he was someone other than whom he was. Scholars and writers from Europe and America passed through the Congress, unaware of who was financing them, and Josselson was not allowed to reveal anything. To satisfy his own interests, he was working on a historical book about the Russian leader Bagration during the war with Napoleon, which points to Russia as the focus of his interest, and also to his identification with an unfairly disgraced hero. He also suffered from a heart ailment. After he left the Congress, he settled in Geneva, where he died.

CONNECTICUT RIVER VALLEY. My first enchantment probably occurred in 1947, when I came to Smith College in Northampton to give a lecture. My professor from Wilno, Manfred Kridl, was on the faculty there for a while. The surrounding countryside was populated by Poles, who had arrived after the Irish started leaving for the big cities. The second time I was there was when my friend Jane Zielonko taught at the college. Then, years later, I taught at Mount Holyoke for one semester while living in Joseph Brodsky's home. And each time, the splendor of autumn, the indescribable multicolored foliage— which is why that valley remains a paradise for me, with its invigorating cold and various hues of gold. And also transitoriness. Kridl, Jane, Joseph—all are in the realm of shadows. And very soon Tola Bogucka, the girl with whom I once fell in love in Krasnogruda, and then met in Northampton as a psychiatrist, will be among those shades.

CRUELTY. It is possible that a tendency to macabre jokes, to black humor, is characteristic of the culture of the Polish intelligentsia in this century, which would be explained by the accidents of history in a given part of Europe. Before the last war, the humor in such magazines as *Szpilki* (Pins) or the cabarets was quite cruel, and the poets Janusz Minkiewicz and Światopełk Karpiński stood out in this regard. The war years, with their daily familiarity with roundups and executions, the cheapness of human life, intensified this tendency. Quite likely, various anecdotes when related to a foreigner as comic meet with a lack of understanding or a kind of distaste. True, we should also take note of significant inroads of sadism in Western literature and film, which is not unconnected to market-driven shock value. Shortly before the war, one of Sacha Guitry's films opened with a funeral procession: a dozen or so coffins are being carried, and behind them walks one lone boy, the only survivor of his family. They had all eaten poisonous mushrooms for supper, except the boy, who was denied supper as a punishment, because he had misbehaved. However, when the Yugoslav director Makavejev introduced real photographs of corpses from Katyń into his surrealistically comic film, he went too far.

When the audience at one of the first performances of *Waiting for Godot* in Paris burst out laughing while watching Pozzo torment Lucky, his slave, the philosopher Lucien Goldmann, with whom I was sitting, was offended: "What are they laughing at? The concentration camps?"

Where is the boundary between intensification of description dictated by empathy, and intensification which is, as it were, revenge against the world for its cruelty? And is not that revenge at the heart of the Marquis de Sade's novels? I personally suspect that I have been infected to a significant degree by the frivolous Polish sense of the macabre, and I consider this a disease for which I should seek a cure.

In the student and literary milieu of Wilno there was a well-known young giant, very handsome, from a wealthy family who were landowners somewhere up north, from the Bracław region. He even published a beautifully printed play at his own expense. It so happened that soon after the Soviet army entered Wilno, after the end of neutral Lithuania, the three of us—he, his beautiful wife, and I—were sitting together and deliberating: to go or not to go. To go was a great risk. Not to go—the fate of becoming a Soviet citizen. I decided to cross the border, although I would not have done so had Janka not been in Warsaw, because I would have been afraid. They stayed.

Janusz Minkiewicz, who was surviving in Wilno at the time by performing his "Xantippe" cabaret, constructed a macabre story out of the couple's experiences after his own return to Warsaw under German occupation, and read it, laughing, at underground literary evenings. No one who has not experienced it really knows about the great fear under Soviet rule, so perhaps Leszek B.'s decision to save himself from deportation by lecturing on Marxism-Leninism at courses for workers only seemed comical, considering that he didn't have the foggiest notion of what Marxism was. He appears in Józef Mackiewicz's novel, *The Road to Nowhere*, as an example of the way people adapted at that time. Janusz Minkiewicz takes the story farther. The Germans arrive. Leszek claims to be Belorussian (no one knows if this is true) and is given an estate, after which he parades around with a whip and threatens the peasants: "I'll show you Communism!" (again, no one knows if this is true). He was shot through the window while he was eating his supper. Who shot him? From the story it appears it was peasants, but a powerful Soviet partisan group was operating in that area and one might, instead, suspect Leszek B.'s collaboration with the Belorussian administration, against which the partisans were conducting a war.

Sympathy for people who are caught, without regard to their wishes, by systems which are alien to them, and who tried to save themselves by whatever means they could, ought not to tolerate making use of their truths for humor. I regret that I have already repeated Minkiewicz's story somewhere, and I write this now to make amends.

CURIOSITY. As a child, everyone has tried catching sunbeams in a mirror, although perhaps not everyone has thought deeply about the facts. A sunbeam can move in a defined field; when it travels outside that field, it disappears. An observation like that appears to bear witness to the young scientist's mental inclination toward deductive reasoning, but not necessarily. He is simply amazed that the world is ordered in that way. Truly, wherever one turns, there are similar surprises everywhere, and the world appears to be a collection of a limitless quantity of details to be taken notice of.

The world is so organized that it is endlessly interesting; there is no limit to the discovery of ever newer layers and strata. It is like a journey through a maze which is pulsating, changing, growing as one moves through it. We make this journey by ourselves, but also as participants in the common undertaking of all humanity, with its myths, religions, philosophies, art, and the perfection of science. The curiosity which drives us cannot be sated and since it does not lessen with the passage of time, that is a sufficient argument against dying. Although, to be sure, many of us enter the gates of death immensely curious, expectant, eager to learn what it is like on the other side.

The opposite of curiosity is boredom, but all opinions leading to the conclusion that nothing remains to be known, because there is nothing new under the sun, are false, dictated by bore-dom, or sickness.

Can you assure me, sir, that when we grow older, ever newer sights open up before us, as if around each bend in the road on a journey? I can. It seems as if everything is the same, yet differ-ent. Without a doubt, we do grow old; that is to say, our senses desert us, our hearing grows duller, our eyesight weakens. Yet our mind finds ways to balance these losses with an acuity that is inaccessible in our younger years. All the more so, then, does de-feated old age deserve our sympathy, when the mind, following the senses, sinks into sleep.

I respect and feel sympathy for those thinkers and poets whose hunger for knowledge reaches beyond the borders of death. Swedenborg's heaven rests upon unceasing acquisition of knowledge and its transformation into "uses" (*usus*), for how else could the diligent assessor of the Royal Mining Commission imagine it? The seventy-year-old William Blake died singing hymns, believing intensely—not only believing, but knowing—that he would be transported into the land of eternal intellectual hunts and no more wasted energy or imagination.

Curiosity must be a powerful passion if so many people for thousands of years have tried to discover, touch, name, under-stand an elusive reality of "n" dimensions. How wise was the person who said that we are like flat, two-dimensional figures on a sheet of paper, to whom it would be difficult to explain that something exists one centimeter above that paper in a third di-mension, not to mention other dimensions.

DĄBROWSKA, Maria. During the war we saw each other frequently, either at her place on Polna Street or at Zygmunt and Futa Poniatowski's apartment at No. 16 Kielecka Street, where our discussion groups met. (*Nota bene*, it was at the Poniatowskis' that we spent the first two weeks of the Warsaw Uprising, which caught us by surprise near their home, and we crossed the fields on foot with them to Okęcie.) I am guilty of a terrible gaffe vis-à-vis Dąbrowska, and although her comments about me are cold, I got off lightly, considering the enormity of my crime: although I treated Maria Dąbrowska with appropriate respect, it never entered my mind that one might look at her as a woman. That vaguely cross-eyed little dwarf, with her mane cut pageboy style, was the last creature on whom I could focus my erotic passions. I knew nothing about what would eventually become general knowledge among the readers of her diaries, that is, about her erotic side, so to speak. She notes in her diary that her companion, Stanisław Stempowski, did not like me, but I don't really believe that, because he was friendly toward me and sent a letter through me to a prominent Mason in Washington.

Later, Dąbrowska apparently was offended by me because I compared her in one of my writings to the nineteenth-century novelist, Eliza Orzeszkowa. That was actually a compliment, but she considered herself a much greater writer—something that I was not then, and still am not, convinced of.

D'ASTRÉE, Anka. Her surname was Rawicz, her husband's name; I no longer recall her maiden name. Her family was from the little town of Druja, Miłosz family property, once Sapieha's, so we had something to talk about. I had no other close ties with her, other than that she used to attend the evening lectures at the Pallotini Fathers' on rue Surcouf. Her Polish was excellent; she had graduated, after all, from a Polish *gymnasium*. I marveled at her industriousness. Under the assumed name D'Astrée she ran her own film production company in Paris, producing mainly advertisements, and managed it very well. An impeccable hairdo, *maquillage*, clothes—a businesswoman's armor in the daily battle for money. And all this in order to mask her personal dramas. Her marriage to Piotr Rawicz showed every sign of profound love and understanding. They were connected by their studies at the Sorbonne, their common interests, and their common past as a couple of Polish Jews who survived. Piotr Rawicz came from a wealthy family in Galicia, from Lwów, if I am not mistaken; he acquired his high culture and a knowledge of languages in his parents' home. He had gone through the German concentration camps and was still haunted by that experience, which is the source of his novel *Le sang du ciel*, published by Gallimard (in English, *Blood from the Sky*). Recognized in Paris, he wrote for *Le Monde*. He was friends with Kot Jeleński. His marriage to Anka was made up of a series of unbelievable scenes, separations, and reconciliations. In the end, they separated.

During one of my stays in Paris, most likely in the seventies,

Anka invited me to her newly purchased apartment in a very wealthy neighborhood on the upper reaches of Boulevard Saint-Michel. The apartment was truly lovely and beautifully appointed, with sculptures and new furniture. Why must one furnish such an apartment only to die immediately afterward? The bond between her and Piotr must have been very strong, and when he shot himself shortly after her death, it was impossible not to think about that. And also that no one comes out of the Shoah without psychological wounds. The story of this couple would make a moving film script, which no one will write.

DEMBIŃSKA, Zofia. Yes, she was a fanatic. If she had not had absolute faith in the cause, however, she could not have slaved away as she did, working with Jerzy Borejsza to organize the Czytelnik publishing house and an entire publishing empire. Her sister also had a powerful belief, but the other one, Catholicism; she was a nun.

The so-called Wilno group had a great deal of influence in Poland during the early postwar years. Various important Party personalities emerged from it. Let me name them: Stefan Jędrychowski, Jerzy Sztachelski, his wife, Dziewicka-Sztachelska, Muta Dziewicka, Jerzy Putrament, Druto or Drutas, a Lithuanian who became Poland's ambassador to France, and his wife Guga Sawicka, Kazimierz Petrusewicz, and finally Zofia Westwalewicz, whose married name was Dembińska. There was no stronger individual among them than Henryk Dembiński, who was killed by the Germans in Hancewicze in Polesie, where the Soviet authorities had sent him to assume the position of principal of a Belorussian *gymnasium*. Since the Wilno group supported its own and displayed a great deal of solidarity, the various non-Party members from Wilno gathered around her, for example, Władysław Ryńca, and the Żagary poets Czesław Miłosz, Jerzy Zagórski, and Aleksander Rymkiewicz—in a word, all of Rabbit's friends and relations.

Historians will no doubt study the Wilno group some day. There were very few non-Jews among the leading Communists in those days, and one of the distinguishing characteristics of this group was that its members came from the gentry or from middle-class Christian families. Often, they were very Catholic, as in Zofia's case; after all, her deceased husband had left the Catholic organization Rebirth, and they had traveled almost the same path to Marxism. So, the group's characteristic feature was the tension between religion, which they took from their homes, and revolution. This was somewhat similar to the experience of Jewish Marxists, except that in their case the argument was with Judaism, and often with Zionism, too.

Dembiński had something of the fiery social reformer in him, a revolutionary from a bygone era, the 1848 Spring of Peoples. In the years immediately preceding the outbreak of the war he was enthusiastic about Schiller and used a great deal of Romantic rhetoric in conversation. He was absolutely correct in his complaints about the wrongs done to the people in a capitalist system, about Poland's drift toward fascism and the politicians' inability to see the security threat posed by Germany, but his "sublime fervor" disposed me to look upon him with skepticism.

In the ruins of Warsaw, Wiejska Street was like an island in a sea of rubble. Borejsza and Zofia sat there at Czytelnik. When Julian Tuwim returned from America, Borejsza gave him an apartment on the other side of the street, facing Czytelnik (I've seen some of Tuwim's letters, written to Borejsza in New York).

In her work, which probably occupied fourteen hours a day,

in the countless memoranda written by her, Zofia was like a character from a nineteenth-century novel, because, after all, there were no other models for the behavior of a female social reformer and strong woman in Poland. As one of the authors in Borejsza's and her stable, I feel called to remind people that we should not ascribe the beginnings of People's Poland to a purely political game. Communists like those two obviously aspired to control thought through the press and through publishing houses, but at the same time they were proud of the state's role as a patron of the arts. The long list of painstakingly edited classics of world literature, published with government funds, is a sufficient argument against the wholesale condemnation of Polish writers for "treason." After all, they translated and edited countless volumes by contemporary Western writers, with the result that people in Moscow and Leningrad learned Polish in order to read works that were banned in Russia. Zofia Dembińska played no small role in preparing the later publishing movement.

DISGUST. It was Józef Czapski who told me this story from the Russian Revolution. At a railroad station buffet a man, who was distinguished from his surroundings by his dress and manners and who obviously belonged to the prewar intelligentsia, was eating dinner. He drew the attention of several hooligans who were seated in the restaurant. They came over to his table and began mocking him, finally spitting in his soup. The man did not defend himself at all and did not attempt to drive off his attackers. This went on for a long time. Suddenly, he pulled a revolver from his pocket, placed the barrel in his mouth, and shot himself. Evidently, what he had encountered here was the last drop in a cup that was already full of the revulsion that the unleashing of ugliness had triggered in him. No doubt he was thin-skinned, raised in a gentle milieu which had protected him quite well from the brutalized reality which is accepted as normal by the lower classes. That brutality and vulgarity had reached the surface along with the revolution and became an attribute of Soviet life.

In 1939 the population of Wilno and Lwów suddenly discovered the grayness and ugliness of this life. I shall risk proposing the thesis that Stanisław Ignacy Witkiewicz committed suicide less out of terror and more from disgust at what he knew would happen, which he had already described in the concluding chapters of his novel *Farewell to Autumn*. George Orwell, who had not read Witkiewicz, after all, depicts daily life under the rule of the new order in just the same way in *1984*: the grayness, dirt, boredom, smells from cheap cafeterias. Calling this type of sensitivity "aesthetic" does not get us very far. It is better to ponder what it is that is unbearable in human existence and the convergence of these features under certain conditions. Which leads to the conclusion that it is necessary to protect man, even, if necessary, by wrapping him in a cocoon of illusions.

DOSTOEVSKY, Fyodor. I taught a class on Dostoevsky and have been asked many times why I have not written a book about him. I have always answered that an entire library in various languages has been written about him and that I am not a literary scholar; at most, I am a distant cousin to one. To tell the truth, however, there is another reason why.

It would have to be a book based on mistrust, and one cannot do without trust. That great writer had an influence like none of his contemporaries, with the exception of Nietzsche, on the thinking of Europe and America. Neither Balzac, nor Dickens, nor Flaubert, nor Stendhal are names as universally known now. He used a form of the novel such as no one had ever succeeded in using before (or after) him, although George Sand attempted it—to present a diagnosis of an immense phenomenon which he himself had experienced from the inside and had thoroughly comprehended: the erosion of religious belief. His diagnosis turned out to be correct. He foresaw the results of this erosion in the minds of the Russian intelligentsia. The Russian Revolution found its prediction in *The Possessed*, as Lunacharsky openly admitted, and in "The Legend of the Grand Inquisitor."

Undoubtedly a prophet. But also a dangerous teacher. Bakhtin, in his book on Dostoevsky's poetics, proposed the hypothesis that the polyphonic novel was that Russian writer's invention. Polyphony makes Dostoevsky such a modern writer: he hears voices, many voices, in the air, quarreling with each other, proclaiming contradictory ideas—are we not all in the present phase of civilization exposed to this raucous chaos of voices?

His polyphony has limits, however. Behind it is concealed the fervent man of faith, the Russian millennialist and messianist. It is difficult to think of anything less polyphonic than the scene with the Poles in *The Brothers Karamazov*, a crass satire which does not fit the seriousness of this work. The treatment of the character Ivan Karamazov produces a far stronger emotional effect than polyphony would allow.

Dostoevsky the ideologue has been distinguished from Dostoevsky the writer in order to protect his greatness, which is marred by unfortunate pronouncements, and Bakhtin's hypothesis has proved a great help in this effort. In point of fact, however, one can say that had there been no Russian messianist and his passionate concern for Russia, there would have been no international writer. It was not only his concern for Russia that gave him strength, but also his fears about Russia's future that forced him to write in order to issue a warning.

Was he a Christian? That is not clear. Perhaps he thought that he would become one, because he saw no salvation for Russia outside of Christianity? But the conclusion of *The Brothers Karamazov* allows us to doubt whether the destructive forces, which he observed, had found an effective counterweight in his mind. The pure youth Alyosha, at the head of his twelve schoolboys, like a Boy Scout troop, as a projection of Christian Russia capable of saving her from Revolution? That's just a bit too sweet and kitschy.

He fled from kitsch; he sought strong flavors. The sinners, rebels, deviants, madmen of world literature first inhabited his novels. It seems that descending into the depths of sin and shame is a condition in his works for salvation, but he also creates the damned, like Svidrigailov and Stavrogin. Although he is all his characters, one in particular was given the type of understanding that is closest to his own: Ivan Karamazov. That is why Lev Shestov suspects, justifiably so, in my opinion, that Ivan expresses Dostoevsky's ultimate inability to believe, despite his positive characters, the Elder Zosima and Alyosha. What is it that Ivan declares? He returns the Creator's "ticket" because of a single tear of a child and then relates the legend of the Grand Inquisitor, which he himself has composed, and whose meaning leads us to the conclusion that if it is impossible to make people happy under the sign of Christ, then one must try to bring them happiness by collaborating with the devil. Berdiayev wrote that Ivan is characterized by "false oversensitivity" and no doubt the same could be said of Dostoevsky.

He wrote in a letter to Mrs. Fonvizin that if he were ordered to choose between the truth and Christ, he would choose Christ. Those who would choose the truth are probably more honorable, even if the truth appears on the surface to deny Christ (as Simone Weil argued). At least they are not relying on their fantasy and not constructing idols in their own image.

There is something that would incline me to make a softer judgment: it is the fact that Lev Shestov found the inspiration for his tragic philosophy in Dostoevsky. Shestov is very important for me. It was thanks to my reading of him that Joseph Brodsky and I were able to understand each other intellectually.

DREMA, Vladas. Painters did more for Wilno than writers. Drema was my classmate at the university, a student in the Department of Fine Arts. That department had preserved virtually unchanged the traditions of the predecessor university from the early nineteenth century. Drema was a co-founder in 1937 of the "Wilno Group," whose members were Polish, Jewish, and Lithuanian painters. *Nota bene*, internationally acclaimed artists who were trained originally in Wilno include Chaim Soutine, the sculptors Antokolski and Lipschitz, and the somewhat less famous Ferdynand Ruszczyc, Ludomir Ślendziński, and Vytautas Kairukštis, but I am also moved by looking at reproductions of paintings and engravings by many other productive and often very fine artists.

Drema has remained in my memory more as a physical presence than a particular face. He was drawn to Communism for a while, like his friend Adamovičius, a Lithuanian poet who wrote under the pen name Kekštas, which explains Drema's relationship with *Żagary*, in which I believe he published a short note.

When I returned to Wilno in 1992 after fifty-two years' absence, I met not a single person who had once walked its streets.

They had been murdered or deported, or they had emigrated. But I found out that Drema was alive, and I decided to visit him. I was given an address in Literary Lane. But that was the very same gate inside which I once lived, only it was yawning wide open, for the ancient doors, with their heavy metal ornaments, had disappeared (were stolen?)! The stairs to the right? It was there, after all, that I rented a room in 1936 from an old lady who was ensconced in her apartment, crowded as it was with étagères and figurines. It turned out that later on Drema had lived in this very apartment for many years. Finally, I was given his new address.

He was lying in bed, paralyzed from the waist down, tenderly cared for by his wife, son, and daughter. It appears that his illness was not the only reason he was marginalized. He wasn't honored as he should have been for his service as a historian of the arts in Wilno, as the author of a book on the painter Kanut Rusiecki (of the artists' colony in Rome in the 1820s) and of numerous essays and articles. Above all, he was the author of a monumental work which moves me so profoundly that I wish its creator would be remembered forever. Wilno has an amazing characteristic which is difficult to explain rationally, a certain magic that makes people fall in love with this city as if it were a living being. For more than two centuries, many painters and graphic artists have taken as their theme the architecture and views of Wilno. Drema collected these brush and pen works in an album celebrating the city's past, titled *Dinges Vilnius* (Vanished Wilno), published in 1991 in a print run of forty thousand. It is neither more nor less than a four-hundred-page history in pictures of Wilno's architecture, with old maps, so colorful and beautiful that they have no relation at all to the countless monographs about cities that are printed on glossy paper. Poles,

Lithuanians, Jews, and Russians—among the latter, true lovers of the city, like Trutnev in the second half of the nineteenth century, painted and sketched Wilno.

DRUŻYNO, Anna and Dora. Miss Anna was short, almost a dwarf, with a huge head and a very ugly face in which the enormous wart on her nose was the most prominent feature. She carried out her profession as a teacher proudly and sternly; in her youth, it was a patriotic activity to teach the language which was looked at askance by the tsars and to spread knowledge about the Polish Romantic poets. Many manor houses in Lithuania and Samogitia employed such teachers and the respect for Miss Anna in our family derived from her having been my father's teacher once upon a time. When independent Lithuania was formed in 1918, for a while Miss Anna carried out the duties of director of the Polish *gymnasium* in Poniewież. Later, however, during my student years, that is, she lived with her sister in Wilno, subsisting (poorly) on her meager savings.

She came from a backwater gentry family; she did not find a husband and became a teacher because there were very few ways for a single woman to earn money in those days. Miss Anna's spinsterhood embittered her and hardened her character traits, her resoluteness taken to the point of dictatorial rages, her easily triggered anger. She had no one, however, on whom to unload that anger other than her sister, Dora. Dora, who was certainly born to be married, also remained an old maid and had no one in the world other than Anna, whom she obeyed in every detail; she never insisted on her own opinion. Rather stupid, almost retarded, she fussed about her sister, doing the marketing, cooking, and cleaning.

They rented a room on Embankment Street and I used to

visit them there, not quite sure why. It was one of my family obligations, like visiting relatives. These visits never took place without conflicting emotions: the sisters were from a long-past era, they were old, poor, and helpless; my twentieth century, my youth, and my education made me superior, and from that came pity, empathy, and something like sorrow for the world, because human fates could turn out like that. I have never stopped seeing those two old women, defenseless against historical time, and simply time itself. No one but me remembers their names anymore.

ECONOMY. I don't understand a thing about it. It's common sense that a person should plow his fields and raise animals, and thereby produce his own food. But that people in a particular country should live off this, that they should buy and sell among themselves—that's already too much. And then there's the whole branch of knowledge dealing with the laws of supply and demand. By devoting oneself to this science (?) one can even receive a Nobel Prize, as did two of my colleagues at the University of California in Berkeley, Debreu and Harsanyi (one of them French and the other Hungarian).

And yet, I ought to understand at least a little about economy because I did pass an exam on this subject in Wilno. It was taught by Professor Zawadzki, who was more a practitioner than a theorist; at any rate, he had once held the office of Minister of Finance. His habit of looking into a pocket mirror and checking to see if his tongue was white was explained by his nighttime libations. He was rather corpulent, black-eyed and black-haired, like all the Zawadzki descendants of the Wilno bookseller who had published Mickiewicz's first volumes. People said they were Jews. My classmate, Jurek Zawadzki, bore a physical resemblance to the professor, because he was a brunet with a tendency toward excess weight; his pretty sisters also resembled him.

Their father was a bank director, I think; whatever he was, their house was rich, the polished parquet floors shone, and I felt uncomfortable there in my homemade clothes. The Zawadzkis lived in the city, but they also had a country estate, which I mention because that pattern was of long standing in the highest circles of the local intelligentsia, as one can deduce from various literary works—from Mickiewicz's "City Winter," for example.

After graduating, Jurek studied at the Polytechnic Institute in Warsaw. He perished in 1939, after Soviet troops entered Poland.

I exaggerate my ignorance of economy, because earlier in my life I came to know it from an entirely nontheoretical side, as an insufficiency of money. Already as a twenty-year-old, I had discovered its ominous power, like the power of Fate, disposing of people's destinies despite their wishes and desires. The great American crisis of 1929 drove Polish immigrant laborers out of the mines and factories of France and into the streets, and I moved among crowds of them during my first visit there. In Germany, by depriving millions of people of work, the crisis prepared them to vote for Hitler. How fragile is the social organism; how easily its activity can be disrupted, I discovered in America, where at least since the sudden collapse of the market in 1929 people live as they do in California in relation to an earthquake: it could happen at any moment. There is no certainty that plans and intentions for the next year won't be suddenly thwarted. So it's no wonder that the science (or art?) of economics, which is based for the most part on attempts at foreseeing catastrophes, is highly valued, and that one can receive a Nobel Prize for it.

EDIFYING READINGS. In my selection of edifying readings I was the true grandson of my Grandmother Kunat, and it is irrelevant that her intellectual reach was narrower and mine a little broader. Here I must make a distinction: I read books for a thousand different reasons, but the readings which I call edifying I undertook with a distinct goal—to fortify myself. The majority of literature which was contemporary with my life did not fortify, but weakened one, so it was inappropriate for this goal. For the same reason I was not particularly fond of the novel and what is generally classified as belles lettres did not help me much.

Everything that enlarges man fortifies us; everything that depicts him as a multidimensional being. The idea that man is not only flesh, but also an inhabitant of a superterrestrial sphere which he frequents through prayer, comes to us with some difficulty. Therefore, I selected pious tracts of various religions, Christian and non-Christian—the writings of St. Augustine and Emanuel Swedenborg, the Zohar and other selections from Kabbalah, the lives of holy individuals. Also philosophy, if it was sufficiently pious. In this connection, my knowledge of French served me well. Before the war, my favorite author was the religious philosopher Louis Lavelle; after the war, French theologians like Gaston Fessard. In English, immediately after the war, in America, I discovered *The Cloud of Unknowing*, a fourteenth-century handbook on contemplation.

Living abroad, I read the Catholic periodical *Znak* (The Sign), which was published in Krakow. I found a great deal of material in it to mull over, and I respected its editors, who may have been unaware of how far-reaching their influence was.

One can detect in what I am saying a very pragmatic attitude toward truth, since such varied and incompatible texts have fed my imagination. I will not object. *The Varieties of Religious Experience*, by William James, himself a pragmatist, which I read in Wilno during my *gymnasium* years, affected me powerfully. But I must add immediately that the tolerance which is natural to pragmatists definitely does not have to result in the syncretic mixture of beliefs and faiths that took place in the New Age movement. It appears I was able to protect myself from this.

Among my edifying readings I would also count several not very rigorous philosophers who were, nonetheless, invigorating: Schopenhauer, several of Nietzsche's works, Shestov.

ENGLISH. World War I, it seems, brought an end to the period of French cultural influence in Europe when knowing the language meant that one belonged to the upper classes. French survived, however, more or less throughout the interwar period and only toward the end of those two decades did people begin to study English. I dipped into various self-instructional texts and valued those slim bilingual books with their easy plots—Kipling, for instance. Real study, however, began in Warsaw during the war. Janka and I were tutored by her colleague from the Start film studio, Tuś Toeplitz, who was later to become the director of the Łódź film school. He wandered around Warsaw, giving lessons as if nothing was wrong, not allowing himself to think that as a Jew he was in grave danger, and he was so successful that we, too, put out of our minds the thought that he was in danger. Just in case, he carried Italian identity papers. Our next teacher was Mary Skryżalin. An Englishwoman, a Quaker, who came to Poland after World War I with a Quaker charitable organization and married a Russian émigré. She had two children; her son thought of himself as Russian and her daughter as English. Mary's drama began with the outbreak of the German-Soviet war, because her son joined some Russian units attached to the German army in order to fight against the

Bolsheviks; she never heard from him again. Mary Skryżalin was a good, kind woman. She probably died in the Warsaw Uprising.

My improved command of English gave me the courage to accept a commission from Edmund Wierciński to translate Shakespeare's *As You Like It* for the underground Theater Council. True, I was helped by existing French and Polish translations. I was most successful with the translation of the songs, and singing them made us and our friends happy. My translation of T. S. Eliot's *The Waste Land* dates from the first half of 1944.

Living in America I confronted the problem of translation head on. It is obvious that any country's literature and vocabulary are shaped to a considerable degree by translations into its language. That was the case in Poland with Latin and French. Unavoidable contact with technological civilization and its English terminology forces us to consider what should be kept, what should be Polonized; for example, should "mass media" be translated as, literally, "means of mass communication"? I am afraid that I am the one who introduced that Polonized form when I translated the essays in the volume *Mass Culture* published by *Kultura* in Paris.

At the University of California in Berkeley I taught a seminar on poetry translation, utilizing what I had learned in my Wilno *gymnasium* in Adolf Rożek's Latin classes. This was a democratic method of collective translation work. My work with the students resulted in an anthology of postwar Polish poetry, but I preferred translating other poets, because translating myself was harder. For the longest time I was known in some circles as the author of *The Captive Mind* and in others as a translator of poets, especially of Zbigniew Herbert. I began to be known as a poet in my own right only in the late 1970s.

[**F**]

FAME. Dreaming about fame would be pitiful and deserving of sympathy as one of those human follies, were it possible to view it from a height, detaching oneself from among mere mortals. That one is free from that weakness does not prevent us from being amazed. Once upon a time it was possible to earn distinction among one's neighbors from the same village or county. There were no newspapers, radio, or television to spread the news of someone's eminence. Although often the fame of athletes, eccentrics, and exceptionally pretty girls did spread beyond the county; for example, the eccentric glutton, Bitowt, was famous throughout Lithuania. Somewhat less famous was another lord, Paszkiewicz, or Poszka, who wrote poems in Lithuanian in praise of an oak tree which grew on his estate, to which he gave the name Baublis. The fame of that oak was enduring, however, because Mickiewicz immortalized it in *Pan Tadeusz*. Song has always served to immortalize names, even the names of the kings of obscure little Greek states, as in *The Iliad*. Usually they were war heroes, although, thanks to Homer, we also remember the names of Helen and Cassandra.

Things have been entirely different ever since individual man became a part of the multimillion mass of people who all resemble him in their anonymity. He finds in his newspapers and sees on screens the faces of film stars and athletes, which makes his own anonymity painful. The desire to manifest his separate existence in some way can be a true passion and may take various forms. "Here am I!" he cries in a slim volume of poems put out in a tiny edition; he writes a story which is intended to bring him renown; we may also suspect that eccentric acts, including crimes, often are caused by the desire to draw attention to the actor.

The game, however, is not so much between him and the crowd, as between him and his closest milieu, his family, classmates, the profession to which he belongs. Here I draw upon my own experiences, my school in Wilno and my literary beginnings. It appears that in *gymnasium* I wrote intelligent papers, but I remember nothing about this, except that earlier in my life I was interested in biology. I also won a literary competition, apparently for a sonnet; again, zero memory. Then came the university, the Creative Writing Division, and Żagary, with anxious attempts to win my colleagues' praise. That's what I needed, because what did I care about the public at large if it knew nothing about poetry; I wanted confirmation of my worth by those who were knowledgeable. I accorded the title of connoisseur to a few of my friends.

The desire for approval is so elementary that one could study various societies from this perspective, asking what means they use to ensure the fulfillment of ambition—orders, titles, the granting of land, money? In the wars that they fight with each other, are soldiers' daring acts of courage not performed in order to be better, or at least not worse, than their fellow soldiers in their units?

The essential characteristic of fame is its illusory nature, for what does a famous name mean if those who mention it are not well-informed about why it is famous? That, after all, is the fate of the majority of monuments in every large city; they turn into signs from which the content has evaporated. The greater the number of people, the more does fame become specialized; that is, an astrophysicist is renowned among astrophysicists, a mountain climber among others who have climbed the peaks of mountains, a chess master among other chess masters. Pluralistic civilization abets division into groups, clubs, circles, lodges, poetry readers or, even narrower, lovers of haiku or limericks, photographers, or kayakers. Certainly, the Nobel Prize confers a certain amount of fame, but one should not forget that relatively few people understand why someone was awarded one, since the percentage of poetry readers is not very great—just a trifle larger or smaller, depending on the country.

FEDOROWICZ, Zygmunt. Rotund, chubby. Fedorowicz was an activist in the Nationalist Party, especially active in the underground during the war. Director of the King Sigismund August Gymnasium for Boys in Wilno. It was a humanities *gymnasium*, which means it offered Latin. On an equal academic level with our school were the Eliza Orzeszkowa Gymnasium for Girls, also specializing in the humanities, and Lelewel Gymnasium for Boys, without Latin. Almost as exclusive were the schools run by religious orders—by the Jesuits for boys and by the Sisters of the Nazarene for girls; the schools named after Mickiewicz, Słowacki, and Epstein had a somewhat lower status, as did the schools in which the language of instruction was not Polish, but Yiddish or Russian, along with one school each for Lithuanian and Belorussian (the latter was repeatedly closed down as a "seedbed of Communism").

That old Wilno is not only a city of memories for me, but a

continually present political problem. Scouting was conducted in a nationalistic spirit. There were two famous troops—Black No. Thirteen and Azure No. One, in which, terribly anxious about it, I passed my exam and received a Golden Lily. In the lower grades, I had all the makings of a good citizen, whereas now when I consider Wilno in those days I am taken aback. Catholic and patriotic, in 1919 the city welcomed with a great ringing of bells the Polish uhlans who had liberated it from the Bolsheviks, was grateful to Piłsudski, and during the phase of Central Lithuania voted for annexation to Poland (Jews and Lithuanians did not take part in the plebiscite). A moderate nationalist, Fedorowicz did not stand out particularly despite the dominance of Piłsudskiists, as their press organs showed: the conservative *Word* and the liberal *Wilno Courier*. The nationalists' *Wilno Daily* had a smaller press run.

The city had acquired the habits of a besieged fortress in which loyalty and preparedness for heroic deeds are most highly valued. In fact, that patriotic and scouting upbringing bore fruit during the German occupation in the unyielding underground organization, resulting, after the entry of the Soviet army, in mass arrests and executions of prisoners at Ponary. One aspect of the psychology of a besieged fortress is constant preoccupation with the enemy and spotting treason everywhere. The enemy was identified, with varying degrees of intensity, as Russians, Germans, Lithuanians, and Jews (because they were inclined to favor Russia in 1919).

The armed force of the city was the Home Army (the AK), which had defended the integrity of Poland's pre-1939 territory and thus found itself in a desperate situation when no one, including the allies, recognized the prewar borders.

During the interwar decades, the "localists" drew accusations of treason because they dared remind people of the multiethnicity of the lands belonging to the Grand Duchy, thereby erasing the image of "eternally Polish Wilno."

The 1936 trial of the group connected with the periodical *Po prostu* (Without Ceremony), which had emerged from the Żagary group, divided opinions in the city. The right-wing majority condemned them as agents of the Comintern (as a matter of fact, *Po prostu* was discreetly supervised by the Polish Communist Party).

When the Lithuanian authorities took control of the city, Józef Mackiewicz's *Daily News* drew accusations of collaboration with the occupier, as he was faithful to the ideology of the "localists." The later slanderous accusations against this writer (that he had cooperated with the Germans) in my opinion were unfounded and grew out of that first suspicion of treason, which the "nationalists" in the underground, Fedorowicz and Ochocki, maintained with special fervor.

The Daily News was not the only Polish-language paper under the Lithuanian authorities. *The Wilno Courier*, which was considered the organ of Polish opinion, was also published. Its liberal editor, Kazimierz Okulicz (from the Tomasz Zan Masonic lodge) left for London; editorial responsibility was taken over by an older classmate of mine from Sigismund August, nicknamed Plumbum—Józef Święcicki. He was deported to a camp in Vorkuta, where he died. Prior to Fedorowicz, the director of our *gymnasium* was Żelski, who held similar views, I believe. Many graduates of Sigismund Augustus would become well-known. I shall name a few: Czesław Zgorzelski, a professor of Polish literature at the Catholic University of Lublin; Stanisław Stomma, a

Catholic journalist and law professor; Tolo Gołubiew, a novelist; Jan Meysztowicz, author of books about the history of the twentieth century; the novelist Tadeusz Konwicki; the author of this ABC book.

FEUER, Kathryn. A Russian specialist and my colleague at Berkeley, she taught mainly Tolstoy. Very wise, kind, considerate, collegial. But how did a girl from a Canadian, French, and therefore Catholic, family come to study Russia? First, she had to rebel against her family and parish, choosing Marxism and looking longingly at the dawn in the East. I don't know when exactly her vision cleared—as a result of the Moscow trials or of the Hitler-Stalin pact. But her direction was set, which meant studying Russian culture, writing a master's thesis, learning the language, and somewhere along the road acquiring a Marxist husband, Lewis Feuer, who would soon overtake his wife in his revulsion against Marxism. There followed a doctorate and a position at Berkeley for both of them, his as a professor of sociology. They were really a pair of poor rebels and gypsies, who were granted a miraculous adventure—professorships at Berkeley. The stability of domestic life was alien to them; for me, the proof of that was Lewis's appalling mistreatment of the institution of the fireplace when I used to visit with them. To my way of thinking, that institution demands knowledge of the type of kindling used and the logs to be laid upon it. Lewis burned newspapers in his fireplace.

Kathryn knew everything about the Soviet system and empathized with the slaves of that hideous tyranny. She and Lewis had read *The Captive Mind* in English and understood it perfectly, because it could, after all, have been a book about them. I don't know what my other professorial colleagues thought about it, if they even read it. Gleb Petrovich Struve, the son of an activist in the Russian emigration in Paris, had never had any direct contact with Soviet reality, although as the publisher of Mandelstam's poetry he was well acquainted with those problems. One could not say the same of the other Russians. All I know is that when the question of granting me tenure was up for consideration, the major objection put forward by someone in the university was *The Captive Mind*, which was said to have been written in order to justify the Left.

The idea of inviting Aleksander Wat to Berkeley originated with Struve, if I am not mistaken, whom Wat had charmed at a seminar in Oxford. Struve, however, should not be mentioned as the only initiator. I believe Kathryn, who was very well-disposed toward Wat, was the main actor in this, with some help from me. It was difficult for him to travel because of his many physical and psychological ailments. Formally, he was invited by the Center for Slavic and East European Studies, whose then chairman, Gregory Grossman, showed Wat a great deal of compassion. It was he who came up with the idea of taping conversations with him.

Kathryn and Lewis left Berkeley because his department treated him, an anti-Marxist, with a great deal of contempt during the "revolution" of 1968. They found employment at a couple of other universities, and finally at the University of Virginia. I visited them there.

Kathryn is no longer alive, but I often think of her as a person who combined intelligence and goodness—and what more can one want in a human being? Probably, such a combination cannot occur with impunity, because I think of her as an unhappy individual. I am not distributing laurel wreaths, so I shall not neglect to mention her heavy drinking (in which I often accompanied her), which developed into alcoholism toward the end of her life.

FRANCE. Love of France, although not mutual love, characterized the culture in which I grew up. Perhaps that inequality was partially obscured. Only gradually did I become convinced that my part of Europe is a blank spot in the consciousness of the inhabitants of France, and that Alfred Jarry was simply confirming this when he set the action of *Ubu Roi* "in Poland, which is to say, nowhere."

In school, we were fed on the Napoleonic legend and the romanticism of pilgrims. To tell the truth, we did not understand then how very isolated those unfortunate pilgrims from an agricultural country were in bourgeois France. Just like their successors, landowners who cherished messianic myths in their souls while journeying in their bodies to the Riviera or Monte Carlo. France attracted the snobbery of the intelligentsia like a magnet; it—not Germany, not Italy, not England—was synonymous with the culture of the West. That is why the defeat of France in 1940 was so depressing for occupied Warsaw. It was read as the end of Europe. And was it not the end? Europe had to be reconstructed by powers that did not belong to it.

I am ashamed of my Western snobbery, but I received it along with my upbringing. Two sojourns in Paris weakened my image of France as a country of literature and art and strengthened another image—of a country in which every sou is counted, and whose truth is known by the hardworking Polish immigrant laborers. I wrote a poem about the barracks for the unemployed in Levallois-Perret. Whatever were the conditions there, however, the fact remains that my good knowledge of French shaped my readings in the late thirties and during the war. In my literary circle, Jacques Maritain's books were definitely influential. And it so happened that from one of the members of the circle of Maritain's admirers in Laski, from Maria Czapska, I think, I obtained a typescript of his book *À travers le désastre*, written when he was already in America. The typescript had been smuggled in from Holland. A book aimed against collaboration, in support of de Gaulle and the Free French. It appeared in my translation in 1942 as an underground miniature book, under the title *Along the Roads of Defeat*. For the preface, in which I defended the honor of a France humiliated by the Germans, I should have received the Legion of Honor, especially since the underground edition of the original in Éditions de Minuit in Paris appeared a year and a half or two years later than the Warsaw edition.

I mention this in order to soften the impression of my anti-French attitude. I do not conceal the fact that I harbor this feeling and that it is traumatic; it derives from the postwar years of my existence as a political émigré. It makes no difference to me that the French intellectuals later confessed to their great political error. The extent of that error is such that I have stopped believing in any subsequent "isms" if they are of Parisian derivation.

So, should one agree with the opinion (expressed by a Frenchman), that France would be a wonderful country were it not for the French? With the revulsion of one who has been spurned, with gratitude for what I received from French culture, with gratitude, too, toward several individuals, with attachment to a couple of Paris streets and a number of landscapes, I have an ambivalent attitude toward that country.

FRENCH. I was a witness. It happened over several decades, during my lifetime. First, individuals from the higher social classes were able to speak French somewhat, if only enough to communicate in the presence of the servants so that they would not understand. During the two interwar decades, the *gymnasia* offered a choice between French and German. For me, the choice of French was obvious. In literature, the interwar period was focused on France, although knowledge of the language among the younger generation was already doubtful, and access to books was limited. In essence, the French publishing empire—those novels in yellow jackets, sold along the Volga, Danube, and Vistula—came to an end in 1914.

Paris's position as the cultural capital of the world was unquestioned before World War I and remained constant until the thirties. That is where the American expatriates first turned their steps, as did Polish artists and writers. The list of members of the Society of Polish Artists in Paris could serve as a roster of people elected to a nonexistent academy. Someone ought to investigate how indebted the Little Green Balloon Café was to the Parisian cabarets. The songs which Leon Schiller and Teofil Trzciński sang to our group during the German occupation, accompanying themselves on the piano, had imported French melodies, including this famous one:

> *The wind is laughing outside the panes,*
> *Damn it, this life is rotten.*
> *No, I won't drink anymore,*
> *I'll start my life anew in the morning!*

Boy's translations are the crowning achievement of French influences. In interwar poetry, Guillaume Apollinaire was honored in translation by Adam Ważyk, and those poems assisted at the birth of such poets as Józef Czechowicz, Anna Świrszczyńska, Miłosz—despite the Kraków avant-garde.

I didn't put much effort into studying French in school, but the textbook aroused my curiosity and made an impact on me. I found in it a poem by Joachim du Bellay (from the sixteenth century), which I liked so much that I began to practice writing poetry, using it as a model and not, as might have been expected, the poems of Leopold Staff.

I learned the language thoroughly only later, in Paris in the spring of 1935, when I used to walk every morning across the Luxembourg Gardens to the Alliance Française on Boulevard Raspail. It was a regular school, very rigorous, especially for those people who, like me, were taking the *cours supérieur*. Grammar explanations, dictations, lectures on literature. After a couple of months there was a fairly difficult written exam, and a diploma with an overly impressive title, which gave one the right to teach French in school. That was a useful wringer that I put myself through; as I realized later, I was one of a very few writers of my generation who knew French to that degree. I used it for my readings. As the sole reader—or almost that—of the monthly *Les Cahiers du Sud* in Poland, I was initiated into the latest literary developments. I profited the most, however, from reading French religious philosophers such as Louis Lavelle, and theologians. Their prose retained that classical balance and clarity that my professors at the Alliance had praised. Soon, however, the French of scholars and philosophers succumbed to an astonishing and rapid change, as if confirming thereby the loss of its superior place in Europe. It became unclear, convoluted, inflated with professional jargon, elevated to the heights of that babble which guarantees prestige.

The French Institute in Warsaw, housed in the Staszic Palace, was destroyed by a German bomb. I was hired, along with Stanisław Dygat, to rescue books from the rubble, and thereby added a great deal to my French reading. Probably that sort of reading is responsible for what Gombrowicz said in Vence when, as was his wont, he steered the conversation to philosophy: "It's strange; when we speak French, you are precise, and when we change to Polish, you become vague."

I would choose 1938 as the date when everyone in Warsaw began studying English. The era of French, like the era of Latin before it, was coming to an end in Europe, after the temporary vacillation or interregnum that began in 1914. It is easier to explain this change as a whim of the *Zeitgeist* than as the military dominance of the Anglo-Saxons, which was still to come.

FROST, Robert. I write about him, who is recognized as the greatest American poet of the twentieth century, not with admiration, but rather with amazement that such a figure is possible. Because it is difficult to understand how one country could produce three such different poets as Walt Whitman, Emily Dickinson, and Robert Frost.

Born in 1874, a contemporary, more or less, of Paul Valéry (1871), Leopold Staff (1878), and Bolesław Leśmian (1878), he was already formed intellectually when the twentieth century began. America at that time was far removed from Europe, whose cultural capital was Paris. I can think about Frost comparatively, knowing, as I do, poets who are very different from him—French and Polish poets. Not only Europeans thought of America then as a country of shallow materialism; her citizens did, too, and if they valued culture they looked longingly across the Atlantic. Frost, too, when he was a young man, spent a couple of years in England, where he published *North of Boston* (1914), which also earned him recognition in America. But he built his entire, unusual career after his return to the land of the golden calf. How did he do it?

He changed his clothes and donned a mask. He put himself forward as a rube, a New England farmer, writing in a simple language, full of colloquialisms, about his environs and the people who lived there. A real American, digging in the soil, and not from any big city! A self-made talent, a country sage in daily contact with nature and the seasons! Helped by his acting and declamatory talents, he carefully maintained that image, playing on the appeal of the simple country philosopher. His readings attracted large crowds. I saw that bard with my own eyes when he was already an old man: blue eyes, a white mane, sturdily built, deserving of sympathy and trust with his openness and simplicity.

In fact, he was someone entirely different. His childhood was spent in San Francisco, not in the country outside of Boston. Among his various means of earning his living there were also a couple of years of managing a farm in New England—the oldest part of the American continent to have been colonized by whites. He felt the landscape there, the people, the language; he knew their work because he had done it himself—mower, digger, lumberjack. His readers valued him, however, for his idyllic mood, which was only a disguise. Beneath it was concealed a grim, hopeless vision of man's fate.

A powerful intellect, unusual intelligence, well-read in philosophy, and such enormous deceptiveness that he was capable of hiding his skepticism behind his constant ambivalence, so that his poems deceived with their supposedly wise affability. I am amused by the thought of a French poet reading Frost—for instance, Paul Valéry. He would probably have snorted contemptuously at those little story-plays taken from life and written down with the pen of, you know, a simpleton, a cowboy. At the same time, one should remember that both poets, despite their will and their knowledge, were connected to the language's moment, to its current—descending, in the case of the French, and ascending, in the case of American English.

Frost struggled with the scientific world view of the nineteenth century, enthusiastically reading Darwin, who was, *nota bene*, not only a scientist, but a thinker, aware of the influence of his discoveries on his contemporaries. For Frost, this meant a break with Emerson, with American faith in the benign power of nature, and acceptance of the ungrounded nature of individual life, which is caused solely by chance. That is to say, he pondered evolution, and also borrowed from his reading of Bergson's *Creative Evolution*, but I won't delve into his philosophy. All I want to say is that Leśmian's poetry has a similar underpinning of skepticism, and that his balladic simplicity is also different from what it appears to be on the surface. His gods and other worlds are a conscious description of the Buddhist veil of maya. Like him in his skeptical world view, Paul Valéry promoted constructions of the self-creating mind which admires its own creations. In Leśmian, however, Nature takes on fairy-tale shapes, it swarms with fantastic creatures, and an almost Christian Heaven opens out into a universe of poetic imagination, redeemed by its own beauty. Constructed out of crystals, the autonomous edifice of intellect in Valéry also finds its ultimate realization in the perfection of metric verse, and several lines from *Le cimetière marin* have always remained with me. Why then, I ask, do I find Frost so disturbing and depressing?

It is not that he dissembled. He decided to become a great poet, mercilessly condemned his rivals, but also knew that he would not achieve greatness pursuing his philosophical bent. Quite simply, he discerned what would be his strengths: rural New England and his superb ear, registering the variants of colloquial English. He had to limit himself to what he knew well, cling to his seeming provincialness. His poetry is not lyrical, but tragic, for his narrative poems about the ties between people are mini tragedies; or else it is descriptive, or, more accurately, moralistic. I feel that it is cold.

To think at one and the same time about that poetry and the biography concealed behind it is to descend into a bottomless well. No one will learn about Frost's own wounds and tragedies by reading his poetry; he left no clues. An appalling chain of misfortunes, numerous deaths in the family, madness, suicides, and silence about this, as if confirming his Puritan heritage, which demands that one conceal what is private behind a stoic façade. The worst part of all this is that in concerning oneself with him one is menaced by a sense of one's own particular existence. If the boundaries of the human personality are so fluid that we truly do not know who we are and are constantly trying on different changes of costume, how did Frost manage? It is impossible to grasp who he really was, aside from his unswerving striving toward his goal of fame, in an attempt to exact revenge for his own defeats in life.

I confess that I do not like his poetry and that in calling him great I am only repeating what others, Joseph Brodsky included, have written about him. Brodsky seems to have valued him as a master of metrical poetry. Frost said of free verse that it is like a game of tennis without a net. I, however, am absolutely on Walt Whitman's side.

In Frost's defense, I should add that he did not soften the cruel truth about human life, as he perceived it, and if his readers and listeners did not understand that very well, all the better for them. There is, for example, one poem about how very alone man is in relation to nature, which is absolutely indifferent to him, even though he wishes to receive some sign of understanding. Alone, not only in relation to nature, because each "I" is isolated from all others, as if it were the sole ruler of the universe, and seeks love in vain, while what it takes to be a response is only the echo of his own hope. I cite this poem because it also demonstrates Frost's allegorical and moralistic methods:

THE MOST OF IT

He thought he kept the universe alone;
For all the voice in answer he could wake
Was but the mocking echo of his own
From some tree-hidden cliff across the lake.
Some morning from the boulder-broken beach
He would cry out on life, that what it wants
Is not its own love back in copy speech,
But counter-love, original response.
And nothing ever came of what he cried
Unless it was the embodiment that crashed
In the cliff's talus on the other side,
And then in the far distant water splashed,
But after a time allowed for it to swim,
Instead of proving human when it neared

And someone else additional to him,
As a great buck it powerfully appeared,
Pushing the crumpled water up ahead,
And landed pouring like a waterfall,
And stumbled through the rocks with horny tread,
And forced the underbrush—and that was all.*

*Complete Poems of Robert Frost 1949 (New York: Henry Holt and Co., 1967).

GOLD. The first novel about the mythic island of California, inhabited and ruled by warring women under the leadership of
Queen Calafia, was written in Spain. On this island all objects
and furnishings are made of gold, so abundant is that metal. The
legend of the golden land lured adventurers from across the
ocean, who defeated the Aztecs and Incas with the intent of
looting their treasures and then ending their lives in civilized
Madrid, which not many of them managed to do. The majority
of them died in battles or from disease, or were unable to return.

Then it turned out that California was not an island. But it
also turned out that it did have gold. This was in January 1848,
when nuggets of gold were found in a stream during the construction of a mill on Sutter's land. Johann August Sutter, from
Switzerland, had founded New Helvetia and a defensive fort in
the vicinity of what would later become the city of Sacramento.
He was the richest and most powerful man west of the Sierra
Nevada mountains. The discovery of gold, which he was unable
to keep secret, ruined him. The construction of the mill, work on
his other enterprises, and cultivating his fields all became impossible. Anyone who drew breath threw himself into digging
and panning for gold, and the hordes of people who were attracted to this paid no attention to the boundaries of his private

property and murdered his Indians. Soon they were joined by crowds of Yankees and Europeans who arrived by ship. The journey by sailboat around Cape Horn took many months. The ships brought their passengers to the isthmus of Panama and, on the other side, from the isthmus; the passengers were left to traverse the isthmus by whatever means they could muster. Thus, the city of San Francisco grew, although its harbor was soon filled with disabled vessels whose entire crews had run away in search of gold.

The height of gold fever came in the year 1849. For me, this date coincides with the Spring of Peoples. Mickiewicz's *The Tribune of Peoples* was still being published, but would soon burn itself out. I remember Aleksander Herzen's descriptions of the torpor and apathy in Europe after the defeat of those great hopes. All that was left to those starving Europeans was to dream about sudden riches.

The white men who swarmed over the camps in the foothills of the Sierras were a collection of all sorts of professions, nationalities, and educational levels. They agreed on one thing, though: the conviction that the horse thieves (i.e., the Indians) deserved no mercy. Their self-imposed, punitive labor brought a lot of gold nuggets and gold dust to only a very few, but they, too, squandered their money on alcohol, gambling, and women. The merchants and the enterprising owners of bars acted rationally, supplying the camps with food and implements, as well as the sought-after (in this predominantly male society) women who traded in their own charms. Several of these, in San Francisco, made a fortune. Doctors also prospered, especially those who treated venereal diseases. One of those doctors was a Pole who lived in San Francisco, one Felix Wierzbicki (1815–1860), who had emigrated to America earlier, in 1834. He was the author of the first book published in California, under the title *California as It Is, and as It May Be.*

The Wild West; it's practically movie folklore. It appears to have been in the distant past, but I lived a large part of my life in this Wild West and it is hard not to think about the people who once walked this land. About the tragic history of Johann August Sutter; about those who traveled around the continent only to die by a knife, a bullet, or illness, and who lie in the many cemeteries near the abandoned gold panning operations. About the Indians, whose hunting grounds were destroyed, and who then were killed themselves because they got the meat they needed by stealing horses and mules.

Of all the riches won and squandered, the moments of triumph and drama, the most lasting thing turned out to be a song. Sung to this day and used in films, it is a song about a placer miner in 1849 and his daughter, Clementine. To spare the reader the effort of finding this text, here is the first stanza and chorus:

> *In a cavern, in a canyon,*
> *Excavating for a mine,*
> *Lived a miner, forty-niner,*
> *And his daughter, Clementine.*
>
> *Chorus:*
> *Oh my darlin', oh my darlin',*
> *Oh my darlin' Clementine,*
> *You are lost and gone forever,*
> *Dreadful sorry, Clementine.*

This is not a sentimental song, but rather a humorous one. Because when a heroine dies, having fallen into a raging river, is it right to say "Dreadful sorry, Clementine"? The description of her beauty isn't particularly high-flown, either, since, like an elf, she wore size nine shoes, which means she was a giant. And when she drowned, her rosy little lips blew "bubbles soft and fine," and the man remembering her confesses,

> *But alas I was no swimmer,*
> *So I lost my Clementine.*

> *Oh my darlin', oh my darlin',*
> *Oh my darlin' Clementine.*

GRADE, Chaim. The Nobel Prize for Isaac Bashevis Singer was cause for violent controversies among Yiddish-speaking New York Jews. Grade was of much better background than Singer; in America, it's best to come from Wilno, worse to come from Warsaw, and worst of all from Galicia. Above all, however, in the opinion of the majority of the disputants, he was a much better writer than Singer, but little translated into English, which is why the members of the Swedish Academy had no access to his writings. Singer gained fame, according to this opinion, by dishonest means. Obsessively concerned with sex, he created his own world of Polish Jews which had nothing in common with reality—erotic, fantastic, filled with apparitions, spirits, and dybbuks, as if that had been the quotidian reality of Jewish towns. Grade was a real writer, faithful to the reality he described, and he deserved the Nobel Prize.

Wilno was an important center of Jewish culture—not just a local center, but on a world scale. Yiddish was the dominant language there, and literature in that language had its main support in Wilno, along with New York, as the number of periodicals and books published there demonstrates. The city was better off before World War I, when it belonged to Russia and profited from its position as a key railroad junction and trading center. This came to an end when the city was transferred to little Poland, although in terms of culture, the interwar period was a time of blossoming. Something of the vitality of past years, especially 1905–1914, also continued. Political parties that had been founded in tsarist Russia were still active, with their prime concern the needs of workers and a socialist revolution—most important of all, the Bund, a separate Jewish socialist party, which wanted to be a movement of Yiddish-speaking workers. It was a counterpart of sorts to the Polish Socialist Party, which, however, since it was considered to be exclusively Polish, had relatively few adherents in the city. It would not be accurate to link the creation of the Jewish Historical Institute with the Bund, and yet in its aim of preserving the cultural heritage of the cities and small towns where Yiddish was used in daily life, one can detect the spirit of the Bund. The Communists were rivals of the Bund and grew stronger with the years; in 1939, they apparently had a majority of followers. Both these parties, in turn, were at war with the Zionists and the Orthodox.

This Jewish Wilno recognized the attractiveness of Russian culture, but was separated from Soviet Russia by the state border. The border was quite close, however, and this produced a phenomenon peculiar to Wilno. Many young people, dreaming of taking part in the "building of socialism," crossed the eastern border without appropriate documents, enthusiastically ensuring their near and dear ones that they would write from there. No one ever heard from any of them again. They were sent straight to the Gulag.

Chaim Grade belonged to the group of young poets called Yung Vilne. In addition to Abraham Sutzkever, I remember the name Kaczerginski. The attitude of this group toward the older generation, somewhat like Żagary's, inclined us to make an alliance with them. We were exactly the same age, and their "Young Wilno" used to come to our readings.

The poet Grade was a descendant of an officer in Napoleon's army named Gradé, who, wounded, and nursed back to health by a Jewish family in Wilno, married into it and converted to Judaism. Chaim's mother, who was very poor, was a street peddler whose entire stock fit into a basket. Grade devoted many moving pages of his oeuvre to that pious, hardworking, good woman. She appears against the background of a milieu which followed all the religious customs, and whose common characteristic was extreme poverty.

Chaim's youth in Wilno did not pass without political and personal conflicts. His father, Rabbi Shlomo Mordechai, an advocate of Hebrew and a Zionist, who held strong convictions and was not much inclined to compromise, engaged in heated arguments with the conservative rabbis. He raised his son to be a pious Jew. Chaim's later history shows that he remained faithful to Judaism, in contrast to the emancipated Singer. As a poet, Chaim quickly achieved recognition and local fame, but he was distinguished from the majority of young people who read Marx and sang revolutionary songs. The Communists' attempts at attracting him to their side were not successful, and Grade became the object of violent attacks. Worse yet, he fell in love with Frumme-Liebe, who was also the daughter of a rabbi and from a family of Zionists who emigrated to Palestine. His Communist colleagues tried in vain to interfere with their marriage.

These details can be found in his four-hundred-page novel-memoir called, in English translation, *My Mother's Sabbath Days*. There he tells in detail about his wartime experiences, beginning with the entry of Soviet troops into the city. His friends' enthusiasm contrasted with the stony sadness of the crowd at the mass in the Wilno cathedral, where he went out of compassion. The chaos of the German invasion in June 1941 separated him from his beloved wife. They were supposed to meet a couple of days later, but he never saw her again. She died, as did his mother, in the Wilno ghetto. A wave of fleeing refugees carried him to the East. After many peripeteia (once, they wanted to shoot him as a German spy) he made his way to Tashkent. After the war, he emigrated to New York. He always writes about the Russians with love and respect. He insists that he never encountered any signs of anti-Semitism in Russia.

His colleagues from the Yung Vilne group, Sutzkever and Kaczerginski, were in the ghetto and then joined the Soviet partisan troops. Sutzkever wound up in Israel, where he edited the only quarterly devoted to poetry in the dying language of Yiddish, *Di Goldene Keyt* (The Golden Chain).

In America, the poet Chaim Grade developed into a prose writer, and like Singer, who attempted to recover the vanished world of the Jewish towns of Poland, he immersed himself in the past, writing about the shtetls of Lithuania and Belorussia. Singer engaged in fantasy and offended many of his readers; Grade was attentive to the accuracy of the details he recorded and has been compared with Balzac or Dickens. His main theme appears to be the life of the religious community, which he knows well, especially the problems of families in which the wife works to earn money and the husband pores over holy books. One collection of novellas is even called *Rabbis and Wives.*

I became interested in Grade thanks to my contact with his second wife, his widow. After his death in 1982 (he was seventy-two years old), she began energetically promoting his work and collaborating with his English translators.

[**H**]

HATRED. My life story is one of the most astonishing I have ever come across. True, it lacks the clarity of a morality tale, as in Joseph Brodsky's story: he was tossing manure with a pitchfork on a state farm near Arkhangelsk, and then, just a few years later, he collected all sorts of honors, including the Nobel Prize. It does not lack similarities with the Polish fable about stupid Jaś, however, because it required a great deal of stupidity to act differently from my colleagues in literary circles and to flee to the West, which was convinced of its own decadence. The dangers of such a flight are described very well in these lines from *Hamlet*, applied to the Cold War:

> *'Tis dangerous when the baser nature comes*
> *Between the pass and fell incensed points*
> *Of mighty opposites.*

To be despised and triumphant in the course of a single life, to wait for the time when it would become apparent that my enemies who made up disgusting things about me had made terrible fools of themselves. What interests me most in all of this is the difference between our image of ourselves and our image in others' eyes. Obviously, we improve upon ourselves, while our opponents seek to strike even imaginary weak spots. I muse over my portrait that emerges from songs of hatred, in verse and prose. A lucky guy. The sort for whom everything goes smoothly. Incredibly crafty. Self-indulgent. Loves money. Not an iota of patriotic feeling. Indifferent to the fatherland, which he has traded in for a suitcase. Effete. An aesthete, who cares about art, not people. Venal. Impolitic (he wrote *The Captive Mind*). Immoral in his personal life (he exploits women). Contemptuous. Arrogant. And so forth.

This characterization was usually supported with a list of my shameful deeds. What is most striking is that it is the image of a strong, shrewd man, whereas I know my own weakness and I am inclined to consider myself, rather, as a tangle of reflexes, a drunken child in the fog. I would also be inclined to take the side of my enemies when they track down my insolence as a nonconformist, because the polite little lad and Boy Scout is still quite firmly inside me, and I really do condemn the scandals I caused in school, and in each of my violations of the social norms I detect an attraction to brawling and psychological imbalance.

My tendency toward splitting hairs, and toward *delectatio morosa*, the label used by monks for masochistic pleasures such as those they suffered by recalling all their sins, argues against my alleged strength. It is not exactly pride, but as for arrogance, it is well known that it usually masks timidity.

I count it as great good fortune that I never fell into the clutches of the political police. A talented interrogator would immediately have guessed my general sense of guilt and, playing on it, would have led me to confess, in a great act of contrition, whatever crimes he named. So many similarly unfortunate people were broken in this way, and I feel profoundly sorry for them.

HOOK, Sidney. Born in Brooklyn, he experienced poverty in his childhood. Like "all of New York," in the thirties he believed in the end of capitalism and the world victory of Communism. Educated as a philosopher, originally as a Marxist, he later turned to the pragmatism of Dewey. He broke with the Communists early, and their press called him a "counterrevolutionary reptile." Although he was not a Trotskyist, after the Moscow trials he and Dewey organized a committee to study the alleged crimes of Trotsky and to clear his name.

I became acquainted with him during my first postwar Paris period. I had been following his activities for a long time and met him in Palo Alto, where he settled after retiring from the university. He struck me as a dry, unyielding intellect. From the perspective of time, I see that one was supposed to honor him for his obduracy. He was a fanatic of reason and hated lying, so that his life was an incessant struggle with admirers and sympathizers of Soviet Russia. He founded the Committee for Cultural Freedom in New York in the beginning of 1950, before the June congress in Berlin and the opening of the Congress of Cultural Freedom in Paris. His and his committee's relations with the Paris Congress are a story of shifting tactics toward the Eastern ideology. The creators of the Paris Congress represented the NCL, the non-Communist left, and were critical of many events in America, throwing ballast overboard, as it were, in order to draw closer to the universal criticism in Europe of the American system (racism, the Rosenberg trials, McCarthyism, the war in Vietnam). Hook and his colleagues in New York, confronting the well-organized propaganda of anti-Americanism, attempted to study each accusation separately and adopt a considered position. They maintained a sober evaluation of the "revolution" of the sixties and the politicization of the universities, and defended professors who resisted it and were, therefore, unpopular. When the Congress was dissolved and transformed into the Association pour la Liberté de la Culture in 1968, after it was revealed that it had been financed by the CIA, Hook no longer had any points in common with the organization, whose main personalities were Pierre Emmanuel and Kot Jeleński, and the only person who shared his uncompromising stance was Leopold Łabędź, the editor of the London journal *Survey*.

Hook's most famous essay was titled "Heresy Yes, Conspiracy No"; it defined his stand as a defender of democracy.

HOPPER, Edward (1882–1962). A classic of American painting whom I find so disturbing that I intended to write about him either in verse or in prose. Standing before his paintings, one cannot escape the question: What can a painting tell us about the country and the era in which it arose? A difficult and practically impossible question, because, for example, the light in Vermeer, and in Dutch painting in general, seems a witness to religious harmony and domestic tranquility, but we know that it was precisely then that Holland's wealth derived to a great extent from slave ships, which were practically floating concentration camps. Similarly, who would dare to discern bourgeois France from the canvases of the Impressionists? And yet there is a tie, even if it eludes language.

Hopper painted during the first half of the twentieth century. He differed from his contemporaries by his lack of susceptibility to the fashions emanating from Paris. He was there a couple of times before World War I and admired French painting, but he rebelled. He insisted that France inhabited every inch of French art, and declared, "We have been apprenticed to them for thirty years, and that's enough." He understood, then, that an American painter had to stand on his own feet. According to him, the turn to deformation and abstraction meant that priority was granted to the means and not the end, resulting in an escape into decorativeness, which can only impoverish art. The aim of painting was, for him, faithfulness to experience, to life, contents, internal truth, nature—he defined it variously. He considered the movements of the brush and the discovery of shapes as means to that end. Some of his pronouncements on faithfulness to nature sound as if I were listening to Józef Czapski, although Czapski, that observer of small cafés and suburban night trains, did not strive for generalizations, whereas Hopper deliberately wanted to create a portrait of America.

His America is, above all, New York and the East Coast. He faithfully portrays the architecture of the great cities and the wooden houses of the coast, the bridges, highways, gas stations, and only rarely scenes in which a couple of figures appear, most often a lone woman who is blond, naked, about forty years old, and staring into space or at the wall of the tenement building outside her window. Emptiness is one of his frequent subjects— as in *Sunday*, where we see a row of identical lower middle-class houses and one idle little man, who clearly does not know what to do with the time on his hands. Or the emptiness of a great city at night before dawn: *Nighthawks* portrays a couple who are seated in a diner, a pimp and an old prostitute, both of them smartly attired when viewed from a distance, but up close one can see their devastated, truly ghastly faces.

Everyone who looks at Hopper's images will say, "Yes, that's

America," and will insist that they could not have arisen in any other country. But there's something in them that weighs upon the heart, and they could have served as illustrations for some of Henry Miller's texts about the empty canyons of the New York streets. Is Hopper a satirist engaged in social criticism, perhaps in the spirit of Marxism? No, not at all. He is trying to convey his own experience. That experience does not embrace the entirety of American life; for instance, there is nothing of the horror of the Negro ghetto in them, or of the migrant life of black agricultural laborers. So, it's white America, and even so, just barely touching the rural expanses of "white poverty." No, Hopper most definitely is not conducting any sort of social analysis; the content which he tries to grasp evades words, especially since an important element is simply pity. As far as I know, the Marxists never used Hopper's canvases for their anti-American propaganda. And no wonder, because they would make a mockery of their aims: Here's what you are striving for, for prosperity, the loneliness of people who seem to be made of plastic. Hopper's content or his truth, which is so hard to name, still has something in common with the Marxists' beloved concept of alienation. He paints alienation, wary of any program, attempting to make the most decent use possible of canvas and pen, this portrait painter of reality.

HULEWICZ, Witold. For today's readers just a name, nothing more, and this is somehow unjust. For me, however, it is also the face and presence of a large, somewhat heavy man, dark-haired, not lanky but, rather, broad-shouldered, with a prominent nose and olive complexion. I see him in the studios of Polish Radio or bent over the handlebars of his heavy motorcycle, with a beautiful woman on the rear seat (they would always say the same thing: "Shake before using"). He was a well-known figure in Wilno, but a newcomer, and now I ask myself, how did those newcomers fare among us? There was a clear division into "ours" and "other"; the latter were referred to in general as "Galicians," whether they came from Galicia or not. In my *gymnasium*, only Adolf Rożek, the Latin teacher, was obviously a Galician. But at the university it seemed it was half and half, and those who were products of a Viennese education were conspicuous, like my Roman law professor, Bossowski, who stood ramrod straight, as if he had swallowed a stick, and wore stiff collars like a former hussar officer.

Hulewicz came from the Poznań region. During World War I he fought in the German army on the Western front. After the war, he co-edited, with his brother Jerzy, the journal *The Source* in Poznań. He wrote and published volumes of his own poetry. Although he belonged to the Skamander generation, fame passed him by, as it did many of his contemporaries, perhaps because *The Source* just did not catch on. In contrast to *Skamander*, it remained on the border between Young Poland and the new in its use of language.

For Wilno, where he was active in the twenties and thirties, he was a precious discovery. It was he who founded the Union of Polish Writers and invented a humorous institution named Smorgonia and also CAWA, or the Council of Associations of Wilno Artists; he worked with Osterwa's *Redoubt* as its literary director, and later was the director of the Wilno Transmitter of Polish Radio, to which he lured Tadeusz Byrski away from *Redoubt*.

Why, then, was such a rabid campaign conducted against him, in which Stanisław Mackiewicz's *Word* took the lead? What was the issue? No one today remembers. Vicious feuilletons were written about him, and the permanent illustrator of *Word* and habitué of Wilno coffee houses, Feliks Dangel, was constantly mocking him in his caricatures (*nota bene*, immediately after September 1939 Dangel appeared in Wilno in a German officer's uniform). Hulewicz ought to have shrugged off these attacks as the manifestation of jealous localism, inclined to dividing people into the "we" of the Grand Duchy of Lithuania and the "them" from outside. He was so upset by this, however, that he allowed himself to be provoked and it came to a duel with sabers between him and Mackiewicz. There was a great to-do, scandals, until finally the central administration of Polish Radio recalled Hulewicz in 1934 and named him chief of the Literature Section in Warsaw.

Hulewicz translated Rilke, which I think is important, and maintained personal relations with him from the time when he met him during a stay abroad in the 1920s. His is the sole Polish name, it appears, in Rilke's biography. I shall not attempt to evaluate the quality of his translations in comparison with others which were done later, mainly by Mieczysław Jastrun. It would be interesting to study—perhaps students of Polish literature will explore this—why Rilke barely existed in the consciousness of Polish poets of the interwar period. I can cite myself, alas, in this regard, although I did read his prose, *The Notebooks of Malte Laurids Brigge*, in Hulewicz's translation. A search for reasons would probably lead into a thicket of problems connected with language and the sociology of literature— for instance, the spirit of *The Literary News* did not favor such poetry.

Hulewicz, like many newcomers, succumbed to Wilno's

charms, as is demonstrated by his slim volume of verse, *The City Beneath the Clouds* (1931), in which he praises Wilno's architecture, which is baroque and splendidly soaring.

During the first year of the German occupation Hulewicz, always active, was engaged in organizing the underground press. Arrested in August 1940, he remained in prison until June 12, 1941. An admirer of German poetry and music, the author of a book about Beethoven, he was shot at Palmiry on that day.

IMBRODY. I tug at this thread of memory, but I can pull out very little, only as much as remains from Grandmother Miłosz's stories. Imbrody was the beloved place of her childhood, the estate of the Mohls, or von Mohls. In Inflanty, there were families who were descended from the Teutonic Knights and had become Polonized: the Mohls, Platers, Weyssenhofs; there were others, such as the Romer and Puttkamer families, who had moved south to Lithuania, or were Russified, like the Budbergs and many others who made their careers in the tsarist administration. Some of them, like the Todtlebens, for example, I would not know how to categorize.

Imbrody was somewhere in the vicinity of Dyneburg (now Daugavpils in present-day Latvia). Not too far from there is Łukomla, with the graves of the Druja branch of the Miłoszes, now part of Belorussia. Scraps of some foggy stories about a superstitious maid whom the young men liked to play jokes on; about a *bacik* on a lake (who uses that word for a sailboat today?); about travels in a carriage through steep forested slopes infested with bandits; and also about evening parties at which poems were recited and living pictures acted out. Patriotism, reverence for Emilia Plater, because she was a heroine and, in addition, a distant relative. Anecdotes that circulated for a long time in company—for instance, the one about a woman so near-sighted that she mistook her own jabot for a mushroom in her soup:

> *And thinking it a dried mushroom,*
> *She stuffed it into the bowl of white borscht.*

I am moved by the very fact of that woman's existence, of which all that has remained is this verse.

Yes, once, a long time ago, I looked through my grand-mother's album from the time of her youth. She had drawn flowers and fruit, written down some poems—I don't know if they were her own. Her stories featured evening parties in town, in Riga, because that is where she lived; she traveled to Imbrody for vacations. An opera production, a swan floating on stage as if alive, performances by the famous singer Adelina Patti, also a Polish theater's performance of Jules Verne's *The Children of Captain Grant*, arranged for the stage. And Majorenhof, a local-ity on the outskirts of Riga, where one went to bathe in the sea.

Hanseatic Riga of the wealthy German merchant class, a city of stone Gothic and the regional capital, drew people, including my great-grandmother von Mohl, who was given in marriage to a Doctor Łopaciński, who lived there. Doctor Łopaciński appar-ently had studied in Dorpat (Tartu), the oldest (after Wilno) university in those parts, because the Wilno university was closed after the November insurrection. My father was born in Riga and later chose to attend the Riga Polytechnic instead of the university in Dorpat.

I do not know if my great-grandfather Łopaciński had any landed property, or if he practiced his profession as a doctor ex-clusively. From my grandmother's stories I remember that he was kind, treated the poor free of charge, and loved to make jokes; he was quite a wag. I am depressed by the darkness that surrounds an existence which is impossible to imagine: that doctor, his wife (my great-grandmother), yet I can see only my grandmother, no farther. Also, all of Inflanty and the Imbrody estate are submerged in darkness. A question catches my attention: What language did the local peasants speak? Probably Latvian.

INACCURACY. The past is inaccurate, because we cannot determine how it was in fact, no matter how hard we try. We must rely on people's memory, which is treacherous, because memory is constantly juggling and revising the data of experience. Even when people say they were present when something happened, one cannot trust them, but usually they simply repeat as a fact what they heard from other people. In telling about an event, we ourselves cannot avoid revising it, because our narrative simplifies and composes a whole out of selected components, while omitting others. It suffices to compare our knowledge of facts with their depiction in chronicles, journalistic accounts, memoirs, to understand the need for fantasizing that is somehow inscribed in the language itself, and which draws us into the forest of fiction.

Certainly, when I was writing my *Abecadło Miłosza*, I wanted to present real people and problems, without falsifying anything. My good intentions weren't sufficient, however, because my mistakes keep being revealed by news that reaches me: of course, it was probably like this, but not exactly. And this has happened even in connection with the experiences of individuals whom I knew well, such as my friends from school. I wrote, for example, that Jurek Zawadzki served in the cavalry and died in the September Campaign of 1939. As another of our friends, Tadeusz Kasprzycki, informs me, however, Zawadzki never served in the military. In accordance with his profession as a graduate of the Warsaw Polytechnic, he was engaged in building fortifications, and was sent to the Eastern border in 1939 where, after the Soviet invasion, he joined a unit in the forests that was attempting to mount resistance. The circumstances of his death are unclear.

The picturesque character from Young Wilno, Tadeusz Bulsiewicz, was, in fact, deported and then fought in Italy, but he does not rest on Monte Cassino. Sergeant Bulsiewicz, a cultural officer, was the favorite of his brigade: "I had heard him innumerable times. That day, however, he gave a real concert of wit and humor. The audience was simply howling with joy, and tears rolled down my face from laughter," his army colleague writes in his memoir. "He must be a very talented man. He was the author and director of a splendid spectacle performed behind the front lines in Gazala."

The writer continues, "He was so upset by the bloody losses of our division in the battle of Monte Cassino that he reported to his superiors with a request that he be attached to one of the infantry battalions on front line duty. No attempts at persuasion from his superiors, friends, and colleagues had an effect. He insisted. Bulsiewicz was a journalist by profession. Before the war he worked as an announcer for Polish Radio's Wilno station. In addition, he was not so young that he could bear the difficulties of service in the front lines without suffering harm. Furthermore, it had been a long time since he had line experience."

On patrol along the Chieti River he separated from his colleagues and decided to launch a grenade attack on his own at the rear of the German position. Gravely wounded in the mouth by a German mortar shell, he survived, but was disfigured. He could barely speak. "Then he was evacuated to England, where he underwent some kind of special operation. There is information that he died after the unsuccessful operation. Others insist that, unable to make his peace with such a severe disability, he broke down psychologically and committed suicide."

People from Wilno were certain that Henryk Dembiński loaded the Wilno archives onto a truck in the autumn of 1939 and drove them to Minsk. They are so certain that they swore, "We were there; we saw him." This is an example of why one cannot believe eyewitnesses. As Wacław Zagórski reports, "I saw Henryk Dembiński for the first time this year. He is in despair. In the best faith he took over the directorship of the State Archive in Wilno. He was mistaken in his belief that he could save those precious collections from devastation. When he went to work yesterday morning, he noticed Soviet trucks outside the archives. Soldiers were throwing folders of laws into the street through the windows. Some packets, which had been carelessly tied with string, spilled out onto the pavement. He stood to the side and, with impotent rage, watched this barbarous vandalism."

INVERNESS (California). For me, it is an example of those places which we come across by chance and rather reluctantly, but which gradually begin to inhabit us and later take on meaning. I was there numerous times in the company of people with whom I was more or less close, and when I am there now I have to think about them. At the beginning, however, Inverness caused me difficulties because of Tamales Bay. Its one straight street runs between the bay and the almost vertical wall of a hillside covered with a green thicket. The bay is shallow; that may be an illusion, but it appears to be too shallow to swim in. In any case, the wind raises only the tiny waves of shallow water. A few cutters lie at anchor against the pier as if defying nature, although they can sail from there into the Pacific. Perhaps my displeasure or discomfort has something to do with the other shore, which is completely bare—no cultivated fields, not a single tree, nothing. To be accurate, Inverness does not lie on the bay, but actually in the steep thicket of leafy trees, laurels and madrones, which make it difficult to imagine the winding lanes and wooden houses, mainly for vacation use, which are hidden there, so crowded in among the abundant vegetation that they are almost paradisiacal. To live in one of them, as I found out, is to be daily in the company of birds and animals. So, the Inverness area can seduce even a former ornithologist like me. An almost mile-long trail through the redwood forest begins at Olema; I often walked along it to the sea with my family and friends, but in those days there were only meadows, oak trees, and grazing horses at the trailhead. Now there is an enormous parking lot and an information center for nature lovers. Inverness (and Olema) somehow inhabit me, but mainly in connection with the people with whom I spent time there. Whereas in and of itself it still produces a resistance which I do not understand.

[K]

KEKŠTAS, Juozas; actually, Juozas Adomavičius. A young Lithuanian poet affiliated with the Żagary group in the Wilno of my youth. We had better relations with poets writing in other languages than did the older generation. Among the Belorussians there was Jauheni Skurko, who came from the Narocz Lake region, and who published his revolutionary poems under the pen name Maksym Tank. From the Jewish group, Yung Vilne, there were Abram Sutzkever and Chaim Grade, both of whom survived the war (Sutzkever in the ghetto, and then in a partisan group, and Grade in Tashkent).

Kekštas was definitely on the left, though I have no idea what ties, if any, he had with the Party. He was imprisoned for a while before the war, in the same cell as Maksym Tank. When Wilno became the capital of the Lithuanian Soviet Republic he started behaving rather naively, bringing upon himself the accusation that he was a deviationist, which was followed by a trip to the Gulag. Freed by the amnesty for Polish citizens, he joined General Anders's army and was evacuated with it to the Middle East. Later, he took part in the Italian campaign. Severely wounded at Monte Cassino, I believe, he was hospitalized for a long time, but by the time the Allies occupied Rome he had regained his health and was immersing himself enthusiastically in the beauty of the Eternal City, according to the Lithuanian ambassador to the Vatican, Lozorajtis, who encountered him there. Obviously, it was quite an adventure for an inhabitant of an agrarian European province to have survived the Soviet camps and then to find himself in Rome in the uniform of a victorious army. I don't know what considerations caused him to emigrate to Argentina instead of settling in England. He lived in Argentina for many years, employed chiefly, it appears, in road construction.

In Argentina he wrote and translated into Lithuanian. One should consider his translation into Lithuanian of an extensive collection of my poems—from *Three Winters* (1936), *Rescue* (1945), and *Daylight* (1953)—as an act of loyalty to Wilno and love of poetry. Under the title *Epochos Samoningumo Poezija* (Poetry of the Era's Self-Awareness), it was published in Buenos Aires in 1955 in a print run of three hundred copies. The well-known Lithuanian literary critic and poet Alfonsas Nyka-Nyliunas wrote the afterword, which indicates that the community of Lithuanian writer-émigrés, though few in number and scattered across a number of continents, made it possible for the book to appear. *Kultura* maintained contact with that community.

Illness (paralysis as a result of the wounds he suffered at the front?) forced Kekštas to leave Argentina. Apparently moved by solidarity with a fellow Wilno-ite, Jerzy Putrament came to his aid, making room for him in a home for disabled veterans in Warsaw. And that is where Kekštas lived, writing and publishing occasionally in Wilno, until his death.

KISIELEWSKI, Stefan. Before the war, nothing would have predicted his later fame as Kisiel the feuilletonist. He was a young avant-garde composer and music critic. I knew him then, but only as a social acquaintance. Our friendship began during the German occupation; from those times, I thought of him as my "beloved red monkey." He told me that he wrote, and I asked him for a typescript of his novel. Zbigniew Mitzner was buying up manuscripts with his family's money, which they were earning on the black market; I was one of his authors. Then my friend Władysław Ryńca started buying manuscripts and I went over to him, acting as his agent. It was then that Kisiel gave me his novel, *The Conspiracy*. It shocked me, because I hadn't expected such psychological intricacies from him. One could guess who (Panufnik) lay behind the characters described in it. The first two parts are rather heavy going, but the culmination is the splendid third part about the military campaign of September 1939. We signed a contract. Ryńca purchased a private home in Piastów, where he kept all the manuscripts, and the novel survived. After the war, as planned, he founded a publishing house called Pantheon, and issued *The Conspiracy*, but soon afterward all private enterprises were shut down. The novel's "scandalous" contents did not offend me at all, although when Kisiel was writing for *The Universal Weekly* he drew a flurry of criticism about it. The idea was a wonderful one: the hero, who suffers from impotence, is cured by the war, which has put an end to all normality—and to his Poland. How many symbolic meanings!

Kisiel and I used to meet in the writers' cafeteria on Foksal, and we also drank together in my home on Independence Avenue. I think it was February 1945 when he managed to join us in Krakow after the epic uprising in Warsaw.

That was when Jerzy Turowicz was organizing his *Universal Weekly*, and I recommended Kisiel to him as a good pen. Thus began his long career as the jolly man who practically turned somersaults in his feuilletons so that he could smuggle something into the sole independent (even if only partially so) paper.

Our friendship lasted for years, and led to countless meetings: Copenhagen, London, Paris, San Francisco, Warsaw, plus telephone conversations, and my writings about his books. With my encouragement, he wrote his detective novel, *Crime in the Northern District*. My highest praise went to the novel he wrote under the pseudonym Teodor Klon: *I Had One Life*. It depicts occupied Warsaw as seen through the eyes of a man who is in a state of permanent intoxication. I guessed he was concealed under the pseudonym Staliński, but the political novels he wrote under that pen name didn't appeal to me especially; the Party officials in them were like little crabs in a basket, clenched in battle with each other.

Kisiel and I quarreled frequently—for example, in the period when he had political ambitions and even held a seat in the Sejm. The most important thing that he did was writing his feuilletons for *The Universal Weekly*, for there he expresses ordinary common sense which is offended by the sight of absurdity. For a man who loved his country—and Kisiel was a patriot— what happened in Poland after 1945 seemed like one immense act of destruction and prodigality. Of course, he could not go beyond pointing out facts, behind which was concealed the truth about a little satrapy controlled from outside.

I think that if Kisiel and I had been able to spend time together in conditions of freedom (true, we drained a bottle together in 1991, not long before his death), after a while our views would have diverged considerably. Kisiel, in the end, always appeared in the costume of a jester and a harlequin, but underneath it was concealed an intellectual who was filled with

Polonocentric prejudices. He advised me to read *Thoughts of a Modern Pole* by the early twentieth-century nationalist Roman Dmowski. He understood absolutely nothing about our eastern neighbors' situations and in this he was dramatically different from Jerzy Giedroyc, with whom he often quarreled. He considered my Lithuanian sentiments to be an eccentricity, and he ascribed to me the desire to be recognized as a Balt. Most likely, had he found himself among the émigrés in wartime London, he would have shared their imperial illusions and would not have wanted to hear about any Lithuanians, Belorussians, and Ukrainians, and would also have planned the extension of a Polish protectorate over Lithuania.

Although he traveled and read a great deal, I believe he was not very different from those émigrés in his assessment of the West, and this is a severe criticism in my view, because it means that he always stood outside the life of the Western countries, without attempting to get a sense of their specific problems.

I criticize him, but I also admire him. The only independent paper between the Elbe and Vladivostok, and in it the "free voice, guaranteeing freedom," of sad Kisiel in his jester's outfit.

KISIEL'S DIARIES, 1968–1980. He insulted many people, but I have no cause to complain. Kisiel was a martyr for the truth: lying drove him into rages, and since he lived a long life and remembered a lot, living in Communist Poland—in that great enterprise for the falsification or erasure of history—he lived in a constant state of irritation. Lying, according to him, was the very essence of Communism, and in that regard the Communist press was even worse than the economic system.

He was a patriot, and like the poet Kniaznín after the partitions, he was in despair at the fate of Poland, handed over at

Yalta to Moscow's authority. The country was ruled by little Party despots installed by Moscow, and a lackey-like tone of fawning and flattery in relation to everything Russian was obligatory. Kisiel had no hope; he considered the division of Europe to be permanent, and he mocked the "Prince of Maisons-Laffitte" (Jerzy Giedroyc, the editor of *Kultura*), who insisted that the imperium would soon disintegrate from within. The new Poland was like the Czech lands after White Mountain, in his opinion: it had lost its intelligentsia of gentry origins through emigration, the execution of thousands of officers at Katyń, the Warsaw Uprising, the security organs' executions. Kisiel counted himself among the survivors and anxiously observed the new generations who no longer remembered, and for whom the reality of Communist Poland, which for him was as absurd as can be, seemed completely normal.

Very intelligent, he understood that he should not concentrate on one thing, Communism, all the time. But he could not restrain himself; he simply had to. Music saved him occasionally, but when he wrote his feuilletons, the censors' constant corrections reminded him of his lack of freedom, while his novels, published abroad under the pseudonym Tomasz Staliński, served his obsession, which is probably why they are boring.

The *Diaries* contain a catalog of Polish positions toward the West, or rather, of invectives hurled against it, most often, "blockheads, idiots," and frequently, "cynics," "cowards," and "scoundrels" (that one in regard to the French). Because a war for the planet was under way, he judged all phenomena in the West according to the necessities of war. Whatever tended to weaken it was evil: people with long hair, drug addicts, Maoists, anarchists; whatever favored a hard line against Moscow was good. He believed, after all, that it wasn't only Poland which had lost; he was inclined to believe that the West would lose through its naiveté and egotistical absorption in its own troubles. His attacks on Jerzy Turowicz, the editor of the respected Catholic *Universal Weekly*, are mainly connected with Vatican II, which had liberalized and softened Catholicism. Why did Turowicz come out in support of Vatican II? It was a Western affair, unnecessary for Poles, since the Church in Poland had other troubles.

The *Diaries*, despite such extremism, offer an exact image of Polish hopes and disappointments; they explain, too, why the most popular American president in Poland was Reagan, with his hard-nosed policies toward the "evil empire."

Despite all our differences, Kisielewski and I belonged to the same generation, and our reactions were often similar. My cast of mind, however, was entirely different from his. Most important, I was able to resist being politicized. Finding myself in the West, I was obliged to inform people, to tell them about Communism, about what they did not know and did not want to know. I performed my duty with a couple of books, but then I told myself, "Enough," and did not take it further. What would have happened had I not restrained myself in this way can be seen in the example of Leopold Tyrmand, Kisielewski's friend. In America Tyrmand poured out the truth about Communism, but it was as if his voice was resounding in an abstract space, and not in a society that had its own divisions and banners. It was mainly extreme conservatives who listened to him and he became the editor of an extremely conservative journal, and thus could no longer exert any influence on a broader range of public opinion.

I was restrained by tactics, certainly, because such an example was not productive, but also by my consciousness of another calling. Had I become a political writer, I would have narrowed and impoverished my possibilities.

In his pessimistic prognoses Kisiel, fortunately, was mistaken, but he was not the only one. His truth-telling, however, is magnificent, and he expresses opinions about Poland and the Poles which no one else has had the courage to put into writing.

KNOWLEDGE. I have had the experience of being on top and on the bottom. I have trembled before examinations, certain that I really was incapable of doing anything, and then later I was the one who looked at students trembling with fear, a professor aware of his power. What remains from these dual experiences is skepticism as to the stock of knowledge we have acquired. As students taking an exam do we not tiptoe like tightrope walkers across a wire stretched across the abyss of our ignorance? Or, administering examinations, do we not cautiously avoid asking questions which we, too, who supposedly know our subject well, would be incapable of answering? Until, as has happened to me, we become comfortable with our own inadequacy, which is beneficial, for why should we burden our memories with something that is no longer useful? My old philosophy professor in Wilno, encountered years later in California, remembered which eighteenth-century English philosophers I had discussed at my examination. To which I replied that I no longer knew a single one of their names.

My professor of civil law was undoubtedly a wise man. He said that it is impossible to know civil law and that only the good Lord might perhaps deserve an A; he himself deserved a C, so what could he expect of his students? After which he handed us a list of questions and answers: "Learn this and that's your whole exam."

Pretending to have knowledge is, however, an important social ritual, and one can doubt that the solution of our civil law specialist would be acceptable. On one side of the barrier the student pretends that he knows, and gets a good grade if he does this adroitly; in other words, skill at conducting this operation, rather than knowledge itself, is rewarded. On the other side is the professor, draped in a toga in the splendor of his authority, concerned with maintaining appearances, although often he is so doubtful about the meaning of all this teaching, that he has a desire to confess to the class, "I myself understand nothing of this."

On written exams on humanistic subjects the ability to use appropriate language is decisive. An appropriate language is the one which the "ism" professed by the examiner uses. Changing fashions of "isms" bring with them their own lexicon, their own jargon, and woe to the student who does not display a readiness to apply it. When writing, one must take into consideration the views of the person who will read what you have written, and at the very least not irritate him with some heresy. Ingenuity and conformity are valued as a part of the ritual.

Make use of your personal qualities, dear children. Since I am pulling the rug out from under myself, I can confess that I was not always objective in grading, because I would give good grades to attractive female students.

KOESTLER, Arthur. The first international best-seller immediately after World War II was probably Koestler's short novel *Darkness at Noon*, published in French translation under the title *Le Zéro et l'infini*. As is usually the case with fame, it was the sensationalism of the theme that made an impact. We should recall that Communism was fashionable at the time, that historical events were understood as a struggle of the powers of progress against Fascism. On one side were Hitler, Mussolini, General Franco, and on the other democratic Spain, the Soviet Union, and soon, the Western democracies. Koestler's novel horrified people by its breaking of a taboo, for it was forbidden to speak other than affirmatively about the socialist system as it was known in Russia. Poles who had passed through Soviet prisons and camps, and who tried in vain to explain something about this to the West, certainly learned this. Russian socialism was protected by an unwritten comradely pact; that is, by uttering any warnings against it, one committed a faux pas. The millions of fallen Soviet soldiers and Stalin's victory, also the West European Communist parties, who were now practically the only ones on the playing field with their service in the resistance movement, supported a reality which no one dared to denigrate. Anti-Soviet meant Fascist, so that, for example, the Party newspaper *L'Humanité* wrote about the French government's inexplicable tolerance of Anders's Fascist army, which had its cell in the Hôtel Lambert, directed by the (Nazi) major Józef Czapski.

And now here was a book that spoke of the terror of Stalin's governments, which took up (belatedly, to be sure) the secret of the Moscow trials of the 1930s. Immediately dread, the odor of betrayal, hellfire, formed around the book, and that is what makes for good sales.

Koestler wrote many books after that, including a lengthy autobiography, so I can refer to them. He was of a generation that entered the international arena from German culture, in the orbit of Vienna, or still in the traditions of the Habsburg monarchy. Like Kafka in Prague, like my friends Hannah Benzion, who was born in Czech Liberec, and Arthur Mandel, who was born in Bielsk, like Georg Lukács from Budapest—they all wrote in German. Koestler was born in Budapest but studied in Vienna, and from there he went everywhere. One can say of him that because of his voracious, inquisitive intellect he visited, one after the other, all the intellectual fashions and currents of his century. First Zionism and emigration to Palestine as a *halutz* contributing to the building of a Jewish state, then a passionate engagement with science and editing of the science section of a large Berlin newspaper, and right afterward, in Weimar Germany, Communism. From 1933 to 1939 he managed to work in Münzenberg's central office for Communist propaganda, in Paris, to serve as a correspondent during the Spanish Civil War, to spend time in one of Franco's prisons, and to break with the Party. His later emotional engagements included anti-Communist activity among intellectuals (the Congress for Cultural Freedom), a campaign against the death penalty in England, and finally a return to the interests of his youth, to the history of science, with sideways leaps, such as the mystery of the creative mind, or the Khazar roots of East European Jews.

I read *Darkness at Noon* (in English) several years before I met the author. Its theme is an investigation in the Lubianka prison. A true Soviet, the hard-headed Gletkin, is assigned to interrogate the old Bolshevik Rubashov, so that the latter should confess to crimes he did not commit, because in the trial that is to take place, he is supposed to receive the death penalty. In other words, the novel is an attempt to answer the question asked by many people in the thirties: Why did the old Bolsheviks confess that they were guilty and repent publicly? It must have meant that they were truly guilty, that Stalin was correct to kill them, because how else could these confessions be explained? In the novel, Rubashov yields to Gletkin's arguments: as a Communist he is obligated to place the Party's interests in first place, above all other interests, such as his good name or his desire to save his friends. The Party demands that he should publicly admit to being guilty and accuse his colleagues, because that is necessary during the given era. A record of his dedication to the cause will be preserved in the archives, and after his death, when the proper time comes, the truth that he was innocent will be brought to light.

Thus, an explanation in terms of ideology, as befits an intellectual. It seemed exceedingly recherché, and later, many people simply insisted that those people were broken by torture during the trials. Aleksander Wat, however, cites a conversation with the old Bolshevik Steklov, right before that dignitary's death in Saratov prison. According to Steklov, they confessed out of disgust at their own past: they each had so many crimes on their account, that it cost them nothing to demean themselves once again, and torture was not necessary.

No doubt both Koestler and his critics captured a portion of the truth. I am writing about him because he provides a link to the period of the civil war in Spain. People went there to fight out of the purest ideological motives, and perished at the front as the result of a sentence executed by Stalin's agents. Spain was at the center of the "anti-Fascist" propaganda carried out on an international scale by the Paris bureau, and one of its closest collaborators was Koestler himself. They made use of so-called "useful idiots" in many countries, naive people who wanted to do good. To what extent Münzenberg, the director of the bureau, was aware of Stalin's double game is unknown. In Spain, Koestler, Dos Passos, and George Orwell came to understand it.

I met Koestler in Paris, probably in 1951. His physical form explained a great deal. He was harmoniously built and handsome, but tiny, almost a dwarf, and this may have contributed to his Napoleonic ambitions and pugnaciousness, which made it difficult for him to function in any group. It was he, after all, who came up with the idea of working among the West European intellectual circles in order to cure them of Marxism, and the Berlin Congress of the Defenders of Cultural Freedom in 1950 was his work, and from it evolved the American Congress of Cultural Freedom in Paris, but Koestler himself was swiftly maneuvered out of there. Later, living in England, he limited his interests in Eastern totalitarianism to creating a fund to help émigré writers. He dedicated some of his royalties to that end.

My relations with him were eminently collegial, although superficial. We never got into a serious conversation. During the 1960s, he traveled in the United States with his much younger girlfriend or wife. They paid us a visit in Berkeley. As on many similar occasions, I was in an uncomfortable position. For him, I was the author of *The Captive Mind*, a book which he had read and valued, but in my own mind I was someone entirely different, the author of poems which he knew nothing about. I don't ascribe my bad behavior during their visit, however, to this divergence in our fields. Simply I, the host, drank too much and fell asleep, which I confess with a sense of shame, and it seems to me that I offended him without meaning to at all. Were it not for his small stature, with its attendant excessive pride, perhaps he might have seen this in a better light.

He was, it seems, above all a man of nineteenth-century positivism, whose two branches—the nationalist and the socialist—both attracted him for a certain time. His strong humanitarian sentiments made him work against the English penalty of death by hanging, and later he fought for a law permitting euthanasia.

He was an adherent of euthanasia and proved it in practice. He and his young wife were found together, seated side by side in armchairs, dead.

KORZENIEWSKI, Bohdan. We wore janitors' coveralls and, seated on one of the metal levels of the library stacks, we sorted books. We did this in the University Library in Warsaw and also in the Krasiński Library. We took breaks to rest and to talk, but Pulikowski, sneaking around in his rubber-soled shoes, would catch us sometimes despite our precautions. It was he who oversaw our work, not Witte, the short Slavist from Breslau, who just sat in his office. Witte (Pulikowski probably put him up to this) had devised an ambitious plan for dividing up the Warsaw book collections according to genres and transferring them to appropriate depositories: Polonica would be in one building, foreign languages in another, works on the theater in yet another. Absolute insanity in the middle of a war, but necessary to protect the developer of the plan from going to the front. He was assisted in this by Pulikowski, who was a musicologist, a German from the Reich, married to a German.

Korzeniewski and I were connected not only through this work, which we did for the soup we were given in the afternoons and for the *Ausweise*, the official work permits that came with the job, but also through our meetings and theatrical discussions with Edmund Wierciński, Leon Schiller, and, on occasion, Stefan Jaracz. Korzeniewski was mainly engaged in the practical affairs of the underground Theater Council, for which I was writing some pieces at Wierciński's invitation. Did Pulikowski, creeping around, hope to overhear some conspiratorial whispering, or was he simply making sure that his workers weren't lazing about? We shall never know who he was beneath his martinet's façade.

It is possible that the illegal newsletters and weapons, too, which were hidden in the libraries were there with his knowledge. He had helped in rescuing Korzeniewski. Korzeniewski landed in Auschwitz in 1940, because when the Germans surrounded his housing block in the Żoliborz district in the great roundup, he obeyed their orders and went downstairs. He had one of the lower numbers tattooed onto his arm in the camp. Efforts to get him out continued for several months, and their success, I think, owed not a little to Pulikowski, who campaigned for his employee. So, Korzeniewski was one of those people in occupied Warsaw who were familiar with the concentration camp, like Schiller and Jaracz, who were rescued from it with great difficulty. This did not dissuade him from continuing his underground activity. As for Pulikowski, he died during the Uprising; the particular circumstances of his death are unknown.

Korzeniewski belongs to the history of the theater in Poland, as an organizer and a director. But today only professionals know his name, and that is not likely to change in the future. I am writing about him, however, absolutely convinced that at some time in the future this man of the theater will be recognized as great in his other incarnation. Toward the end of his life he wrote down his experiences as a prisoner in Auschwitz, as the man who saved the University Library in Warsaw after the Soviet troops marched in, and finally as a delegate and detective in pursuit of books taken out of Poland by the Germans. His account, published under the modest title *Books and People*, first appeared in 1989, and was reissued in 1992. In it, the entire rationalistic temperament of this admirer of eighteenth-century writers came to fruition in splendid, spare, laconic prose. Since reality had exceeded the bounds of probability, one might take the faithfully recorded details as the inventions of a surrealist—

for example, the boy in the uniform of the Hitlerjugend (the Auschwitz commandant's son) drilling his little brother, or the vain attempts to warn the Soviet soldiers, who broke into jars of specimens preserved in formaldehyde and drank the liquid in them, and then had to be buried the next day. Or the train loaded with wartime booty—just clocks, all of them ticking in their own rhythms. No one could have imagined that, and Korzeniewski's prose has preserved the unique details of great history. The truthfulness of this prose exceeds even Tadeusz Borowski's descriptions, because there is no trace of sado-masochistic delight in them. It will take its place in textbooks and will become a lasting part of Polish literature.

In the summer of 1949 in Obory, at a session on the theater, Korzeniewski was attacked for the "unrealistic" costumes in a play he was directing by the nineteenth-century Russian writer, Sukhovo-Kobylin—*The Death of Tarelkin.* A Party member by the name of Jerzy Pański was the most vociferous of his attackers. I took the floor and thought I would try to defend the director, but my defense was more dangerous for him than the attack. He told Małgorzata Szejnert that the worst attacks on him were because of me. I feel very bad about this. He defended himself against the accusation of "grotesqueness" by pointing to illustrations from the era of Tsar Nicholas I. That was exactly what the uniforms and hats of the tsarist police looked like at that time.

KOTARBIŃSKI, Mieczysław. Really, my book must not turn into a list of benedictions. Considering that people usually act out of their own interest, the disinterested help that I received on many occasions should surprise me. But Mieczysław, the younger brother of the philosophy professor Tadeusz Kotarbiński, a painter and director of the studio in the Academy of Fine Arts, was a radiant figure and whatever he did was, I swear, on the side of good, if we can still place faithful service to art on that side. I would define my feelings toward him not as gratitude, but as tenderness. I owe him my introduction to Stanisław Michalski (an unusual figure in the preindependence underground work), the director of the Fund for National Culture, from which I received a scholarship that made possible my stay in Paris in 1934–1935. No one knows, however, that after I returned from Paris I became a powerful figure as an advisor to the Fund, despite the rather right-wing views for which Michalski was known.

His fingers black from nicotine, enthusiasms that he seemed almost ashamed of, and a passion for art: Mieczysław wanted to help his fellow man, including Jews. For that, he was incarcerated in Pawiak prison and was executed in 1943.

KOWNACKI, Stanisław (Staś). It would be difficult to invent a character as peculiar as Staś. I was able to get to know him well, because we went through practically all of Sigismund August Gymnasium in the same class. He was from Ukraine. The son of a Polish father and a Russian mother, he spoke both Russian and Ukrainian well. In Wilno he was looked after by his cousin, Piotr Kownacki, the editor of *The Wilno Daily*. Here I shall permit myself a digression. That newspaper, one of three Polish-language papers in the city, represented the Nationalist Party. *The Wilno Courier*, under the editorial direction of Kazimierz Okulicz, who was said to be a Mason, was Piłsudskiite with a democratic slant; *The Word*, under Stanisław Mackiewicz's editorial direction, was seen as the organ of the conservative "bisons" (the great landowners). *The Wilno Daily*, patriotic and devout as it was, left itself open to cutting witticisms because it occupied the second floor in a building whose ground floor housed a well-known public house, or bordello. The Nationalist Party in Wilno exuded hatred for the Piłsudskiites. And not without reason. I shall cite only the beating by military officers of Assistant Professor Stanisław Cywiński (the man who initiated me into the writings of Cyprian Norwid), one of their activists, because in one of his articles he had expressed himself none too flatteringly about Piłsudski. The disastrous defeat in 1939 did not put an end to this enmity; on the contrary, it provided an occasion for settling scores. Piotr Kownacki wrote a pamphlet then in which he poured out all his rage over the defeat, assigning responsibility for it to the rulers. The other author of the pamphlet was, wonder of wonders, Józef Mackiewicz, *The Word*'s associate, who had had nothing in common with the nationalist Kownacki before the war. What united them was their fury and despair in the face of the country's misfortune. But their attack on defeated interwar Poland was not taken kindly in Wilno and, in my opinion, the series of accusations of treason that would dog Józef Mackiewicz had their origin in that pamphlet.

Piotr Kownacki somehow evaded deportation during the Soviet occupation. (Stanisław Cywiński was deported and died in the Gulag.) During the German occupation, he worked in the underground, was arrested, and was tortured in Auschwitz. When I tell Americans about such cases, they cannot understand that the Germans murdered programmatic anti-Semites. But it's true; they did.

In school, Staś did not show any interest in politics. He was completely devoted to one passion—building shortwave radio receivers and transmitters, and was thoroughly absorbed in conversations and also correspondence with a large number of similar amateurs throughout the world. His room looked like a laboratory. He devoted only a minimum amount of time to his school studies; he had good grades, but nothing exceptional. He also joined in our athletic enthusiasms. In the winter, because the city is nestled among rather steep hills and gets a lot of snow, we had intense luge competitions. During one of them, a sled crashed into a tree and Staś was taken to the hospital, where he was diagnosed with a crushed spleen, which had to be removed. Despite his doctors' expectations, Staś lived on and on, into his eighties.

After high school, Staś studied electricity at the Warsaw Polytechnic, and then, after receiving his diploma, he spent a year in England. That came about as a result of a certain wiliness on my part. After I returned from my year's scholarship in Paris, the Fund for National Culture used me as one of its advisers in the field of literature. To support Staś's application, I employed this strategem: Why, I asked, is there such an imbalance? Why give scholarships to humanists while young engineers get nothing? The argument worked and Staś went off to Cambridge, which was not inconsequential in his later adventures.

After the 1939 defeat Staś found himself in Bucharest where, thanks to his knowledge of English, he was hired by the British Embassy to enroll Polish pilots and send them to England. In turn, he himself followed that track and joined the Royal Air Force in England. He took part in the Italian campaign, flying as a radio operator in two-man observation planes, and later, stationed in Algiers, he fell in love with Arabs.

Wanda, whom he had married before the war, remained in

Warsaw. She was an office worker in a metallurgical factory in Praga, the industrial, working class district across the Vistula River from Warsaw proper, and the *Ausweis* documenting me as a worker in that factory was her doing; she produced it for me when I had no documents after the destruction of my Wilno passport. Perhaps that *Ausweis* wasn't much protection, but it was better than nothing. Immediately after the conclusion of military operations she managed to get to Germany, and from there to England, where she and Staś took various jobs—anything to make survival possible; for example, for a time they traveled among the Polish encampments like a mobile shop, selling kielbasa. After that phase, they emigrated to the United States, where Staś began his amazing academic career. Not at just one university. He was a fine lecturer, but he never lasted more than one year in any position, and by moving around all the time he traversed the entire continent. Staś had a peculiar sense of humor. It manifested itself in his expressing, with a perfectly straight face, opinions which drove his listeners to distraction, because they never knew if he was speaking seriously or joking. He could, for example, tell his Jewish colleagues how Jews collect Christian children's blood to make matzoh. If that particular story testified to his love of cruel jokes, some of his other anti-Jewish pronouncements probably expressed his true feelings. He always took the side of the Arabs and railed against the state of Israel. His anti-Semitism became more and more pronounced. His constant provocations, with total indifference to the consequences, usually led to his fellow professors becoming sick and tired of him after just a couple of months.

In addition, Staś also conducted his provocations through litigation, as illustrated by his suit against the federal government when he worked as an engineer for Lockheed. Since this was part of the defense industry, in certain divisions it was necessary to have high security clearance—permission to have access to state secrets. Staś originally was granted the highest level of clearance, but then he was lowered one step because, as was noted in his personnel file, he subscribed to *Kultura*. But it's an anti-Communist journal! Who bothered to inquire about such things—all that mattered was that it was written in an Iron Curtain language, and that was proof of its unhealthy interests. It happened that soon afterward, Staś took part in a government conference in which participation was granted only to those with the highest level of clearance. That is when he initiated his suit against the government for permitting an individual with insufficient clearance to take part in that conference.

Because of his clowning and playing the buffoon even with his friends, I never really knew what the man actually thought. I believe I can take his measure from his numerous letters to the editor, demonstrating his anti-Israel obsession.

By dedicating himself to the pure art of sticking out his tongue and thumbing his nose, Staś kept exposing his family to poverty whenever he lost a job. But when he was truly badly off, he could use his knowledge of technical terminology in five languages (English, Polish, French, Russian, and Ukrainian) and take on scientific translation jobs. Ultimately, he made it. He bought a house in Los Gatos and put his two daughters through college.

Our 1962 vacation: the two of us at Eagle Lake in the Sierra Nevada mountains. A tent, cooking equipment, a folding kayak, in the morning a walk down a meadow path to bathe and swim out beyond the bulrushes, although the water was quite cold. If only Ignacy and Bohdan Kopeć were there, it would have been like that time in the Rudnicka Wilderness after we passed our *gymnasium* graduation exam, but Kopeć was in Poland and Ignacy Święcicki was on the other coast of America.

KRASNOGRUDA, or Krasnohruda. It was not the Kunats' hereditary estate; it was purchased from relatives in the nineteenth century. I don't know the first name of my great-grandfather, who had two sons: Bronisław and Zygmunt. The former became the master of Krasnogruda; the latter studied agronomy in the Central School in Warsaw, emigrated to the north, to Lithuania, married Józefa Syruciówna, and became my grandfather. The photograph of him as a little boy still amazes me. What intensity of the joy of living, and at the same time a jocular sense of humor and intelligence. A very sweet little boy; everyone must have loved him, and that was confirmed when he grew up.

Not far from Krasnogruda, in Sejny, is the grave of Bronisław Kunat; Zygmunt's grave, however, is in Kiejdany county, in Świętobrość. When he traveled to Kaunas, the capital of independent Lithuania, to take care of various matters in the government offices there, his family name was a great help, because it seemed so native, since in Lithuanian *kuna* means "body," "strength." In fact, all it could prove was that the Jadźwing tribes spoke a Balt dialect, something between Prussian and Lithuanian; according to family legend the Kunats were descended from Jatwież. Their roots, then, are where there are the most excavations testifying to the existence of Jadźwings—in the Suwalski region. But how it came about that they were driven out in the Middle Ages, I do not know. They did not go beyond the condition of an Indian tribe; they did not unite into a state. So is it true that one great battle which ended in slaughter was sufficient to put an end to their existence? And that the leader's young son, taken into captivity, was accepted into the clan of the Axe and raised as a Pole? This smells a bit like the fantasies of historians from the era of Romanticism.

For a couple of centuries, an unpopulated wilderness stretched between the settlements of the Teutonic Knights and Lithuania; it began to be settled late, by Poles from the south, Lithuanians from the north. Where was the seat of the ennobled Kunats? The library of Stanisław Kunat, an economist, and after the November uprising an émigré in France, a professor at the École de Batignolles, was in Krasnogruda. If I could find out where he was born, that would be an indication.

The heirs of Krasnogruda—Bronisław's daughters, my cousins Ela and Nina, and also Ela's husband, Władysław Lipski, and, symbolically, their son Zygmunt, who died in a German concentration camp—rest in the Catholic cemetery in Sopot. There, too, lies Weronika, Zygmunt's daughter and my mother. But her sister Maria is buried in Olsztyn. So many bare facts, which we carry with us wherever we go, although civilization seems to be less and less congenial to memories of these foggy tribal concerns.

KRIDL, Manfred. In Wilno, I was briefly a student of Polish studies, the "matrimonial department," populated almost exclusively by young women. That would have been an interesting topic: the influence on youngsters of the circumstance that in school, Polish literature is taught almost exclusively by women. Studying law, however, I still belonged to the Creative Writing Circle, which is the source of my acquaintance with the Circle's patron, Professor Kridl.

The peculiarity of Polish studies as a discipline: after all, it arose in the nineteenth century, primarily with the help of Romantic poetry, as an academic discipline for patriotic indoctrination. The discipline was based on chewing and digesting the bards, which was understandable in a country ruled by foreigners after the partitions. A certain doctrine was already potentially present in the very division into the nation (one's own) and the state (foreign). Europe, composed of tribes who spoke various languages, was fairly cosmopolitan up until the end of the eighteenth century. A change ensued along with the spread of universal written culture, because until then oral culture, or folklore, was dominant. That is what Ernest Gellner argued, writing about the origins of nationalism, and he was probably right. The leaders of this change were the first generation of the intelligentsia—the student-literati—and Wilno's Philomaths confirm this thesis perfectly.

Is indoctrinating patriotically the same thing as indoctrinating nationalistically? Not exactly. But it was the same with such professors as Ignacy Chrzanowski. If Polish literature is difficult to understand in countries which developed more harmoniously, in any event without the experience of partitions, it is because at its center lies the absolute concept of a near-goddess: the Nation. This was caused by the messianists and their heirs, professors who maintained a messianic fervor. It is only a single step from this to a political program. In essence, Roman Dmowski's Nationalist Party entered Polish thought in the most natural and logical way. Dmowski was a very intelligent man and it seems difficult to refute his program. Unfortunately, he studied biology, and in attempting to ground the messianists' far too lofty ideas about the Nation, he resorted to Darwinism, although instead of individuals fighting for survival, he introduced nations. His thinking lacked generosity. And it was probably that flaw that predestined him to be a graphomaniac (he wrote bad novels).

This digression is not unconnected to Kridl, because it was precisely in the two interwar decades that a change took place in the discipline of Polish studies, leading to a renewal in the way literature was studied. Kridl contributed to this change, although he also had predecessors. Born in Lwów in 1882, he studied Polish literature there and also was attracted to the intellectual rigor of philosophers. He named them: Twardowski, Łukasiewicz, Kotarbiński, Husserl. Then he studied in Freiburg and in Paris. After World War I he taught at the Free University in Warsaw and at a university in Brussels. In 1932 he became a professor at my university, succeeding Stanisław Pigoń, and there he created his own circle, frequently citing in his articles the writings of the Russian Formalists. He was conscious of contributing, with his students, to a scholarly revolution, and later he described it in *The Struggles Between Wilno and Warsaw for a New Science of Literature.*

Western Structuralism is derived directly from the Russian Formalist School. But that happened later. Kridl's group can be called pre-Structuralists. I did not belong to it; one of its members was Jerzy Putrament, one of the new male Polonists. But Kridl, as patron of the Creative Writing Circle, reacted positively to the *Anthology of Social Poetry*, which Zbigniew Folejewski and I edited. (He was the son of Wilno's mayor; later, a professor in Sweden, the United States, and Canada.) Professor Kridl wrote a preface for the anthology in which he responded sympathetically to our leftist extremism, but also with a skeptic's smile. In any event, he was open to the new and he situated himself politically among the free-thinking democrats—entirely differently from Professor Konrad Górski, for example, a messianic nationalist with whom he was in continual conflict.

My excursion to Troki with Irena Sławińska and Kridl's family bears witness to a certain closeness to the professor. We squeezed into one boat, which was painted in bright colors, as was the style. I sat at the oars, rowing vigorously out beyond the island, to the open expanse of the lake.

Kridl and his family managed to leave Lithuania at the beginning of the war and to travel via Sweden to Brussels, where he had old friends. From there to America. I met Kridl when I myself wound up in America after the war. For a while, he taught at Smith College in Massachusetts, a fine institution, but in general things were going badly for him even though Slavists knew of his scholarly articles and books, and that Roman Jakobson "himself" supported him.

At this point, a great scandal begins, not instigated by me, but with my considerable participation. I am the Polish Embassy's attaché, and Professor Simmons, chairman of the Department of Slavic Studies at Columbia University in New York, has been talking with me. He reveals a proposal from his university. They will create a chair of Polish literature and will name it the Adam Mickiewicz Chair if we will give them the money—$10,000 annually. At that time, that was a significant sum. To my question, Who will be the lecturer? Simmons says, somewhat timidly, that they have a candidate, Professor Kridl. I reply that I know and value Kridl and will do what I can.

A wealthy American university is not ashamed to seek a subsidy from a poor Communist country! But there had never been a chair of Polish literature in America and so I, a traitor, a collaborator, have the opportunity to create one, despite all of Polonia, which declaimed patriotically, but had never managed such a feat. Obviously, my guilty conscience as a collaborator gave me added energy. Simmons's motives became clear only later. It may be true that he had Communist sympathies. But above all, he wanted to get rid of Coleman. That American of Irish descent had taken a liking to Poles and was teaching something or other in the department; he was insufficiently qualified, however, to become a full professor. Simmons reasoned, completely logically, that instead of Coleman he could have a serious Polish scholar who was without a permanent position.

Our Minister of Foreign Affairs at the time was Zygmunt Modzelewski, an old Communist who had spent many years in emigration in France, from where he had gone straight to Moscow when summoned—straight to the Gulag, that is. A quick-witted person, he immediately saw the benefits of this proposal, including the political ones, since Red Poland would appear as a protector of Polish culture. The subsidy was awarded and the Mickiewicz Chair, occupied by Kridl, was created in honor of the one hundred fiftieth birthday of the poet, in 1948.

All hell broke loose in the Polish-American press (Kridl as a Bolshevik, a Communist plant at Columbia), and it was in-flamed nonstop by Coleman. The poor guy had submitted his resignation in protest against the creation of the chair; it was accepted, to his horror, and that was what this was all about. The president of Columbia at the time was Dwight Eisenhower, and Polish protest demonstrations against the Communist infiltration of his institution took place in front of his residence.

The piles of press cuttings sent to Warsaw contributed to my reputation there. Pride in founding the first Polish chair in America would not, however, have been appropriate, because there was something unseemly in this whole noisy affair. The genial Coleman and his wife, Marion, wanted to do good; they tried to translate Mickiewicz, but they didn't have the right "level." Their Polish friends were ordinary people who had not the slightest notion of what Kridl represented. Polonia was made up of hardworking laborers, who were often illiterate when they migrated from their villages, and they had no conception of a university; they simply did not know that influences come together there. Now, here is a conspiracy of the educated against the common people. And what did Mickiewicz have to do with this? He made quite a lot of mischief by arming the educated Polish stratum with messianism, which barely trickled down to the common people. They disarmed the participants in the 1863 uprising and handed them over to the Russians, and later emigrated to the mines and factories of America. In these circumstances, the chair in Polish literature acquired a class-based aura: "We, the intellectuals, know better what is good for you."

Kridl, Józef Wittlin, and I worked on a Mickiewicz volume in English—a symposium by the pens of various authors, edited by Kridl, and subsidized by the Embassy. It appeared, not in the anniversary year of 1948, but behind schedule, in 1951.

I did not follow the ensuing years of the chair, because I left America. After the professor's death, the chair was discontinued; the university did not think it useful to invest its own money in it.

Kridl was more than just a serious scholar. He is remembered by everyone who knew him as a just and kind man, too trusting and noble, perhaps, for an age that did not favor humanists.

[L]

LENA. This happened in 1917, on the Yermolovka estate on the Volga River. I was six years old and a refugee. Every morning a carriage driven by a uniformed coachman drove up to the Yermolovs' palace and twelve-year-old Lena would get in to be driven to her school in Rzhev, which was about one kilometer away. In my old age, that scene has become very clear, enriched by knowledge that neither I nor Lena had at the time. For only a few days later the end would come for the carriages, the coachmen, and the palaces, and Lena would grow up in a different Russia, which neither her parents nor her *babushki* could imagine. I have often thought about what happened to her, attempting to picture her in various situations of revolution and civil war.

But that boy looking at Lena's neck, taken together with his later musings about her fate, is really a highly erotic knot. The first of my fascinations. Because then there was the smashed coffin of the princess, her ribbons, her satin slippers, in the tomb on the road to Kaunas near Poginie. And the events of the 1920s, when beautiful Barbara terrified people after her death in Świętobrość. And I at a Pirandello play in Paris, when Ludmilla Pitoëff, a very famous actress at the time, changes in the course of just a few minutes from a young girl to an old woman—and the Parcae, the goddesses of Fate, sprinkle ashes into her hair, draw wrinkles on her face. It is always the same: woman and time the destroyer. Desired perhaps because she is so fragile and mortal. Yeats comes to mind:

> *Does the imagination dwell the most*
> *Upon a woman won or woman lost?*
> *("The Tower")*

Lost, it would seem.

LEVERTOV, Denise. I remember that dinner, in an Italian restaurant in Greenwich Village in lower Manhattan. An international circle of poets sat at the table. It was probably the late nineteen-sixties. Denise was good-looking, and also famous. Eugène Guillevic, whose poems she had translated into English, was always at her side. Guillevic, a bearded Breton, muscular, short, sturdily built, looked like a satyr or Priapus. He was a member of the French Communist Party, but his poetry had nothing political about it, other than a similarity of assumptions, because it was possible to view them as the result of his materialistic philosophy. I kept my distance from him and we became friendly only later, in Rotterdam, where we both took part in an international poetry festival. Guillevic had a marvelous sense of humor, as did Vasko Popa from Belgrade, whose poetry resembles his, and who was also our Rotterdam companion. Popa, a Party member, stiffened, however, when Guillevic, who couldn't control his foul mouth, made fun of his own party.

But let me return to that dinner. Guillevic's companionship was perfect for Denise, whose fame, independent of her talent, contributed to the rise in left convictions and participation in pacifist actions. I found her physically very appealing, less so in her opinions, but we all were drinking a lot of red wine, and those red-checked tablecloths, the aroma of the food, the smoke and laughter, left a joyous memory. I did not expect that I would become friends with Denise years later in entirely different circumstances.

An unusual person, she differed from other American poets in the high culture she had acquired in her home, which was noticed by Kenneth Rexroth, the California promoter of poets. She was born in England to a rather strange set of parents. Her father, the descendant of a famous Hasid, came from "northern Belorussia," as she put it, and began as a rabbi. Before World War I he decided to study at a German university and chose the nearest one, in Königsberg. He changed his religion to Christianity and from then on spent his entire life reconciling Christianity with Judaism, writing and translating from Hebrew and into Hebrew. He became an Anglican priest. Her mother, a Welsh woman, was descended in a direct line from "Angel Jones of Mold," a small-town tailor and mystic. Their home in England, filled with books, was the site of continual discussions about religion, philosophy, and literature. They did not send Denise to school; she studied at home.

Born in 1923, Denise debuted as a poet in England, but shortly after the war she married an American soldier and moved to America. There she changed her way of writing, switching to free verse, measured only by breathing, as in William Carlos Williams. Actually, she experimented from one volume to the next.

Always, despite her agnosticism, she remained her parents' faithful daughter—a mystic. She stumbled across the difficult problem of reconciling her personal, and often excessively metaphorical, style with her allegiance to Revolution. Her ardent heart could not bear what was happening in the United States and beyond its borders. Racial discrimination, nuclear weapons, the prisons and terror of the military juntas in Latin America, the war in Vietnam. She attached herself to the rebellion of the younger generation and became the standard-bearer of the movement of the sixties, taking part in demonstrations, traveling to North Vietnam, everywhere, in fact, around the globe, where a voice of protest was needed. The only place it was not needed, certainly, was in the countries of the Soviet bloc.

Her attentive readers were not surprised by the numerous changes her poetry underwent. In the final analysis, she always preserved the same personal tone; as she aged, she paid more and more attention to contemplation of nature and writing in its defense. I included her poems from this phase in my anthology, *A Book of Luminous Things*, and also translated them for the Polish edition.

No one, however, could have foreseen that Denise Levertov, the revolutionary, would become the one and only fine woman poet of orthodox religious poetry of her time—poetry about Christ, the Incarnation, the Crucifixion, and the Resurrection. It was not a sudden conversion; on the contrary, this turn toward her parents' faith occurred gradually, over a couple of decades, leading eventually to her acceptance of Catholicism. She collected her religious poems in a separate volume, *The Stream and the Sapphire* (1997). Their uniqueness rests in her use of modern poetic devices, similar to what Rouault did, for example, in his religious paintings.

In her last years, chronic illness made it impossible for her to travel outside of Seattle, where she lived. We often spoke by telephone. When I translated a number of her Christian poems with the intention of sending them to the Catholic *Universal Weekly* in Kraków, I wrote to her to ask for permission. Her letter, written in the hospital, the last one she managed to write, reached me at the same time as the news of her death.

LOS ANGELES. This collection of towns, settlements, suburbs, should not really be called a city. It should not even exist, because cities are not founded in areas that are dry as dust, where everything depends on water that is brought in from far away. There was no reason to think that it would become the capital of America, and who knows, perhaps of the entire world.

Los Angeles horrifies me. In our imagination money is still steel and the production of factories; it is difficult to accustom oneself to the great change, the complete reversal, that has granted a marginal human activity, entertainment, its central position as a source of money or power.

Who could have anticipated this? When I used to go to the movies in Wilno, they were still silent films, with Mary Pickford, Chaplin, later with Greta Garbo and Sylvia Sidney; I was unaware that I was participating in the future. Going to the movies meant entertainment, no more than that, and in Los Angeles, where those films were made, I can lose myself in thought about the development of a technological curiosity, a trifle, a way of spending one's free time, into the dimensions of a world power.

LOURIE, Richard and Jody. Richard was one of the thirty students in the first class that I taught at Berkeley in 1960. Unkempt and disheveled, he heralded a change in mores; he deserves the label of one of the first hippies. He had written some nonsense on an exam and instead of simply giving him a bad grade, I invited him in for a conversation in order to explain to him why he was mistaken. That was the beginning of our friendship. He told me about his earlier career. During his high school years in Boston he had earned a lot of money as a chauffeur for a famous local gangster, which carried the risk of his being riddled with bullets by a rival gang, but also put him in the position of a little king of life.

In Berkeley, Richard quickly became acquainted with the culture of pot or grass, and of LSD. He fit in very well on this colorful campus, about which a certain dumbfounded and horrified Bulgarian professor once said, *"Eto postoianny karnaval!"* ("It's a nonstop carnival!") Jody, a sculptress whom he married, also adapted in the same way to the customs of the Berkeley folk. Richard's grandparents had emigrated to America from a Lithuanian Jewish town. Jody, on the other hand, still maintained contact with her Catholic family in Italy.

Richard developed differently from what one might have expected. Industrious and systematic, he did well on his exams, earned a master's degree and then a doctorate in Russian literature. He also learned Polish. His example demonstrates that the disintegrative influences of the environment on a person who possesses an inner compass are limited. Furthermore, Richard, instead of choosing teaching as his means of earning a living, decided that he would make his living as a writer of prose, but above all, as a translator. Over the course of many years, I have watched him do this with the greatest admiration. He became the leading translator from Polish in the United States (translating, among other works, my books and Aleksander Wat's *My Century*); he also frequently translated from Russian. Since translations are too poorly paid to make a living from, he needed truly iron discipline and efficiency. Jody, whose ceramic sculptures are highly praised, equaled him in willpower. Richard made use of his knowledge of Russian and his travels in that country in several books of prose that are on the borderline between reportage and fiction.

Now they are both of retirement age and we are connected by decades of untroubled friendship. And also by comic episodes, like the time when I received an honorary doctorate from Brandeis University and invited them both to the reception. Evening dress was required. Richard, not particularly comfortable with this since he still maintained his bohemian habits, showed up in a tuxedo and yellow shoes.

I produced a good translator in him. Another one of my students is Louis Iribarne, who published a translation of Witkiewicz's *Insatiability*; also Catherine Leach, the translator of Pasek's *Memoirs of the Polish Baroque*. I can also make a partial claim to Bogdana Carpenter. Madeline Levine studied with Professor Wiktor Weintraub at Harvard. Translators from Polish can be divided into Weintraubists and Miłoszists.

LOVE, First. Where I was born, the Niewiaża River flows beneath high plateaus to either side, and on the slopes of the ravine the green parks of the manors could be seen at intervals of one or two kilometers. Not far from Szetejnie, across the river, right near Kałnoberża, was the Suryszki manor, a name similar to Syrutyszki, which was probably once upon a time the property of the Syruć clan, although they are closer to Kiejdany. Considering the small size of that tiny region, no larger than a quarter of a county, you would think that everyone would know everyone else in the neighboring area; there isn't a single trip you could take by car that would last longer than ten minutes. That, however, is a delusion stemming from our habits of today.

Muddy roads, a lack of horses (because they are needed to work in the fields), a lack of telephones to make arrangements, did not encourage lively neighborly relations.

My grandparents took me along once on a visit to Suryszki. The manor belonged to the Kudrewiczes. They are an old noble family, probably of Lithuanian descent, because the word *kudra* means "pond" in that language. I was, I think, eight years old. The old folks gossiped and entrusted me to a young girl, who was to show me the park. We walked along the paths, crossed some little bridges which had railings made of birch poles—I remember that well. Then it happened. I looked at her thin bare shoulders, the narrowness of her arms above the elbow, and an emotion I had never experienced, a tenderness, a rapture, unnamable, welled up in my throat. I had no idea that this is called love. I think she must have said something, explaining, but I said not a word, struck dumb by what had suddenly come over me.

She surely had a name, but I have no idea what it was. No doubt she, like her entire family, was deported to Siberia in 1940. What happened to her? Most likely the Jan Kudrewicz who was released from the Gulag, joined the Polish army, and lies buried on Monte Cassino was her brother. In Kiejdany in 1992 I was told that a Kudrewicz from that family who now lives in England wanted to reclaim the estate, but only on condition that he be given sufficient land to make farming it financially feasible.

MANORS. There have been too few studies on the essence of the manor, considering that this was a fundamental part of gentry culture. Still, some distinctions have to be made. It seems to me that manors in Lithuania were a little different—both because their peasants fared better than in Poland, and because the masters were less lordly. It suffices to recall how Jakub Gieysztor fulminated in his memoirs against certain wealthy gentlemen (Prince Ogiński, Czapski), which meant that they were the exceptions. It is well known that contrary to what happened in Poland, peasants in Lithuania supported the 1863 Uprising, referring to it, of course, as a "Polish uprising," but nonetheless supplying the rebels' forest encampments with food and aid. In the very center of Lithuania, in my Kiejdany district, that is, they were armed participants. True, I think that Father Mackiewicz, a superb preacher in both languages, attracted chiefly the petty squires of Lauda to his detachments, but peasants joined him, too. Without insisting on the idyllic nature of relations there, it still must be said that the end of the manor in the twentieth century took place there without any acts of cruelty.

But the manor is from a bygone era, and everything that came from it was outmoded. When it came up against urban modernity from the West, only degenerate little scions of the gentry—like Gombrowicz, Jeleński, Miłosz—were able to squeeze something out of it. This distinguished them from, for example, Melchior Wańkowicz, an old-fashioned, nattering spinner of tales. The literature of the manor should include not only the novels of Orzeszkowa and Rodziewiczówna, but also novels by Dąbrowska, Iwaszkiewicz, and many others.

For people like me, the difficulty arose from the absence of a firm foundation. The Polish part of Wilno, a city of several dozen synagogues and forty churches, was truly a branch of the manor, with people who spoke in "simple talk"—another word for shaky Polish. Rebellion against it could not be like James Joyce's big-city rebellion against Dublin. Jewish Wilno, in contrast, was growing closer to the great cities to which it exported talent: Petersburg, Paris, New York.

The old-fashioned, respectable novel of the manor assumed a clearly drawn opposition between good and evil. The good was here, on our native soil; evil was external, in the lands of great cities. Virtue was represented by the lord of the manor, a good farmer who somehow made ends meet despite obstacles and held on to his land. Evil was embodied in members of the family who were squandering their money in some foreign country, wastrels and slaves of foreign fashion (even, tee hee, of morphine, as in Orzeszkowa's *On the Banks of the Niemen*).

Probably the most amusing late variant of this model is Emma Domowska's novel *The Manor at Haliniszki* (1903). This time, the foreign land is the Rome of churches and priests, where the mistress of Haliniszki sojourns with her daughter. The daughter has religious visions and is convinced that she has received a commandment to found a new holy order. The mother (not for completely noble reasons) helps her in her attempts to win the consent of the church hierarchy. They need money. The despairing lord of Haliniszki tries in vain to convince the women that they could work for the Lord in their own country. In other words, what is satirized here is not sitting around in Paris or on the Côte d'Azur and squandering money in Monte Carlo, but the devotion of a young miss, who is totally unaware that by praying and seemingly fulfilling the will of the Mother of God, she is on the side of evil.

Move Haliniszki several decades into the future, into the interwar period and World War II; show the manor from a completely different perspective. The action of the novel *God's Lining* by Teresa Lubkiewicz-Urbanowicz takes place somewhere in the neighborhood of Ejszyszki. It is a psychological novel; the manor intentionally provides only the setting. Perhaps despite the author's intentions, it is this setting that is most interesting, because for the first time modernity has intruded into observations and descriptions of the manor. In Haliniszki, at most, men and women held hands. Here, there is the sexual life of a small community, the pressuring of the peasant girls, even the first description in Polish literature of a woman masturbating. The war is cruelly, if obliquely, present in this backward forested province. Reading this well-written and by no means naive book, I wondered if this might not be at last the final entry in a long line of novels about the manors, large and small.

MARGOLIN, Juliusz. I made his acquaintance in Alsace, in Mittelbergheim, in the autumn of 1951, when he came from Israel to take part in a small conference that was being held there.

Margolin was from Pinsk. As a member of the Pinsk intelligentsia his language was Russian, not Yiddish. He became a Zionist as a young man, joined the *halutz* movement, and emigrated to Palestine. In the summer of 1939 he came back to

Pinsk to visit his family and was caught there by the war. Despite all his efforts and his documents confirming that he was a resident of Palestine, he was unable to get back. He was arrested and deported to camps in Vorkuta, where he managed to survive for a couple of years. Finally, freed, he found himself back in Palestine where he wrote a horrifying book in Russian, which was also translated into French. The images of his first day in the world of the Soviet camps are as vivid to me today as they were in 1951 when I received an inscribed copy of his book from him.

That was a brief and very friendly meeting. Many years later in San Francisco I met his son, a well-known attorney, who had studied in Israel and then in the United States, and had settled here. By then, Juliusz Margolin was no longer alive.

MARITAIN, Jacques. I picked up one of the fifteen volumes of the writings of Jacques and Raissa Maritain. For me, Maritain is a great name, but for how many other people who walk this earth?

Jacques Maritain studied philosophy at the Sorbonne before World War I and came upon Bergson's lectures, which turned out to be decisive for him. He was a Protestant. His conversion to Catholicism coincided with his interest in medieval philosophy and his intention of returning Thomist thought to a central place in the twentieth century.

His marriage to Raissa, a Russian Jew who had converted to Catholicism, resulted in these two thinkers' lifelong work in the service of the Church. Perhaps they will even be canonized one day.

I don't think I had intended to renew my acquaintance with Maritain's writings, although his attempt at resuscitating

Thomist thought appears to have been successful. He and Raissa also wrote a lot about poetry and during the interwar period they were read by artistic circles. Politics also enters here. Saint Thomas Aquinas was the beloved philosopher of Catholic totalitarians, i.e., those who contrasted the corporate state (Mussolini, Salazar) to the abomination of liberal democracy and Bolshevism. In Poland, articles praising the use of force in politics were often supported with the name of Saint Thomas. Maritain was not interested in political polemics (just like that other neo-Thomist, the medieval historian Étienne Gilson), but his treatises, applying Aquinas to the needs of the twentieth century, in no way supported the fashion for violent methods. He also spoke out against collaboration with Hitler in his book *À travers le désastre*.

The small group of Polish Catholics grouped around the journal *Verbum* and the home for blind children in Laski referred to Maritain in opposition to the nationalistically inclined majority of the clergy, which was expending a great deal of energy on anti-Semitic propaganda. At the invitation of *Verbum*, Maritain visited Warsaw; I don't know if he came alone or with Raissa. In Poland, his influence on one man from the *Verbum* circle would have lasting results: Jerzy Turowicz would edit *The Universal Weekly* in the spirit of Maritain's writings.

Other narrow circles in Poland read Maritain. They were young writers; the most talented among them, the critic Ludwik Fryde, died during the war. I personally, to a significant degree, owe my distrust of "pure poetry" to Maritain (and also Oscar Milosz). So-called modernity ordered the elimination from poetry of everything that belongs to "prose," leaving it with just a lyric extract. In painting, the theory that corresponded to the avant-garde was Witkacy's Pure Form. Somewhere, Maritain cites Boccaccio, who said in his commentary on Dante, "Poetry is theology." According to Maritain, perhaps it is more like ontology, or knowledge about being. In any event, it cannot replace religion and become the object of idolatrous worship. My religious readings at the time did not help me very much in making sense of myself, but recognizing the modest place of the poet as opposed to the "priesthood of art" (which the avant-garde had continued under another name) ought to be considered a benefit.

Did Maritain triumph as a renewer of Saint Thomas's thought? It is too soon to answer that question. Today, even religious seminaries have entered the orbit of Nietzsche and Heidegger. It is very difficult to read the subtle *distinguo* of the medieval sage, even through the filter of his intelligent student. I do not know how much my late friend Thomas Merton took from Thomism (Maritain visited him in the Gethsemane Monastery in Kentucky). Merton used to speak of his attachment to another medieval philosopher, Duns Scotus.

MARTINIQUE AND GUADELOUPE. On these islands one can learn a great deal about light and dark skin colors. The small aristocracy, known as the *colons*, or descendants of the colonists, is white. Lower in the hierarchy is the middle class: lawyers, bureaucrats, merchants, with skin the color of *café au lait*—mulattos, that is. The islands are a part of France and benefit from numerous subsidies, so there are no pockets of urban poverty there. The life of their middle class is very similar to life in provincial France; the circumstances in which their village residents live are probably better than that of black Americans. They attend school and speak French without an accent, which in itself distinguishes them from American blacks, who are often recognizable by the way they speak. They evince friendliness, without the depressing hostility to whites that we find in America. They speak Creole among themselves, and here is the problem of the whole movement. Should Creole be introduced as a language of instruction? Or perhaps as the state language of independent Martinique? Should the masterpieces of world literature be translated into Creole, which is spoken by around eight million people on various islands? Parents who send their children to French schools do not react very favorably to this program, asking what can be done with Creole outside their own island.

On the neighboring island of Guadeloupe, I thought about the poet St. John Perse, or Alexis Léger, the Nobel laureate whom I knew in Washington. He was born on this island in a family of white *colons*, spent his childhood here, and sang its tropical nature and his black nannies in his first volume of poetry, *Éloges* (1911), a cycle which I would personally rank highest among all his work. His father was a high functionary in the administration, so his home was well-to-do, bourgeois, with many servants. Alexis Léger pursued a diplomatic career after he completed his studies in Paris, finally becoming secretary to the Minister of Foreign Affairs, which is a high position and which caused him to seek asylum in Washington after France was occupied by the Germans. Even though after the war he used to fly to France from the American continent, often flying over his island, he *never* visited it, which astonished the literary critics. His native home was appropriately mythologized by him in *Éloges*, transformed into a country estate amidst tropical vegetation, whereas in actuality it was on a street in the island's capital city. I assume he wanted to avoid a confrontation with himself or with journalists.

MILLER, Henry. Twentieth-century American literature is hermetic, but it was to a significant degree a literature of rebellion against the rat race of making money and publishing. Miller, the son of a German immigrant in New York, earned money by working hard, read Nietzsche, and dreamed of liberation. That liberation was possible only by wrenching himself away from the reach of the generally accepted law that whoever does not work (in an office, a store, a factory) does not eat. His flight to Paris signified a transition to another law, of the colony of artists, a bohemia that was continuously renewing itself. He became an expatriate like Ezra Pound, Gertrude Stein, Ernest Hemingway, Scott Fitzgerald, although in his writing he intended not to be like any of them. Instead of writing novels and short stories, he chose, like Walt Whitman, a "song of myself," but in prose and with all socially mandated rules concerning vocabulary and descriptions of sex gotten rid of. His first-person narrative about his personal adventures, whether true or imagined, turned out to be a harbinger of things to come. I believe that Blaise Cendrars influenced him with his autobiographical short stories, but above all, Miller advanced the Whitmanesque boldness in speaking as "I," in which he was helped by his evident self-love. "I" no longer was identified with America; it celebrated his freedom as a rebel, and in Miller there is already all the poetry of the beats of the 1950s. If there were no Miller, there would probably be no Allen Ginsberg.

In America, Miller's books were banned for a long time on the grounds of obscenity, although their author had returned to his country ahead of the impending war. They were printed in

Paris and that is where I bought them, meditating on the inequality of two languages, because at that time they could not have been translated into Polish simply because of the lack of a corresponding lexicon. They also introduced the image, which has not been achieved as powerfully anywhere else, of the vast urban wilderness of the New York streets. Miller's flight had to be repeated by a younger generation, but differently, as a challenge to the whole social mechanism and against their unfortunate parents, enslaved in the rat race.

After his return Miller wrote *The Air-Conditioned Nightmare*, as he called his journey across America. He settled in a country house in California, in Big Sur, overlooking the Pacific, because it was cheap. His desire to escape having to spend his mornings and afternoons working in an office or publishing house is a genuine part of the American artist's war for independence. If, however, there is no other way, then at least they can send their wives to work (that's what the California poet Kenneth Rexroth did). The colony of artists in Big Sur and other similar manifestations of withdrawal were not without consequences, because the country recognized the value of writers and artists, inviting them onto college campuses. Ginsberg had become a professor by the end of his life.

The immense revolution in cultural norms was the result of the young people's revolt of the sixties, but writers like Miller and the Beat Generation prepared the way for it. It was connected to a rather long history of breaking legal prohibitions which protected the public from obscenity. The trial occasioned by the publication of James Joyce's *Ulysses* took place in 1934–35; it was pivotal, because it introduced the distinction between immorality and the question of taste. From then on one could argue that any particular creation, as a work of art, answers only to the judgment of taste. It was only after the war, however, that there was a gradual end to using legal means against publishers. In 1957 a judge lifted the ban on printing Allen Ginsberg's *Howl*. In the 1960s Henry Miller's books could be purchased everywhere in paperback editions.

Advocates of total freedom of speech considered themselves to be progressives fighting against the hypocrisy of the benighted. Now, when everything is permitted, the whole question of absolutely unrestrained free speech is revealing unexpected negative aspects. Perhaps in conditions of a mass free market this freedom was inescapable, but in that case, writers and artists have assumed the role of unwitting agents of mass culture. Mass culture makes use of the openness which they fought for, but for its own ends, trading in emotions, especially in film, and profiting from full access to areas that until recently were off-limits. Advocates of limits, it seems to me, are correct to speak of the pollution of the public sphere; however, the means at their disposal are limited. One cannot introduce censorship, so all that remains is to appeal to public opinion in the hope that its pressure will produce self-limitations of the powers of film and television.

MINDFULNESS. The Polish word *uważność* appears as early as in the writings of Mikołaj Rej. So it is a good word for translating the English "mindfulness," which, according to Buddhists, encompasses all the teachings of the Buddha. "Mindfulness" means a stance of attentive good will toward nature and people, so that we notice in every detail what is happening around us, instead of passing by in distraction. Reading anthologies of Buddhist poetry published in California, I see that mindfulness has been flourishing in poetry of the past couple of decades, and not only in poetry written by individuals who consider themselves Buddhists. A frame of mind that is the exact opposite of the customs of technological civilization, with its hurried tempo and instantaneous television flashes, certainly facilitates interest in preserving nature, because the mind turns to what is here and now.

Unexpectedly, contemplative poetry appears as a counterweight to disintegrative processes in poetry and art, which means it works against the loss of a sense of meaning. It is, one might say, spirituality's resistance to a one-dimensional world. Often, the inspiration is Christian, but more often Buddhist, although there are also poets who refer to both.

Independent of the enormous variation of form, from one-line notes and haiku to lengthy poems and poems in prose, the poetry of mindfulness has certain traits in common because the aim of those who write it is not purely aesthetic. It is the same as that of humanity's great religious books, and they, after all, respond to the question, "What is man and how should he live?" The poetry of mindfulness is akin to certain books of the Bible, the so-called books of wisdom, such as Proverbs, Ecclesiastes, some of the Psalms. At the same time, in contrast to Christian devotional literature, which usually remains outside the stylistic changes of high culture, it becomes part of what is defined as contemporary poetry.

As an example of observing the world mindfully I choose a prose poem, a little treatise by a Vietnamese Buddhist, Thich Nhat Hanh (there is a large Vietnamese immigrant community in America). He gives his text the title "Interbeing," and attempts to convince the readers that the verb "inter-be" ought to exist in the English lexicon. Polish, however, has a verb like "inter-be"—*wspólistnieć*. The text is very simple and is based on beginning from basics, because what can be simpler than staring at a sheet of white paper? But we can think, instead, about the results, because we feel that something important has been said.

If you are a poet you will see clearly that there is a cloud floating in this sheet of paper. Without a cloud there will be no rain; without rain, the trees cannot grow; and without trees, we cannot make paper. The cloud is essential for the paper to exist. If the cloud is not here, the sheet of paper cannot be here either. So we can say that the cloud and the paper *inter-are*. "Interbeing" is a word that is not in the dictionary yet, but if we combine the prefix "inter-" with the verb "to be," we have a new verb, "inter-be." Without a cloud we cannot have paper, so we can say that the cloud and the sheet of paper *inter-are*.

If we look into this sheet of paper even more deeply, we can see the sunshine in it. If the sunshine is not there, the forest cannot grow. In fact, nothing can grow. Even we cannot grow without our sunshine. And so, we know that the sunshine is also in this sheet of paper. The paper and the sunshine "inter-are." And if we continue to look, we can see the logger who cut the tree and brought it to the mill to be transformed into paper. And we see the wheat. We know that the logger cannot exist without his daily bread, and therefore the wheat that became his bread is also in this sheet of paper. And the logger's father and mother are in it too. When we look in this way, we see that without all these things, this sheet of paper cannot exist.

Looking even more deeply, we can see we are in it too. This is not difficult to see, because when we look at a sheet of paper, the sheet of paper is part of our perception. Your mind is in here and mine is also. So we can say that everything is in here with this sheet of paper. You cannot point out one thing that is not here—time, space, the earth, the rain, the minerals in the soil, the sunshine, the cloud, the river, the heat. Everything coexists with this sheet of paper. That is why I think the word "inter-be" should be in the dictionary. "To be" is to inter-be. You cannot just *be* by yourself alone. You have to inter-be with every other thing. This sheet of paper is because everything else is.*

Perhaps one need not reach as far as Vietnam and California, however, to find an example of mindful poetry. Here is a poem by Janusz Szuber, translated from the Polish, which I quote from his volume, *Ladybug in the Snow*, published in Sanok in a tiny print run. It is a description of a fruit, a plum, from outside and inside, and also a description of awareness through eating the plum:

THE CROWING OF ROOSTERS

The crowing of roosters at the change in the weather:
Under a dark blue cloud the dark testicles of plums
With their ash-gray coating and sticky cracks—
There are sweet scabs of dirty amber.

*Thich Nhat Hanh, excerpted from *The Heart of Understanding* in *What Book?: Buddha Poems from Beat to Hiphop*, ed. Gary Gach (Berkeley: Parallax Press, 1998), pp. 208–209.

The tongue tries to smooth out the roughness of the pit
And years pass. But it still wounds my palate,
Promising that I will reach the crux—the bottom of that day
When the roosters crowed at the change in the weather.

MIRACULOUSNESS. To be a man and live among men is miraculous, even if we know the vile deeds and crimes that people are capable of. Every day we build together an enormous beehive with millions of cells in which we deposit the honey of our thoughts, discoveries, inventions, works, lives. Even that analogy is hardly accurate; it is too static, since our collective work, whatever we name it—our society, civilization, *polis* in Greek—is constantly changing and displaying itself in various colors, subject to time or history. Again, this is an insufficient description, because it ignores the most important thing: that this collective creation is given life by the most private, hidden fuel of individual aspirations and decisions. The oddity of man's exceptional calling rests principally on his being a comical being, forever immature, so that a group of children with their easy mood swings from laughter to crying is the best illustration of his lack of dignity. A few years pass, and suddenly they are adults, taking control and supposedly prepared to make pronouncements on public matters and even—who would have expected this!—to take upon themselves the duties of father and mother, although it would be good if they first had an entire life of their own to prepare for this.

It is they, putting a good face on it, but uncertain of themselves, always visited by a suspicion that their neighbor knows something while they only pretend they know—it is precisely these wavering, tongue-tied beings who carry the gifts of character and talent, who maintain the chain of generations.

If it were only a species of animals who live, die, and perish without a trace, then we might simply repeat after Ecclesiastes: "Vanity of vanities; all is vanity." But as someone once said, "There is something supernatural in man's intelligence." Or, to rephrase this, divinity is inherent in man. Does not the archetype of man, the Kabbalists' Adam Kadmon, not reside in the very bosom of the Everlasting? The Gospel of John on the Incarnation of the Word ("In the beginning was the Word, and the Word was with God . . . All things were made by him"), provides the most complete answer to the question: What was this species created for?

A disgusting tribe of monkeys, making horrible, stupid faces, copulating, screeching, murdering each other. After such an enormous number of deaths administered to people by people in the twentieth century, how can one praise this tribe? Its deeds do not match either the image of innocent children in a classroom, or the ability to achieve the highest knowledge of the soul. But contradiction is no doubt an inseparable part of the human condition, and that suffices as a source of miraculousness.

MISFORTUNE. We cannot just ignore misfortune, comforting ourselves with the thought that it does not exist, when it clearly does. Since we must live with it, what remains is a choice of tactics. Apparently, when a foreign body invades their hive, bees build around it with wax. Alas, this work of building around an intruder must be undertaken anew repeatedly, but it is necessary, because otherwise misfortune will take control of all our thoughts and feelings.

Uncounted numbers of people, both those who came before us and our contemporaries, have known and will know misfortune, although that is cold comfort. As a result of this universality of misfortune, the Book of Job is forever alive. Its first act is the recognition of misfortune as punishment, as Job's friends attempt to convince him. Were it not for the teleological dimension of his argument with them, I would have said that they are right: misfortune descends upon us as vengeance, as punishment, and since we recall our sins at that time, it is justified in a sense. Job objects, citing his innocence, and this should surprise us: What makes him so certain of his own virtuousness? But what could be called the second act of the Book of Job is a defense of God as someone other than a distributor of rewards and punishments. If Job is innocent, then God sends misfortune because it pleases Him to do so, which means that our understanding of what is just and what is unjust does not apply to the accusation which is constantly directed at God and encapsulated in the cry, "Why?" A Providence which looks after individuals and history, as in the sermons of Bossuet, which rewards and punishes, would be logical. Extending this idea to the dimensions of the universe, our demand for good could be satisfied only by a merciful God, who would not have subjected millions and millions of living creatures to pain and death. To create a universe like the one we have is not nice. "And why should I have to be nice?" asks God. "Where did you get such ideas?"

Misfortune simply *is*. And when you wall it off with wax you do not have a clear conscience, because perhaps you are supposed to dedicate all your efforts and all your attention to it. And all you can say in your own defense is "I want to live."

MONEY. My forebears had money because peasants worked for them. My father's mother, however, had to sell first Serbiny and then the rest of her estate, the manor house of Użumiszki, but my father received an education and graduated from the Polytechnic Institute. My mother's family held Szetejnie, a medium-sized estate, but in the most productive region of Lithuania. As a result of the division of the family holdings after the land reform, my mother received Podkomorzynek, our so-called Farm. She ran the farm there, commuting from Wilno, but it was across the new state border, which complicated gaining access to its profits. Yet linen from our own flax was used to make my shirts, and our sheep provided the wool for our clothing and the hides for the sheepskin coats that were tanned and sewn in Kiejdany.

My father did not do well financially and when I went to school in Wilno I was closer to poverty than to wealth, as was in keeping with the condition of the city during the economic collapse. My family helped me when I was at the university, but when I took money from them it was always with a guilty conscience, which led to lean times, meager earnings from writing, scholarships. After receiving my diploma in law I tried for an apprenticeship with an attorney. Somehow, that was not to be, and my rather typical curriculum vitae as a member of the intelligentsia contains another variant—a career as a bureaucrat. My job at Polish Radio from 1935 to 1939 by no means placed me anywhere near a microphone; it was carried out behind desks. I was promoted rapidly and at the end was earning a lot in comparison with the average wage at the time.

I marvel at my good fortune, because I have always landed like a cat on all four feet. Including the period of the German occupation in Warsaw, when there were no opportunities at all for earning money. Jerzy Andrzejewski's theory of "the last złoty" helped me. It stated that when there is nothing at all in one's pocket, *something* has to happen. And it did. I can point to those years in defense of my indifference to material welfare. I really was indifferent, even though fate would make me a person of privilege time and again.

My shame that I came from a family which had lived for generations off the labor of the common people (and had been involved in Polonizing those people) drove me to the left, and in 1945, in large measure because of my color—if not red, then certainly pink—I found myself among the élite that was forming then. True, the very profession of writer, regardless of my views, protected me from having to earn my living by manual labor, and even from sitting behind a desk in an office. Nonetheless, I returned to my career as a government functionary, which had been interrupted by the outbreak of the war, and I served as such from 1946 through 1950, first in the Polish Consulate in New York, then in the Embassy. This does not mean, however, that at a remove from the real America, the one that was subject to the necessities of the daily struggle for the dollar, I succumbed to any illusions that would soften its contradictions. I did not like that system, but I also did not like Communism. And why should we have to like societies that are based on fear—fear of poverty or fear of the political police? I am free to make judgments, in both cases, about pity and sympathy for Adam, driven out of paradise and, one way or another, subjected to torment.

I left America, however; once again, my career as a functionary and, above all, my salary came to an end. The years 1950–1960, in some ways more difficult than the German occupation, because then I was at least among my own people, had to confirm the theory of "the last złoty" or, in this case, franc. Since I survived, having enough to support my family, too, it was confirmed. How did that happen and where, in difficult France, without a job? Thinking about this, I experience fear, but after the fact. There was *Kultura*, of course, but poor itself, it could only manage modest honoraria. In addition, I was possibly the only émigré who refused to write for Radio Free Europe, because I didn't care for its beating of the patriotic drum and its sprinkling of holy water.

Then came my second America. Also not like that of the "Polish rat" immigrants, who have their two hands on arrival, nothing more. Many years spent on an island, the campus, where I discovered my new talent as a teacher. Then honors and awards which, I am certain, I would not have received had I remained in Europe.

NADIA CHODASIEWICZ-GRABOWSKA. When in 1934 I moved into Mme Valmorin's *pension* on rue Valette near the Pantheon, I encountered Nadia Chodasiewicz, who adopted a hyphenated name after her short-lived marriage to a Polish painter, Grabowski. Nadia, a blue-eyed Russian with wide cheekbones, came from an émigré family who had settled in Poland after the 1917 Revolution. She had studied at the Academy of Fine Arts in Warsaw.

The Parisian *pension* figures so frequently in French literature that it is worthwhile to say something about it. Intended for people on a low budget, for students and clerks, it had an aura of poverty and stinginess. The tenants were given a room and dinner, which they ate communally in a dining room, slowly progressing through the ritual three courses, but in carefully measured miniature portions. We often ate *soupe de lentilles*, or lentil soup. The proprietress, Mme Valmorin, was a mulatto from Martinique. My co-tenants were a couple of students, a couple of post office employees, Nadia, and Pan Antoni Potocki.

Potocki (not a member of the aristocratic Potocki family) was once a well-known critic; he had written a history of the literature of Young Poland, a rather eccentric book which was already forgotten by the 1920s or 1930s. He buried himself in Paris as a journalist, grew old there, had no family, and made his living by doing occasional work for the Polish Embassy. A gloomy man with a gray walrus moustache, he was the object of Nadia's ministrations; she selflessly did a lot of good for the old loner. Although she spoke Polish very well, after she and Grabowski were divorced she no longer had any ties to Poland, but she often spoke about her brothers, who had remained in Russia, showing their letters and declaring herself enthusiastically in favor of the socialist state.

As a painter, she strove to follow what she considered the great, splendid model of modernity—not Picasso or Braque, but Fernand Léger, whose paintings of pipes, cauldrons, and mechanized proletarian figures probably matched her imagined view of Communism. Her friend, a young French painter, with whom she often worked and who sometimes stayed for supper, was thoroughly under her influence and painted in the same way.

I thought of Nadia as a strong personality, but I did not anticipate the future direction of her biography. She met her idol, Fernand Léger, won him over, married him, and became curator of his museum in Provence and heiress to his fortune.

NAŁKOWSKA, Zofia. I never liked her novels. As an individual, she appeared on the horizon in the company of other members of the Academy of Literature and as the confidante of the highest Warsaw society, which hardly tempted me to make her acquaintance. Unlike my contemporaries (Breza, Rudnicki, Gombrowicz, Zawieyski), I did not belong to her circle. I met her in Kraków after the war, in the company of Communist officials, but by then she was completely deaf, I think, and her novel, *Knots of Life*, left me cold.

I read volume 4 of her *Diary*, from the war years, and was

stunned. She reveals herself in it with absolute decency and with cruelty toward herself, and the reader thinks that here before him is a human being deserving of the highest respect. Just as she is, with her old woman's laughable femaleness, constantly looking around to catch men's glances and their compliments, with her list of former husbands and lovers, her terrifying enduring love for her mother, enduring beyond the mother's grave, with her truly heartrending pity and sympathy for other people, her clinging to them, with the Warsaw of the ghetto, its liquidation, the executions. A great writer, she came into her own in a way that was surprising to her, since her notes for the *Diary* were only a substitute for real writing, which she missed terribly, while managing a store. That nightmare of necessity turned out to be providential for what became the *Diary*, because were it not for the store, she probably would have sat down and worked on yet another novel. It is worth noting that this book of pain, unhappiness, despair, and willpower is, despite everything, atheistic. Like Różewicz's poetry. And therefore characteristic of a certain phase in the history of Polish literature. It is precisely her conviction that everything ends for a person with his death that gives the *Diary* its heartrending tone.

NATURE. Disenchantment, love. For trees, for a river, for birds. Certainly, in our childhood we do not know that this is called love. Linden trees, oaks, maples simply existed when I was a seven-year-old. Now I know that it is possible for them not to exist and that their fates are connected with people. My great-grandfather Syruć planted them around 1830 and some of them have survived, whereas nothing survived from the library he, like his friend Jakub Gieysztor (the author of memoirs) collected, although on a smaller scale. Gieysztor spent a lot of money on books supplied to him by Jewish used-booksellers in Wilno. Enchantment at a very young age is a sacrament, an experience whose memory acts upon us throughout our life. Having been wounded, I ought to have become a complete pessimist; my ecstatic praises of existence can be explained by that early gift I received through my five senses.

I remember my first encounters with particular birds. For example, the golden oriole seemed like an absolute miracle to me, with its unity of color and its flutelike voice. And it was precisely birds, it seems, that I looked for in nature books as soon as I learned to read—books that would soon become my cult objects.

The colored portraits of birds from the beginning of the nineteenth century were hand painted; I came across some of them, but of course I did not know the splendid albums of the American ornithologists Audubon and Wilson. I liked Mayne Reid's novels about the adventures of young hunters and naturalists in America, in which the Latin name is given beside the name of every animal and bird. Linnaeus imposed this on naturalists with his classification system. I read *Our Forest and Its Inhabitants* by Dyakowski, and soon after that Włodzimierz Korsak's novel for young readers, *On the Trail of Nature*, and his hunting calendar, *The Hunter's Year*. I idolized that author. From there I moved on to scientific ornithological books. I was determined to learn the Latin names of all the Polish birds, and I did.

Reading *The Forest People's Summer* by Zofia Rodziewiczówna was an unavoidable phase, along with daydreams about a preserve of untouched nature. In class, not listening to whatever the teacher was rattling on about, I drew maps of my ideal country in my notebooks; there were only forests there, and instead of roads, canals for small boats. Those were aristocratic daydreams, because only selected enthusiasts were granted entry to this land; today, they would be called ecologists. One should admit that the preservation of nature is aristocratic, no matter what the elect are called. They have been monarchs, princes, dignitaries from totalitarian parties.

By the time I was preparing to take my college entry exams, my naturalist period was behind me, and instead of enrolling in the department of mathematics and natural science, I was soon poring over Roman law, memorizing its formulas in Latin. What a comedown!

I was destined, however, to write—an occupation which was not very different from my childhood efforts at grasping a bird through its name and the information about its appearance and habits. I was fascinated by the words *Podicepts cristatus* and *Emberiza citrinnella*, which served at the same time as incantations capable of calling the birds into being. They also reminded me of the moment of encounter, the first epiphany. I think, though, that always, just as in my mature years, I somehow knew that words are weak in comparison with the thing itself. Certainly, I recognized the influence of sentimental and romantic imaginings about nature. Then nothing remained of all that. On the contrary, it struck me as unbounded suffering. But nature is beautiful; there's nothing you can do about that.

NEMO, Captain. A fighter for freedom, disenchanted, melancholic, and oh, so romantic—that is the hero of Jules Verne's novels, *Twenty Thousand Leagues Under the Sea* and *The Mysterious Island*. A revolutionary fighting for the liberation of his country. Verne made him a Hindu of aristocratic birth. After his defeat he made use of his invention, because he was also a brilliant scientist, and far from humanity he measured the oceans with his underwater vessel, the *Nautilus*. He took the name Nemo, which means "nobody" in Latin. A bitter misanthrope, devoid of any illusions about the human species, he was forever yielding to emotions of pity and empathy, coming to the aid of the shipwrecked in *The Mysterious Island*.

My generation read Jules Verne in our childhood, and Captain Nemo, so like the heroes of Polish Romantic literature, was our favorite character. Which explains the provenance of that name in wartime Poland.

Around 1960 I received a letter from Kraków from a poet whose name I did not know then, Stanisław Czycz. Here is what he wrote in it. It happened during the German occupation; he was fifteen at the time. He was interested in technical subjects and had no literary interests at all. He used to go over to Krzeszowice to visit a friend with similar interests and there, in the attic, they assembled a motorcycle to use after the war. They became curious about a suitcase that was lying in the attic. It turned out that his friend's father, a railway worker, had found it in Kraków in an empty train after the passengers had all been caught in a roundup and sent to Auschwitz. The two friends opened the suitcase. In it was a black cloak, a top hat, and a magician's apparatus, along with a poster announcing a performance by Captain Nemo. Also a roll of paper containing poems under the title *Voices of Poor People*.

"I didn't know what poetry was" (I am summarizing what Czycz wrote in his letter), "but those poems affected me so powerfully that I began to write myself." Soon the war came to an end and the Union of Writers resumed its activities, and then Czycz presented a manuscript of his own poems for evaluation, but intermingling them, to strengthen the effect, as he later explained, with *Voices of Poor People*. He was summoned and bawled out. They asked him where he'd gotten those poems, because they were Miłosz's. He, however, had never heard that name. And that's how I became responsible for making Czycz a poet—who can say, whether to his benefit or harm?

And Captain Nemo? Who was he, from what circles? Probably from Warsaw, because copies of *Voices of Poor People*, a cycle written late in 1943, could only have been circulating there. Somehow, the underwater vessel harmonizes wonderfully with the top hat and black cloak of an itinerant magician. The gradation in the fates of these two figures is horrifying, however: first the struggle of a romantic hero for the freedom of nations, then his disillusionment, and finally death in Auschwitz. Because I have not been able to find a single trace, not one piece of information about Captain Nemo the magician, I have to conclude that it is probable he died an anonymous death there.

NUMBER. When one thinks about how many of us there are, and how many people are born on our planet every day, it is easy to fall into apocalyptic terror. This has a bad side: it idealizes past eras in the conviction that people lived better then, which is obviously not true.

Great numbers, however, cause particular difficulties for our imagination. As if we observe humanity in a way that is not permitted for humans, and allowed only to gods. On film, the image of a metropolis photographed from above is the circulation of thousands of bright dots, or automobiles. We know that people the size of microbes sit in those vehicles. This miniaturization of human beings simply because there are so many of them "must be the favorite amusement of great leaders and tyrants," I wrote in 1939. In other words, they can think in categories of masses.

A million people more, a million less—what difference does it make?

From a distance or a great height the differences between human atoms are erased, but an ordinary observer, even if he places himself somewhere on high, cannot avoid transporting himself there, in his thoughts, among them. He must realize, then, that he is each of them. A blow to his "selfness," to the foundation of individuation, *principium individuationis*. And really, only one's conviction about one's own unique existence, about a fate reserved for oneself alone, supports our belief in the immortality of the soul. A large number not only makes us physically more crowded, because there are people everywhere, in the mountains, the forests, on the seas, but also annihilates us, imposing the conviction that we are all circulating ants, of which nothing will remain.

Certainly, that is a deception of perspective, because all we have to do is reverse the telescope in order to enlarge rather than to miniaturize, and it turns out that there are no two individuals who are exactly alike. Then, generalization loses, particularity wins. Fingerprints are not repeated nor, although this is more difficult to prove, are the features of individual style. It is just that since we move among a great number, we are always inclined to forget this.

[O]

OBLIGATIONS. I felt sorry for them, but they probably took my remaining at a distance as an expression of contempt. Thrown among foreigners, they suffered daily from a sense of inferiority. Calling upon "Polish culture" was supposed to make this better somehow, but that culture of the nobility, with its romanticism and uprisings, was barely comprehensible for them, just as for foreigners who spoke a different language.

Czesław Straszewicz, in his émigré novel *Tourists from Storks' Nests*, chose a sailor, Kostek, as his hero; he travels everywhere with his "constitution," his Polish cookbook, and finding himself in South America, feels that he is better than the natives, since they do not know Polish dishes: "The Indians are a benighted people." In the same novel there is talk of the mainstay of gentry culture in Sienkiewicz. Every night, an officer of the UB (the secret police) in Gdynia quizzes his wife in bed on her knowledge of Sienkiewicz's *Trilogy*.

A cookbook, paper cutouts, the *krakowiak* folk dance—that's not a great deal. The one thing they could really pride themselves on is Polish carols. Let us consider the difficulty of my situation. Cognizant of the élitist nature of Polish culture, which spans an enormous distance between top and bottom, I belonged to the small society of the chosen who carry out our particular rituals. Worse yet, I was the last descendant of a manor house, and for me, the coffeehouse antics of that demon Gombrowicz, who tried to infect his Jewish colleagues with his mania for coats of arms and genealogy, are symbolic of the literary cafés' swallowing up the remains of manor house tradition. I should add that I grew up outside the ethnic Polish area.

So what should I do? How should I "sanctify"? I think Polish folk music is pitiful, the *krakowiak* and *oberek* dances make me laugh, Chopin irritates me because he is dragged out for every occasion, and also because my tastes run to classical music. Those are sufficient reasons not to participate in various ceremonial occasions. But I have been a faithful servant of the Polish language, and of what it will carry into the future. And so a role has been imposed on me (and I am not the first to whom this has been done): if you cannot be *with* them, at least be *for* them. It is unfortunate, but even Piłsudski defined it this way in the end. I respect those who chose to act within the fold of the Polish diaspora, but that was not my place. I preferred to discover if it was possible to remain oneself without currying favor from the West, and yet succeeding on one's own terms. Condemned to reach my audience through translations into English, I felt an obligation to "Polish culture," but not to that crippled one which was divided into exquisite refinement and boorishness.

[P]

PIASECKI, Stanisław. He was someone who had a plan and who systematically brought that plan to life. One could see him, in a certain sense, as the heir to all the Polish reformers, from the end of the eighteenth century on, who believed that it was necessary to begin from the top, by influencing the élite. The Polish élite, in his opinion, did not think right, and the chief responsibility for this was borne by the press they read. Piasecki was a nationalist and an opponent of the "demo-liberals," a somewhat hazy label that included those who had voted for Poland's first president, Gabriel Narutowicz (who was assassinated by a nationalist in 1922). Piasecki thought of *The Literary News* as that camp's paper, so he took upon himself the goal of founding a paper capable of rivaling *The Literary News* and thereby creating a cadre of individuals, at least in Warsaw, who would embrace the "government of spirits." That is why he founded *Prosto z mostu* (Straight from the Shoulder).

In Europe at that time, the future seemed to belong to right-wing authoritarian regimes. There were the examples of Salazar in Portugal, Mussolini in Italy, and soon, Hitler. In various countries, movements of marching youth, dressed in uniform shirts, with their leaders at their head, made no effort to conceal their desire to seize power not through elections, but by a coup. In Romania they were Codreanu's Iron Guard, whose leaders were murdered in 1938, but their comrades later held power for a while with German support. Similar movements existed in Hungary and Croatia. In Poland, the insignia of the ONR (National Radical Camp) was a miniature sword of the eleventh-century king, Bolesław Chrobry, worn on the lapel; its press organ was *Falanga*. Their attempted putsch and seizure of power in 1937 did not succeed, because they did not have the army's support.

The creation in Poland of the OZON (Camp of National Unity) in 1937 signaled a compromise with the extreme right and the desire for at least partial adoption of their slogans. Horthy played a similar game in Hungary, as did the government of Carol II in Romania. In that political climate, *Straight from the Shoulder* acquired more and more readers. It rapidly came to have twice the print run of *The Literary News* and just kept on growing. The paper's "Catholic national" program promoted the idea of a state inhabited exclusively by Catholic Poles. Linguistic and religious minorities were to be Polonized, and Jews forced into emigration. The paper's Catholicism was expressed in frequent citations of Saint Thomas Aquinas. Since the paper was not intended for the masses, the same slogans were voiced by the popular, mass distribution press, chief among them *The Little Daily* and the monthly magazine *Knight of the Immaculate Virgin*, both published in Father Maksymilian Kolbe's Niepokalanów.

At the end of the thirties, the German project of being surrounded on the east by states with a similar ideology seemed close to realization. With some obstacles, the Germans could count on Romania, Hungary, Croatia and, after the partition, on Slovakia, while the occupied Czech lands were transformed into one large weapons factory. Stanisław Piasecki and his comrades, and also the National Radical Camp, which was close to him in orientation, put forward more or less the same program that would soon be adopted in Pavelić's satellite Croatia; in other words, an alliance with Hitler and a common march against Russia would have been logical. Polish history does not obey the rules of logic, however.

I knew Piasecki because my friends Jerzy Andrzejewski and Bolesław Miciński had published in his paper before they broke with him. Piasecki was much more flexible than Grydzewski, the editor of *The Literary News*, in his political stance vis-à-vis the younger generation. He succeeded in enlisting Gałczyński, who published poems in praise of the National Radical Camp and prophesied that a "night of long knives" would come for the Warsaw demo-liberal café society. I must state that Piasecki had already succeeded in creating a cadre which could have replaced the demo-liberals; that is, he already had his specialists in literary criticism, theater criticism, music, art, political science, and so on.

A short, thin man who wore glasses, looking like a typical intellectual, Piasecki in no way resembled his namesake Bolesław, a leader-type and a blond beast. He had a fanatic's thin lips, and was clearly consumed by his fervent service to his patriotic idea. People said he was half Jewish, which was not a rarity among Polish anti-Semites. He hated everyone whom he considered to be an enemy of Poland, internal and external, and no one could have convinced him that by speaking out against democracy he was doing exactly the same thing as Nazi Germany, which he saw as a mortal threat to our country. Immediately after Warsaw was occupied by the Germans he founded both a café which was also a conspiratorial center, and an underground newspaper. Arrested quite early on, he was executed in Palmiry.

POLISH LANGUAGE. There is no way to rationalize one's love for a language, just as one cannot rationalize love for one's mother. They are probably the same thing; it's not for nothing that we say "our mother tongue." Most of my life has been lived outside of Poland; just count it—the Russian years of my childhood, then France, then America. And unlike those whose Polish becomes shaky after ten or fifteen years abroad, I have never had any hesitations. I felt confident in my language and I think that is why I wrote only in it, poems and prose, out of pride, since only its rhythms sounded in my ears, and without them I would have had no hope that what I was doing was good.

My first attempts at learning to read are hazy. No doubt my mother taught me, because it was in the spring of 1918 in Szetejnie. But I remember the garden table (round?) in what I think was a shady bower of lilacs and spirea where I formed my letters under my mother's watchful eye. It cost her a lot of effort to catch hold of me in the garden, because I hated those writing lessons, I wriggled, sobbed, and screamed that I would never learn. What would have happened had someone told me then that I would become a professional writer? I had never heard of such a thing.

The language is my mother, literally and metaphorically. It is certainly my home, which I carry around the world on my wanderings. This is remarkable, because except for brief periods, I was not immersed in a Polish-speaking atmosphere. In Szetejnie Polish was the language of the local squires, but it was peppered with Lithuanian words, since the surrounding village was

Lithuanian. Later, Russia and my bilingualism. Finally, Wilno, undoubtedly pure Polish, if we're speaking of my family, the intelligentsia, the school, although its foundation was a dialect referred to as "simple talk," plus the Yiddish of the Jewish masses and the Russian of the Jewish intelligentsia.

Certainly, prewar Warsaw and the years I spent there during the German occupation. But immediately afterward I was surrounded by English and French. In my rejection of imposing a profound change on myself by going over to writing in a different language, I perceive a fear of losing my identity, because it is certain that when we switch languages we become someone else.

I was a citizen of an ideal land that existed more in time than in space. It was created by old translations of the Bible, church songs, Kochanowski, Mickiewicz, contemporary poetry. How that land compared with the real country is unclear. That whole painful complex of being Polish and wearing, as one's own, the many crooked, caricature-like mugs of the human mass, whose individual features are depressing. Against that complex I set the heroes of my language. In my youth I didn't see this very clearly, since *Pan Tadeusz* existed as a base, the norm. Today I enumerate them: the anonymous monk who translated the so-called *Puławski Psalter* in the fifteenth century; Father Leopolita, translator of the Bible, 1561; Father Jakub Wujek; Daniel Mikołajewski, translator of the Protestant Gdańsk Bible, 1632; Mikołaj Sęp Szarzyński; Piotr Kochanowski, the translator of Torquato Tasso. Next, the classics of the eighteenth century, poets and translators; they normalized the language which Mickiewicz and Słowacki employed. The closer we get to my own time, the more translators there are, since I became aware that translations are of great importance in a language's development and changes. Boy-Żeleński and Edward Porębowicz—even if his *Divine Comedy* is linguistically flawed because it is freighted with the idiom of Young Poland; still, his translations of Provençal, Celtic, and English ballads are important. Among my contemporaries, there are many to whom I would like to bow, and this softens my judgments of People's Poland, because good translators did impressive work then. Thanks to them, people studied Polish in Leningrad and Moscow in order to read Western literature in Polish translations.

By writing in Polish, wherever one may live one is connected to a collective work that has been developing for generations. One also cannot avoid thinking about the appalling history of that country. Aleksander Wat used to say that Poland does not have a literature commensurate with its tragic history; that instead of serious works, it has the literature of a clique. When, during my years abroad, I mentally compared the historical knowledge of my contemporaries who wrote in English or French with my own knowledge, I had to admit that mine was depressingly broad, and that raised the question of what I should do with it. For example, does my *Native Realm* not have the characteristics of a textbook for the Western public, which was inclined to throw the entire "East" into a single bag?

The history of the European countries abounds in misfortune, and I have no intention of entering into a competition over horrors. Still, there is a level of complication where it is difficult to understand anything, and this is the case of the lands of the former Res Publica and the nations who once inhabited it. To confirm this, all one has to do is refer to the mutual accusations in Polish-Jewish conversations or to Polish-Ukrainian mutual accusations.

"And in the Spring, let me see Spring, and not Poland." That cry by the poet Jan Lechoń in 1918 summarizes the way every

Polish writer feels torn, even today. It might seem easy to choose to write exclusively about individual life, about the "universal human" problems of time passing, of love and death, but in the background, whether we are conscious of it or not, that other thing is lurking there, unnamed even to this day, or named only obliquely, as if it were standing on the border. I was acutely aware of this when I was translating my own poems and the poems of other Polish writers into English, or when I was collecting reviews of my anthology, *A Book of Luminous Things*, which first appeared in Polish translation. At long last, no history, contemplation of things that can be seen, distance, medicine for the world of the will or suffering, precisely in accordance with Schopenhauer's prescriptions. Only the question remains: Would I have put that book together were that other thing not present in it by its absence?

PONARY. The most romantic of names, the site of the Philomaths' picnics in the 1820s and then of ours during my *gymnasium* years and in the Vagabonds' Club. Oak woods on the hills outside Wilno, more or less alongside the river, which is where its name comes from. The Wilia River is called the Nerys in Lithuanian—thus, *Po* (along) + *nerai* (the Nerys), or, Ponary.

But the history of human cruelty has completely defiled this name and obscured its old appeal. The Germans chose Ponary as the site for mass executions; around 120,000 people, the vast majority of them Jews (but not only Jews), died there. The role that Lithuanian special detachments played in this is a skeleton in the closet of Lithuanian national consciousness. A precise description of how this took place can be found in Józef Mackiewicz's semijournalistic novel *No Need to Speak Out Loud*. Later, the Soviet authorities executed members of the Polish underground there. How, then, can one draw or film idyllic scenes of youthful festivities under those oaks? For me, Ponary remains what it was during our youth, but I preserve this image with difficulty against the associations that younger generations must have with it.

PREJUDICES. In order to think about the world relatively accurately one should avoid prejudices, or preconceptions about the traits of certain people and things. For example, that redheaded women are untrustworthy, that bathing is injurious to one's health, or that washing down certain dishes with milk leads to twisting of one's intestines. It is possible that preconceptions are related to superstitious rules which themselves are rooted in conventional beliefs. From my childhood in Lithuania, I know what is forbidden: it is forbidden to spit on a fire, it is forbidden to place a loaf of bread upside down, it is forbidden to throw bread into the garbage, it is forbidden to walk backward, because that means you are measuring your mother's grave.

Prejudices are necessary and positive, however, because they simply save energy. It is impossible to race about with one's tongue hanging out, checking out the countless bits of information that surround us. Prejudices permit us to bypass some of them. I don't want to conceal the fact that I have an almost fanatical tendency to prejudices. Thus, I was prejudiced against Poles from the Kingdom of Poland, seeing them as lacking in seriousness; against National Democrats as people who were obsessed; against *The Literary News* because of their gentility, in contrast to my lack of breeding; against the poet Jan Lechoń for his snobbery; against the poet Julian Przyboś for his invariably progressive views. And so on. Stefan Kisielewski tried in vain to get me to read the works of Roman Dmowski, against whom I was intensely prejudiced. I put aside certain types of literature without reading them. That was the case, for example, with a famous best-seller in France in 1954, where I was living at the time—*Bonjour Tristesse* by the very young writer Françoise Sagan. (Years later I read it with very mixed feelings.) The same thing happened when everyone around me was reading *The Painted Bird* by Jerzy Kosiński. We met in Palo Alto and Kosiński asked me what I thought of *The Painted Bird*. When I answered "I have an advantage over others in that I haven't read the book," he nearly choked.

It would have been better had I not deserved to be labeled a man of obsessions and prejudices, but no doubt I do.

PRIMAVERA. A Christian commune founded by Hutterites in the forests of Paraguay toward the end of World War II. There was a time when I wanted to join it. I was working in the Polish Embassy in Washington and neither capitalism nor Communism appealed to me; a Christian commune seemed to be the only solution.

Hutter, a heretic burned at the stake in the Tyrol in the sixteenth century, founded this sect, which proclaimed a return to the original community of Christians and to living in accordance with the Gospel. The Hutterite communes in Moravia were so successful that news of them reached the Polish Arians, who sent a delegation to observe them. "These are not communists, but economists" was the conclusion of the report they wrote in 1569 in which were described the common rooms where families lived separated by sheets. There were private apartments and kitchens for the bosses, but also constant observation: little windows in the walls opening unannounced, and the sight of an ear in them. The Hutterites also left a record of that visit. They did not like the gentlemen in fur coats, mounted on magnificent horses, eager to engage in theological disputes, citing the Bible in Latin, Greek, and Hebrew.

After many persecutions and wanderings, the Hutterites persisted in Canada and North Dakota as closed societies, arousing the anger of neighboring farmers with their collective wealth. They have nothing in common with the sect founded in Breslau in the 1920s or with communes in several cities of Weimar Germany. Persecuted by Hitler, they sought refuge in Liechtenstein, then in England, where they were interned during the war as German citizens. Some of them emigrated to Paraguay and founded Primavera; the rest remained in England.

I met with representatives of Primavera in Washington and that I almost reconciled myself to the thought that I would work with an axe and a shovel in the Paraguayan forests gives some idea of my despair. Janka, however, was sober enough to dissuade me from that intention.

Later, Ernst von Schenk, a journalist from Basel, told me about life in such a commune in Weimar Germany, to which he once belonged. All the men perform physical labor, but all the kitchen work and caring for the children falls upon the women, who are constantly pregnant, overworked, and unhappy.

PROZOR, Count Maurycy. The Prozors owned estates in the Niewiaża valley. I get lost in their genealogy. Józef Prozor (1723–1788) was married to a daughter of the Syruć family and made his career with the help of my ancestor Syruć who, as a courtier of King Leszczyński, "had his brother-in-law Prozor beside him." It seems they lost their estates after the 1863 Uprising. Maurycy, born in Wilno in 1848, grew up in France, attended French schools, and wrote in French. He was the translator of Ibsen's plays into that language. He was not interested in the past, which was the property of the mighty Russian Empire. The fall of tsarist rule took place during his old age. Then Prozor suddenly felt the call of his fatherland. For his parents' generation, the fatherland's name was Lithuania. And when news came of the establishment of an independent Lithuania, he supported it enthusiastically in his articles.

It turned out, however, that such seemingly natural patriotism enraged many people. His Polish acquaintances tried to explain to him that he was not a Lithuanian, but a Pole, and that there could not be a Lithuania separate from Poland because it was only the "rebellious Kowno province" (referred to as Kaunas by Lithuanians).

Lithuania had bad luck with its upper classes—the landowners and the intelligentsia from the ranks of the gentry. They were so thoroughly Polonized that the few among them who thought otherwise were called "Lithomaniacs." In 1918 Lithuanian activists were just the handful of intelligentsia who were of peasant origin and priests. The new little state had enormous difficulty in staffing administrative offices and was completely lacking in people capable of defending its interests in the international arena.

Maurycy Prozor, who had lived in the south of France, in Cimiez, discovered another person in Paris who, like him, admitted his Lithuanian roots—Oscar Milosz. Their friendship developed along two parallel tracks; it was both political and literary. Prozor the reader understood not only his friend's diplomatic activity, but also his difficult, hermetic writings.

The chief obstacle to the Allies' recognizing independent Lithuania was the "unbelievable Polish policy," the Polish delegation's position at the peace congress at Versailles. Oscar Milosz, as chargé d'affaires of the Lithuanian Embassy in Paris, was able to achieve French *de facto* recognition of Lithuania in 1920, and *de jure* recognition in 1923. He also won in the matter of Memel, or Klaipeda, but he perceived Poland's achievement of its right to Wilno as a personal defeat, since he had sought a compromise solution which would have made Polish-Lithuanian cooperation possible. "The childish and destructive intrigues of our enemies, who do not seem to understand that in the future, situated between hostile Germany and hostile Russia, they must be allies of independent Lithuania," he wrote in a letter to Prozor on May 25, 1920.

Drawn into Lithuanian diplomacy by his friend, Prozor shared with him the woes arising from the new understanding of nationhood. In calling themselves Lithuanians, they were not thinking of language, because they did not speak Lithuanian. I don't know what language they used when speaking with each other (Oscar's Polish was perfect); they corresponded in French. Working for Lithuania, they came up against the distrust of "real" Lithuanians. "They don't want to hear about us," Oscar wrote to Prozor once. He voluntarily limited himself to a second-rank position in the embassy, although he was honored for his services with the Order of Giedyminas.

Prozor visited Kaunas and the Niewiaża valley in the twenties. He carried out the duties of Lithuanian Ambassador to Rome for several years. He died in 1928. His daughter, Greta Currat-Prozor, settled in Switzerland.

Very few aristocrats and landed gentry supported a Lithuanian-speaking Lithuania. Oscar Milosz, Count Maurycy Prozor, Stanisław Narutowicz (the brother of Poland's President, Gabriel Narutowicz), Alfred Tyszkiewicz from Połąga, and Michał Romer, a professor at the Witold the Great University in Kaunas, who also served several terms as Rector of the university—that is the complete list, I believe. When they are published, Romer's diaries, which fill more than a dozen volumes, will be an incredible mine of topics for a historian who is capable of understanding the conflicts of loyalty, as moving as they are tragic and grotesque.

[Q]

QUINN, Arthur. He was a Californian. He attended a Jesuit high school in San Rafael, on San Francisco Bay. Robert Hass, my co-translator and Poet Laureate of the United States (1996), and Louis Iribarne, a Polish specialist, my student at Berkeley and translator of Stanisław Ignacy Witkiewicz's novel *Insatiability*, later a professor at the University of Toronto, were his class-mates. In school, Arthur was known for his athletic talent and it was predicted that he would have a great career as a professional baseball player. He gave up sports, however, for philosophy.

He studied the history of science at Princeton University under the direction of Thomas Kuhn, the famous creator of the theory of scientific revolutions, but his interests were far-reaching, his intellectual curiosity and erudition enormous. Upon returning to California, he found a place for himself in the Department of Rhetoric, an academic department at Berkeley that is designed to accommodate faculty members who do not fit into disciplinary boxes. Even there, however, his combination of various fields of knowledge was seen as excessive and drew com-plaints that his scholarship was not scientific, although, as it would turn out, there was method in what he was doing.

When I, already past middle age, taught Dostoevsky at Berkeley, Arthur, who was then a young assistant professor, came to my lectures. A practicing Catholic, he found something for himself in the religious problems posed by the Russian writer. Another way of looking at this would be that he had need of a clear opposition to the Maoist madness of the Berkeley revolution, and my lectures offered this. That is how our friendship began.

The subject of Quinn's first book was a critique of the philosophy of logical positivism; its title was *Confidence of British Philosophers* (1977), although instead of "confidence" he could have used the word "arrogance." It is an objective, solid analysis; one can scarcely sense the author's irony. In general, Quinn as an author is in no hurry to reveal his intentions. After all, he put together (with N. Bradbury) a school anthology of texts from various eras and languages, demonstrating how intentions shape the means of addressing the reader. For several years, his attention was focused on the language of literary utterances, and his book *Figures of Speech* (1982) can be called a humor-filled textbook of stylistics. One would think it a far cry from this work to polemics with Bible specialists, but he published (with I. Kikawada) a study of the Book of Genesis, *Before Abraham Was* (1985), in which, in opposition to the theory of many authors, he defends the unity of the text. According to him, the means of expression in Genesis testifies to a high degree of refinement and a polemical intent toward the Mesopotamian myths.

Arthur's various books could, perhaps, be seen as preparatory, because he was becoming more and more attracted to his own field of history. He was passionate about the past of his native California and the entire American continent. I was particularly taken by his book *Broken Shore* (1981), a monographic study of Marin County, where he grew up. It demonstrates, using the example of this small area, what changes took place in California in the course of only a few decades, so that an old Indian who could remember tribal rituals from his childhood, in his old age (if he had managed to survive) lived in a world of white Americans and their capitalism. In the interval, he could have been a witness to the establishment and collapse of the missions, whose most northern base was the Sonoma Mission in his area. A subject of the Spanish king, he then became a citizen of Mexico, and then of the United States. Perhaps, when Mexico broke away from the Spanish crown, he had worked as a peon on the latifundia established by white Spaniards who had grabbed and divvied up the Mission's properties among themselves.

The Rivals (1994), a volume about California politics in the 1850s, was something of a continuation of Arthur's county history. At the same time, however, in the same year, his five-hundred-page book *The New World: An Epic of Colonial America from the Founding of Jamestown to the Fall of Quebec* appeared. Suddenly, confounding the expectations of his colleagues, who considered Arthur's thinking and writing to be somewhat eccentric, and also confounding his own expectations, he was famous. Reviewers all praised the work, and one measure of its success was the purchase of film rights. For Arthur, who until then was known only to a small circle of readers, this fame was sweet. He could see it as the victory of his unorthodox views. He had never attempted to pander to public opinion. Around him, particularly in Berkeley, radicalism was demanded, or at least "political correctness," which he simply did not worry about. In his history of America he did not oppose noble (because oppressed and suppressed) Indians to thieving whites. His pessimistic vision imposed on him the study of mechanisms that were stronger than people entrapped in events. The Indian peoples engaged in wars with each other, concluding alliances with the French or the English, and thereby preparing their own extermination. The horrifying cruelty of their customs, for example among the Hurons, gave them morally dubious rights against the Jesuits, the chief actors in subduing Canada, who did not quibble about means. Quinn attempts to show the continent's past without illusions.

I permit myself to believe that I contributed something to his understanding of history as tragedy through my lectures on Dostoevsky, on Russian history, and through our conversations, in which Simone Weil occupied much space. Arthur, in turn, helped me a great deal, editing my translation into English of two metaphysical treatises by Oscar Milosz. In addition, together with his colleague from the Department of Rhetoric, the poet Leonard Nathan, he wrote a book about my creative work, *The Poet's Work: An Introduction to Czeslaw Milosz*, which was published in 1991 with a preface by Stanisław Barańczak. The authors divided the material in this way: Nathan wrote about my poetry and Arthur about my essays. My Manichaeanism is very strongly emphasized.

Hell with the Fire Out: A History of the Modoc War (1997) was Arthur's last book. He had time to write a preface in which he referred to his illness, but the book came out a couple of months after his death. His life course was like a morality play. Arthur had a happy marriage, four grown children, but he lacked recognition. Scarcely was he named a leading American historian when he fell ill and the diagnosis was cancer of the brain. The illness progressed rapidly. He had lived fifty-five years.

His last work unites his chief intellectual and emotional passions. California, its past, pity and sympathy for the misfortunes of mortals—the philosophical testament, as it were, of the scholar. Its subject is the war between the small Indian nation of the Modocs and the American army in the years 1869–73, pursued with the combatants' full awareness that it was literally a struggle for the existence or destruction of their language and customs. The consequences follow one upon the other with stubborn necessity, although on both sides there were various attempts at a compromise. Such attempts were made by the Modocs' leader, at least, who was called Captain Jack; he failed, was captured, and hanged. The Modoc Indian nation no longer exists; it left no trace except in the memory of a historian who, more than one hundred years later, pondered their fate and was able to pronounce some general thoughts, while acknowledging with appropriate gravity the intentions of individual people.

Europeans are inclined to accuse Americans of historical naiveté. But the eradication of the Indians and the Civil War, the bloodiest war of the nineteenth century (a greater number of fatalities than in the Napoleonic wars), are ever present in the collective memory, although not many dare to step into that abyss. Arthur Quinn dared, no doubt because, for him, erudition was only a mask for the demands of his ardent heart, which loved God and hated evil.

[**R**]

RAJNFELD, Józio. I believe I saw some of his drawings, probably in *Skamander*, but I did not know him then personally. I now
know that he was born in Warsaw in 1906, into a Jewish family.
His father owned a clothing store. Józef studied in the Architecture Department of the Warsaw Polytechnical School, but he
was consumed by painting. Iwaszkiewicz often spoke of Józio the
painter, who was a close friend of his. After Warsaw he lived in
Paris, in poverty, and then in Italy.

For me, Rajnfeld is my first journey to Italy and San
Gimignano. I undertook my journey of self-education in the
spring of 1937, between the time when I was fired from Polish
Radio in Wilno and when I began working for Polish Radio in
Warsaw. When I lived in Wilno I knew very little about painting. This should be emphasized as a feature distinguishing the
first half of the twentieth century from the second half, when,
thanks to improvements in reproduction and artistic culture, the
most important works of world painting could be known, more
or less, by everyone.

A stipend from the Fund for Popular Culture had allowed me
to spend the 1934–35 academic year in Paris, where I visited the
Louvre on a regular basis and also as part of a group led by the
painter Józef Pankiewicz, who would stop in front of various pic-

tures and talk about a given artist's technique. Józef Czapski was a member of that group (*nota bene*, he wrote a book about Pankiewicz), as were Kazimierz and Fela Kranc, and also on occasion the composer Roman Maciejewski, a German violinist, I think, and probably one other person. So I acquired an introduction to a field that was important (I felt that) for a poet. But I had no money to travel to Italy at that time, so I used my free month only in 1937.

I traveled by train, of course. It wasn't easy to go everywhere by rail. Iwaszkiewicz had talked me into going to San Gimignano and sent me to Rajnfeld, who was living there, but the city was several kilometers from the train station where passengers had to transfer to fiacres. San Gimignano: the famous thicket of towers, steep lanes paved with cobblestones, a city seemingly deserted by its inhabitants, so few people could be seen. No tourists. I found Rajnfeld without any difficulty, even though I did not have his address, because the city, confined within its walls, is tiny. He lived in a *pensione* just beyond the walls with a fair-haired Englishman, also a painter, if I'm not mistaken.

I remember that evening with Rajnfeld and his friend in the garden of their *pensione*. We drank wine, watching the darkness lit up by fireflies flitting over the ravine and the vineyards. Rajnfeld, with his black hair and round face, struck me as attractive and radiant. It was precisely that radiance and a seeming excess of vital energy that remained in my memory, and later, during the war, I tried to picture what might have happened to him. I have a vague recollection that I even thought that if he had remained in Italy, I was glad for him.

During that same journey to San Gimignano I visited Orvieto, the cathedral just outside the city in a meadow with abundant grass which came all the way to its marble stairs. Signorelli's *The Coming of the Antichrist*, which I saw there, seemed timely and was to have a lasting influence on me.

Had Rajnfeld remained in Italy he probably would have survived. For reasons which I am unaware of, he was in France in 1940; after the defeat, he attempted to cross the border into Spain and committed suicide somewhere in the Pyrenées. I have heard that some of Rajnfeld's paintings are in the storerooms of the National Museum in Warsaw.

REXROTH, Kenneth. For a long time, the leading poet of California was Robinson Jeffers. Then, in 1929, Kenneth Rexroth arrived in San Francisco from Chicago. He became the patron and mentor of the younger poets, welcoming all innovations, as opposed to Jeffers the loner whom, *nota bene*, he mercilessly bashed in his essays.

A European poet could not possibly contain as many contradictions as Rexroth did. A revolutionary activist, a Communist, anarchist, pacifist, mystic, pious communicant of the Anglican Church, a Roman Catholic on his deathbed and, in fact, a Buddhist.

He was the hero of poetry as a profession (which is practically impossible in America and, perhaps, everywhere) simply because he had never graduated even from high school, and had no fame to persuade the professors, so no university wanted to admit him. It was only in old age, after he had become famous, that he attained a measure of prosperity and peace as a professor at the University of California at Santa Barbara.

I knew him and was the recipient of much kindness from him, and definitely not because of my surname, although long ago, in 1955, Rexroth had published a volume of Oscar Milosz's poetry in his translation. Kindness toward other poets came naturally to him. I shall leave it to his biographers to produce a not too flattering portrait of the man. They can count his contradictions: he bragged, lied, cheated, prayed, was a bigamist, betrayed every one of his four wives, believed in the sanctity of marriage, was paranoiacally suspicious of his friends. For me, however, he was above all a splendid poet and a splendid translator of Chinese and Japanese poetry.

I showed him the manuscript of my first volume of poems in English translation, translated chiefly by me. He praised it. Asked why he liked my translations since my English was not particularly strong, he responded, "A person who has an ear for one language has an ear for all languages." I don't know if that is true. My volume *Selected Poems* appeared in 1973 with an introduction written by him. Several days after my Nobel Prize he telephoned from Santa Barbara and congratulated me. I assured him of my undying gratitude for his early support.

RIMBAUD, Arthur (1854–1891). He caused his mother and his entire family a great deal of grief. He ran away from home, bummed around, drank, whored, almost died of hunger, wrote manifestos in verse against society, religion, morality, and literature. At the age of nineteen he decided to put an end to everything. From then on, the Parisian literati who had tried to help him lost track of him. After wandering through the countries of Europe, where he tried his hand at various trades, he set out for Africa. He traded in weapons, gold, and ivory in Abyssinia, leading his caravans into inaccessible corners of the Dark Continent. He earned enough to have a palace in Harare and to participate in local political intrigues. So he led the life of one of those white adventurers in Africa whom Joseph Conrad portrayed in *Heart of Darkness* as Kurtz, an agent for a Belgian trading firm.

When he died (from gangrene of the leg) at just a little over thirty years old, he did not know that in Paris his fame was already growing around *Une saison en enfer* and the manuscripts he had left behind. Proclaimed a genius, he became the leading literary myth of the twentieth century.

In the first decades of the twentieth century, three figures vied with each other for the particular attention of Europe's artistic and literary circles. They were Walt Whitman, the "gigantic old man," who was not well-known, though already available in a few translations; Oscar Wilde, "Antinoüs in a velvet beret," the very model of an aesthete and homosexual; and finally Arthur Rimbaud, the symbolic representative of all that is wild, unkempt, rebellious and, most likely, animal-like. Young Poland already knew him; Miriam-Przesmycki printed his own translation of "Le bateau ivre" in his journal, *Chimera*. Good society gossiped in the cafés about the French poet's eccentricities; it was said that he had discovered that vowels have colors, each its own. The ultra-refined writer Józef Weyssenhoff (the author of *Podfilipski*), mocking the *moderne*, describes in one of his poems from 1911, I think, an island on which a gorilla discovers that he can sense "color in a sound, odor in a word." I quote from memory:

> *And listening to the words of Rimbaud*
> *He senses tremors in his hind legs.*

It was only the generation of the Skamander poets, however, who really took to Rimbaud. In 1916, in Kiev, Jarosław Iwaszkiewicz and Mieczysław Rytard translated his *Illuminations*. Iwaszkiewicz adopted the new form of the poem in prose in his *Kassidas*. His "Prayer to Arthur Rimbaud" is virtually a spiritualistic séance, a summoning of his soul. Soon Julian Tuwim and Antoni Słonimski joined the ranks of Rimbaud's translators. One could say that the young Tuwim moved from under the sign of Whitman to the sign of Rimbaud.

Verbal energy, a voluptuousness of language, abundance of colors are signs of a revolution in the Polish language after the linguistic impotence of the *moderne*, and Polish poetry, like the poetry of many languages, owes a great deal to Rimbaud. In this regard, his influence lasted longer than Whitman's, let alone Wilde's.

It is not his artistic innovation, however, that supports the legend of Rimbaud; in the first instance, it is his rebellion against established forms of behavior, against his own bourgeois family, and not only them, but society in general. It is as if by his life course he anticipated and secured a pattern that would be repeated many decades after his death. Does the rebellion of American youth in the sixties not remind us of a multiplication of individual revolts into a crowd of Baudelaires and Rimbauds—including the further adventures of this generation? Rimbaud himself considered his youthful anxieties and despair as good for an adolescent, and went on to serious matters—that is, to making money and to politics. The generation of the yuppies made a similar choice.

Rimbaud was appreciated first by a handful of French writers. They began speaking and writing about him, and the renown of his name reached the artistic bohemias of various countries first, and then spread to a wider public. In a somewhat similar manner, like a wave, the fame of his approximate contemporaries, Cézanne and van Gogh, spread to ever wider circles. Their significance for painting is the same as Rimbaud's for poetry, although everyone knows about them by now, since their paintings garner millions of dollars on the international market.

For a legend to grow up around a particular name, several conditions must be met. Whatever happened in France attracted the attention of the entire world; Europe, at least, read French journals and books. After the period of the domination of Latin, for a long time French was the language one had to know. Certainly, unkempt, rebellious poets appeared in various other countries, but they produced only local stories. What was also necessary was the right moment in historical time, when the inequities of capitalism and revolutionary dreams came together. No one knows if Rimbaud really fought on the barricades of the Paris Commune, but the legend is significant.

Perhaps human societies require names as abbreviations, names that constitute a kind of shorthand, names as substitutes. In Poland these were provided by the Romantic poets; for example, the name Mickiewicz, the trial of the Philomaths, Forefathers' Eve—all fused into one mythic whole. One cannot avoid the question of what will happen to these shorthand names in a culture of fleeting images, a parasitic culture (pop art, postmodernism) which exploits all the achievements of humanity. Most likely their suitability as signs will intensify, while reality will seep out of them. The biography of Rimbaud, the poet who wanted to reach the inexpressible, if only through "unleashing all his senses," who fell silent and transformed himself into a merchant-adventurer, will long be a favorite subject for television screenplays.

RODITI, Eduardo. It was early one autumn day in 1934. I was traveling by metro to Malesherbes from the Polish scholarship students' hostel on rue Lammandé near the Boulevard des Batignolles (the Clichy metro), and at the Malesherbes plaza I found a small plaque with the inscription "Légation de Lithuanie." There, Oscar Milosz welcomed me and said that a young Greek poet from Constantinople who wrote in both French and English would accompany us to lunch. He was, he said, a linguistic phenomenon. Somehow or other, the young man appeared, and I remember the three of us walking together, but I don't remember the restaurant, although it was probably Italian, Poccardi, near the Opéra, because that is where Oscar usually invited his guests.

Roditi would turn up much later among my literary acquaintances, but I did not know that at the time. The moment of that first meeting allows me to reflect on the limitlessness of my (and not only my) provincialism, which no one today can comprehend. Perhaps people who came from Warsaw could successfully pretend that they were not provincials, but those of us from Wilno would have tried in vain. In Roditi I met my first cosmopolitan in the true sense of that word, but the Levant, where he came from, had no shape for me, I had not even heard the name Cavafy at that time, and I also had no idea what problems they had there with Greek and the other languages. Roditi actually came from Salonika and was a Sephardic Jew, which means that his native tongue was Ladino. His English belonged to an entirely exotic sphere, in my opinion, like everything that was English and American. I also could not understand how someone could write in several languages simultaneously.

Roditi first functioned in literary Paris as a French poet, then moved to America, where he joined the brotherhood of avant-garde poets and painters. One of those few people who knew Oscar Milosz's poetry, he remained loyal to his old friend and translated his poems into English. We met a couple of times in Berkeley. We spoke about Natalie Clifford Barney. Roditi was a gay man and, like all men of his type, he upheld the myth of that lesbian who, over the course of several decades beginning just before the war in 1914, conducted a marvelous literary salon in Paris. Miss Barney belongs to the history of both literary Paris and American literature. But I learned of this later while reading the correspondence (which was published in installments) of Oscar Milosz, who was one of the guests at her salon. More than that, because she was his sincere platonic friend and confidante.

I had only just begun to make contact with the labyrinth of interwar Paris and interwar America, and Roditi appeared as an ambassador from those regions, just like Oscar's other friend, the famous Princeton University professor, Christian Gauss, or the writer from two continents, Jean de Boschère.

I used to feel a little envious of the polyglot Roditi, but, provincial that I was, I held to my one language. Strategically speaking, that was not a very smart move, but it worked out well for me.

RUDNICKA WILDERNESS. I am amazed at what a powerful pull the north, and the Rudnicka Wilderness, exerts on my imagination and that of many inhabitants of Wilno. The Rudnicka Wilderness was a vast complex of forests with almost inaccessible marshes in the interior, the habitat of grouse and moose. The wilderness began beyond Lake Popiś, where I once went duck hunting with my father on the feast of Saints Peter and Paul. Jewish youth from the village of Popiszki lounged in the steep ravine, observing the hunters making their way past them in a couple of canoes. My father and I also traveled occasionally to the village of Żegaryno, which was situated in the middle of the forest. We would set out from Raudonka, a wooden cottage and a couple of hectares of land which my father had purchased because it was close to the wilderness, at the sixteenth kilometer on the Wilno-Jaszuny road. The closest villages were Lithuanian Mariampol in one direction, Belorussian Czernica in the other, and somewhat farther along, what I think was the mixed Belorussian and Polish village of Halina. I often drove to Jaszuny in a one-horse cart, with forests on either side of the road, passing on the left the black forests of the Kiejdzie estate, where there were still bears, or so people said, but the woman who owned the estate would not allow anyone to hunt on it. The square in front of the Jaszuny station was usually piled high with stacks of pine logs ready for the sawmill. So, if one were to look at a map (which resides firmly in my brain), to the south of Raudonka is Jaszuny; to the west, the orderly rows of a managed forest, a couple of villages, the railroad track, and beyond it, Rudnicka Wilderness; to the east, a most unusual landscape of hills and groves stretching all the way to the little town of Turgiele. Right there, about one kilometer away by foot, live the Maruszewski brothers, and just a bit farther their brother Józef in his farmhouse. My descriptions of hunting in *The Issa Valley* are definitely not based on the Kiejdany district but on our vacation stays in Raudonka, which was probably given that name because of the rusty water in the stream, since *raudonas* means "red" in Lithuanian. Adders lived in the marshes beyond the stream; indeed, there were plenty of them everywhere.

Right after we passed our *gymnasium* graduation exam Staś Kownacki, Ignacy Święcicki, Bohdan Kopeć and I went on an excursion to the Rudnicka Wilderness. The owner of a small manor house in the vicinity of Rudniki welcomed us most graciously, letting us spend the night in a hayshed and inviting us to have breakfast with her in the morning, but we vanished at dawn, probably impolitely. We swam in Mereczanka, were eaten alive by mosquitoes, made our way to the manor in Jaszuny, where we were treated to potatoes with sour milk in the absence of the landowners (the Sołtans). I remember nothing of this visit other than the romantic name, which was connected with the Śniadeckis and the poet Juliusz Słowacki. Only recently, during one of my trips to Wilno, I visited the park, which has been preserved.

During the war, the Rudnicka Wilderness and the lands to the south of it provided cover for Home Army detachments as well as for Soviet partisan groups operating in the area, mainly composed of Jews who had fled the Wilno ghetto. I discussed this with Abba Kovner, an Israeli poet, when he visited Berkeley. Abba Kovner was a student in the Department of Fine Arts at our university when the war broke out. For a long time, he dressed in a nun's habit; that's how the Polish nuns hid him and several other Jews in their cloister. Then he decided to return to the ghetto, where he became a leader of an armed organization. Only when the situation turned hopeless did he escape to the forest partisans. He told me, "After all, the Home Army was an ordinary army and acted like an army, with actions, battles, and so forth. We had entirely different tactics—partisan tactics. We wanted to give the impression that there were a great many of us, so when we passed through a village at night we tried to make as much noise as possible, as if an entire regiment were passing through, and we aimed for the same effect in whatever actions we undertook."

In the minds of the inhabitants, the Rudnicka Wilderness meant shelter. In Józef Mackiewicz's novel *The Road to No-*

where, when the hero no longer sees any salvation for himself during the Soviet occupation, he loads his wife into a cart and hides in the wilderness, in its southern reaches, near Lake Kiernowo. It appears that the "miracle at Popiszki" described there refers to a different village, not the one on the banks of Lake Popiś.

Toward the end of the war battles raged within the Rudnicka Wilderness between detachments of the KGB and remnants of the Home Army. Then the Soviet Army chose the Rudnicka Wilderness for its permanent military bases and during the decades they were there such devastation took place that I have no idea how much of the forest survived.

RUSSIAN LANGUAGE. I was born in the Russian Empire, where schoolchildren were forbidden to speak in any language other than Russian. Even *gymnasium* classes in the Roman Catholic religion had to be in Russian, although, as my father told me, the catechist in Wilno worked around the ban and told them to memorize one story from the Bible in Russian in the event of an inspection. Then any pupil who was called on would stand up and recite the same verse: "Abraham was sitting in his tent. . . ."

It is not easy to get rid of one's Russian citizenship. The Soviet Union's laws recognized as Soviet citizens all people born within the borders of tsarist Russia. Perhaps this formal principle was unnecessary, since in any case those who arrived with the Red Army in 1944 to set up their rule were Soviet citizens.

Russian penetrated me in my childhood by osmosis during our wanderings through Russia during World War I, and then in Wilno, where Russian-speaking Yashka and Sonka belonged to our band of children in the courtyard of the apartment house at

No. 5 Podgórna Street. I think that Russification had made significant progress in Wilno and its environs, especially after 1863.

I never studied the language formally; still, it sat somewhere deep inside me. I would risk theorizing that people who came from Galicia, for example, had a somewhat different ear; that is, they had a different feeling for Polish, which might also appear in their poetry. In Leśmian, who was born in Warsaw and studied in Kiev, I detect what I think are echoes of iambic Russian, and indeed, he began by writing poetry in Russian. I myself felt a very strong attraction to Russian incantation in poetry. Pushkin, for example, has so much strength and formal power in his lines that they remain as if carved into one's memory forever. Nevertheless, I seem to have realized early that it is a different register from the register of Polish poetry, and that imitating the Russians would be dangerous. The fact is, I have never translated anything from Russian. Even my friendship with Joseph Brodsky, who translated a number of my poems into Russian, could not change that. There is only one of his poems in my translation, but I did write a lot about his poetry in both Polish and English.

A debate about the two languages' different laws was carried on during the interwar decades in relation to Julian Tuwim's translation of *Eugene Onegin*. Adam Ważyk, the author of a competing translation, attacked Tuwim's version. Polish is a language with a constant stress on the penultimate syllable of a word, while Russian has movable stress, with a predilection for iambic feet. In order to imitate Pushkin's iambs in Polish, one had to rhyme monosyllabic words, which Tuwim did very successfully, but the result was rather monotonous. Ważyk renounced this method of rhyming in the main, and his translation breathes more easily; it is more in line with the spirit of the

Polish language. The inequality of the two languages can be seen in Russians' assessments of Polish poetry. Most often, they like poetry that is modulated by rhythm and rhyme, which reminds them of their own poetry.

The Polish language has by now done away with the corset of metrical verse and rhymes without inflicting any great harm on itself. How this would work out in Russian, I don't know. Joseph Brodsky remained a metrical poet.

Before 1914 Russia participated more vigorously in general European civilization than Poland, stunted by the partitions. The Russian intelligentsia was essentially cosmopolitan. Thus, in Polish culture there are imports from the capitals of the partitioning powers: Przybyszewski from Berlin, Jarosław Iwaszkiewicz from Kiev, but actually, thanks to innovations in Russian poetry, from Petersburg. In the interwar period Iwaszkiewicz's Skamander colleagues seem provincial in comparison with him.

Russia in my parents' generation seemed to be only wide open spaces and it was not for nothing that my father received his first engineering post in Siberia. Many people who had to return to the Vistula lands from those wide expanses after the Revolution felt as if they were being cooped up, and there are eloquent examples of their difficult adaptation to the smallness, intrigues, rumors, and the war of all against all. Leon Petrażycki, who was well-known at Petersburg University, where crowds squeezed into lecture halls to listen to him, committed suicide in Poland; the same fate awaited Aleksander Lednicki.

I should add that because of Russian I was almost shot in 1945: "How do you know Russian? Spy!"

[S]

SCHOPENHAUER, Arthur. It would not be right to pass over a philosopher to whom I owe a great deal. His books are on my shelf, for dipping into from time to time. Indeed, he has been a companion to many poets and artists, although the content they discovered in him had changed over time. He was considered the most extreme pessimist. What is he for us now, when we tally the experiences of the twentieth century? If only we had heeded his warnings . . . He fulfilled his duty as a philosopher punctiliously. He did not trust abstract knowledge. According to him, ideas are to observed data as the issuing of bank notes is to gold in the bank for the owner of the value they represent. Humanity moves toward the most monstrous aberrations and crimes by juggling concepts without submitting them to objective assessment. "The tragic side of error and of prejudice lies in the practical, the comic is reserved for the theoretical. For example, if we were firmly to persuade only three persons that the sun is not the cause of daylight, we might hope to see it soon accepted as the general conviction. In Germany, it was possible to proclaim Hegel, a repulsive and dull charlatan and an unparalleled scribbler of nonsense, the greatest philosopher of all time. For twenty years many thousands have stubbornly and firmly believed this. . . ."* Alas, a good deal longer than twenty years!

Errors in thinking have consequences, however, and Schopenhauer, struggling with the German philosophy of his time, was aware of this. "But sooner or later every error must do harm," he wrote, "and this harm is all the greater, the greater the error. He who cherishes the individual error must one day atone for it, and often pay dearly for it. The same thing will hold good on a large scale as regards the common errors of whole nations. Therefore it cannot be repeated too often that, wherever we come across an error, it is to be pursued and eradicated as an enemy of mankind, and there cannot be any privileged or even sanctioned errors. The thinker should attack them, even though mankind should cry aloud, like a sick person whose ulcer is touched by the physician."[†]

Here am I quoting this, I, who once was susceptible to the thinking of Stanisław Brzozowski (who was himself enchanted by Hegel) and later of Tadeusz Juliusz Kroński. However, a lack of consistency has been one of my strengths, and the other pole of my intellect won out—the pessimistic side.

Schopenhauer must have been viewed as a freak by the visionaries who took the upheavals of the French Revolution and Napoleonic wars as an omen of a splendid new Era of the Spirit, and by all sorts of utopian socialists. But he also offended Victorian morality with the openness with which he wrote about the animal urges of the human species. People have had to accustom themselves to the theory of evolution, but he proclaimed this be-

*Arthur Schopenhauer, *The World as Will and Representation,* trans. E.F.J. Payne, 2 vols. (New York: Dover Publications, 1966), 2:70.

[†]Ibid., 2:68–69.

fore Darwin. As I have learned from people who study Darwin's life, he read Schopenhauer and probably borrowed from him. Schopenhauer encompassed the laws governing natural selection and survival of the fittest with the concept of the universal will. The will, "the thing in itself," is expressed in living beings in the urge to exist at any price and in the continuation of their own species; it acts most powerfully in the procreative drive. Will is the very essence of the world; it acts blindly, without consideration for the death of countless millions of creatures. Man, like all animals, is under the power of the universal will and it is the will that supplies the key to both his physiology and his psychology.

In other words, this is simply an image of the world for which we can thank the science of biology. It is not very uplifting, but sometimes it is necessary to swallow bitter medicine. Yet, if the philosopher from Danzig was only one of the nineteenth-century reductionists and unmaskers, he would not attract sensitive, aching souls, artists and seekers of religion. The world as will is, in Schopenhauer, a world of the pain and death of living beings, and we humans cannot think about this without constant empathy, which is sympathetic suffering. Because man is not only a slave of the will, but is also mind, even though mind usually functions only as an instrument of the will. Mind is capable, however, of liberating itself from the pressure of desires that demand to be satisfied, capable of looking at everything from a distance, and then life appears to be an infernal circle of aspirations and fears, which are delusions, phantoms, suggested by the will.

I have known the temptations of "understanding history," which people indulged in feverishly in my century, multiplying ideas and ideologies. Earlier, however, I had a naturalist's interests; that was followed by youthful despair at the merciless laws of Mother Nature, indifferent to the sufferings and extinction of her children. That is when the pessimistic philosophers suited me perfectly. I entered the university when its Rector was Marian Zdziechowski, perhaps the sole Christian pessimist to be so radical as to deny that the world has any meaning, while taking its cruelty to heart. Two other figures in my life course were Simone Weil, who practically discovered the Cathar heresy of Manichaeanism, and Lev Shestov, who rebelled against necessity, against two times two equals four, against the law of cause and effect. I cannot say when it was that I began reading Schopenhauer. He has returned at various stages of my life.

His search for liberation. Connected with his contempt for the majority of mortals, who chase after the satisfaction of their desires like dogs after mechanical hares. He considered the banner of humankind to be its need for metaphysics, which is served equally by religions and by true philosophy, and it was the latter that he wanted to serve. Philosophy, in his opinion, moved along a track that ran parallel to various religions. He appreciated those religions which look at the world without illusions, which understand it, that is, as a vale of tears. He did not like paganism, because it is fundamentally optimistic. The Old Testament was worthy of consideration only as a story about the fall of the first parents and original sin. Christianity took that up and its very core is consciousness of the corruption of matter. He would probably not have liked twentieth-century Christians' flirtations with the pagan world and their avowals that they have never had contempt for matter. Awareness that existence is suffering and empathy for every living thing, not just for human beings' torments, is even stronger in Buddhism, which is why Schopenhauer was attracted to it, although he said he discovered it late, after his system was already worked out.

I think, though, that he had his greatest influence in proclaiming liberation through art. He was concerned with the problem of the artistic genius, who rebels against his submission to the demands of the will: "In accordance with the description we have given of the true nature of genius, it is contrary to nature in so far as it consists in the intellect, whose real destiny is the service of the will, emancipating itself from that service in order to be active on its own account. Accordingly, genius is an intellect that has become unfaithful to its destiny. . . ."*

This is also the reason why all children are brilliant: "For intellect and brain are one, and in just the same way, the genital system is one with the most vehement of desires. I have therefore called this the focus of the will. Just because the terrible activity of this system still slumbers, while that of the brain already has full briskness, childhood is the time of innocence and happiness, the paradise of life, the lost Eden on which we look back longingly through the whole remaining course of our life."†

What is probably most attractive in Schopenhauer for every artist is the conviction that the mind, by extricating itself from the ties of the will, can achieve an *objective* view. "Distance is the soul of beauty," says Simone Weil. That is the same thing. Schopenhauer referred to the example of seventeenth-century Dutch painting. And what about *Pan Tadeusz*? Mickiewicz was transported into that dimension in which striving, passions,

*Ibid., 2:386.
†Ibid., 2:394.

fears, no longer resulted in suffering because they were in the past, and a smile reconciled him with the world of Soplicowo, which was real because it no longer existed.

SIERRAVILLE. Few people go there, because there is nothing to see. Even the name of this little town is too big for the dozen or so wooden homes on a flat plateau beneath the peaks of the Sierra Nevada Mountains. Once I asked a little man who was fussing over repairs to the fence around his house where he came from. He replied that his parents had come here. But from where? He pointed to the east, to the mountains: "From over there."

The hamlet was discovered by hippies; I understand the contents of the tiny bookstore in which I purchased a book about a sect of immortalists to be a remnant of the 1960s. I learned from that book that science frees man from fear of death because it guarantees him immortality. Therefore, both religion and art, which are born of the same fear, will eventually disappear. For the time being, until science is perfected, the bodies of dead members of this sect should be frozen, to await in this state resurrection by people who will one day dispose of more advanced knowledge. This reminded me of the Russian admirer of science, Fedorov, who, in the nineteenth century, proclaimed the imminent victory of science over death. When that happens man will be obliged to resurrect all his ancestors and, perhaps, since the world will be too small, to populate the entire universe with them.

Sierraville was the location of one of Carol's and my adventures. As luck would have it, our car broke down and we had no idea how we were going to get out of there. Then a man we met in a store, who was undoubtedly a hippie, judging from his looks, invited us in the friendliest way to come to his commune a couple of miles down the road if we could make it there by driving slowly, despite whatever was wrong with the engine. The car would be repaired there.

We found ourselves in a land of gentleness. No one was in a hurry; no one raised his voice. They lived in the woods on the mountainside, where there were hot springs channeled into stone containers and baths. The men and women bathed together, absolutely naked, and even when they moved around the building or sat at the table to eat, most of them were naked or barely covered by a piece of cloth. No one forced anyone to do anything, and when we went to bathe while they repaired our car, they accepted it as natural that we did not strip to our bare skin. In the way they treated each other and in their behavior toward us they seemed completely tolerant and laid-back. How they would get on in the long run one could only surmise, but their little community in which no one, neither man nor woman, tried to impose on anyone else by striking airs or making faces struck me as worthy of admiration—the exact opposite of the Gombrowiczean theater.

They fixed the car. They wouldn't accept anything in payment.

SŁAWIŃSKA, Irena. A native of Wilno, Sławińska was my classmate at the Stefan Batory University in Wilno, not in the same department, because she studied Polish and Romance literatures and I studied law, but we both belonged to the Creative Writing Circle (other universities apparently did not have something like that at the time), and thanks to this we were students of the Circle's mentor, Professor Manfred Kridl. I did not know then that one day, far from Wilno (because it would happen in America),

Kridl's fate and mine would intertwine. Today, I can see certain objectively good reasons for my withdrawal from the Department of Polish Literature after just a couple of weeks, because aside from Kridl the department had no professors who interested me.

My relations with Irena were collegial, never closer than that, and we never had any deep conversations in Wilno. I knew some of the other "young Orzeszkowas" better. If I remember correctly, Irena graduated from the Eliza Orzeszkowa State Gymnasium.

When I think about the young Sławińska today, she appears to me against a background of many faces from our class, confirming a certain pattern of the time. Perhaps at other universities students were recruited primarily from the families of civil servants; in Wilno, most in evidence were family origins in large or small manors or gentry backwaters, in the first or second generation, with others representing a low percent, and peasants close to zero. This does not apply to Jews, because they came from merchant families, often very poor ones. The pattern reflected kinship ties in the countryside, which was especially useful during the war. Our classmate from the Division of Original Creative Work, Teodor Bujnicki, who exposed himself to the judgment of Wilno opinion by publishing propaganda verses in the Soviet *Wilno Truth*, spent the German occupation on his relatives' estate near Szawle. Sławińska also lived with her aunt in Samogitia for a while during the war years, and the story that I heard her tell after the war gives some idea of how time was frozen in certain provinces of Europe. The young lady from Wilno struck the fancy of a certain local squire, so he began courting her. Her aunt, offended by his not knowing his place, since he was not a real member of the gentry, just a backwater yeoman, ordered her servants to serve him black soup and to place a pumpkin in his carriage. Thus, this seventeenth-century custom of dismissing a suitor lived on in Samogitia, despite the apocalyptic war that was raging at the time.

That squire had a good eye, because the doctoral student from Wilno, flaxen-haired and comely, was a strong girl, perfect for farming. On the other hand, her passion for sport would have been useless for him, because, taking advantage of the Wilija River and nearby lakes, she had trained to become a terrific swimmer—a fact that should not be overlooked in a recital of her achievements. Her other achievements led to her professor's gown and cap. As a literary scholar she specialized in the history of Polish and French drama and the works of Cyprian Norwid. She received her doctorate only after the war, in 1948, at the University of Toruń, defending her dissertation on "Types of Drama in the Young Poland Era."

Sławińska should attract the attention of historians (and there will no doubt be such) interested in Wilno's contribution to the culture and politics of post-Yalta Poland. As is well known, a left-wing political movement under the leadership of Henryk Dembiński emerged at the university in Wilno in connection with Żagary. That movement once won the elections to the Brotherhood; later it moved farther to the left, publishing the journals *Po prostu* (Without Ceremony) and *Razem* (Together). After 1945 the survivors banded together as the informal but influential Wilno group. The Stefan Batory University also had a Catholic organization, Rebirth, which Henryk Dembiński started out in, as a matter of fact, and in his first political battles he could count on at least some of the Rebirth members, because they were not sympathetic to "national ideology." They did not follow him, however, when he announced his support for the Communist revolution. I associate the following individuals with Rebirth: Stanisław Stomma, Irena Sławińska, Antoni Gołubiew and his wife, and Czesław Zgorzelski. After 1945 these names appear frequently on the pages of *The Universal Weekly*, and Stomma is even its chief writer. There is no doubt that the participation of graduates of Wilno *gymnasia* was especially important in this effort. Sławińska remained ideally resistant to the government's temptations in her scholarly work and pedagogical activity, first at the University of Toruń and then at KUL (the Catholic University of Lublin), which I, for one, by no means an ermine who changed his coat, record with pleasure. I must also loyally add that our ways of thinking always diverged, and I was ready to take issue with several of her books.

I was happy that she found a position and a place for her activities in Lublin. We were not completely cut off from each other in the years of the People's Republic of Poland. After 1956, travel abroad was permitted; I would date our meeting in Paris to 1958, most likely. Irena also made a trip to America, and the Department of Slavic Languages and Literatures at Berkeley, among others, hosted her. It is possible that the information she passed on about contemporary Polish literature had something to do with the university's issuing me an invitation. In her work on theater she was interested in French writers, which explains her stay in Paris, where professors of KUL usually took advantage of the hospitality of the Pallotini Fathers, in the house on rue Surcouf, the headquarters of Éditions du Dialogue. My close collaboration with Father Józef Sadzik on a translation of the Bible, and with the publishing house's *spiritus movens*, Danuta Szumska (a graduate of KUL), meant I was at home on rue Surcouf during my trips from America in the 1970s, and it was sweet to sit at the table with Irena and remember our Wilno days.

The Division of the Humanities at KUL nominated me to receive an honorary doctorate, and in 1980 the University approved the division's decision. It seems to me that Sławińska was the chief mover in this, which I ascribe in part to my literary achievements, but also in no small measure to the solidarity of Wilnoites. In any event, at the grand ceremony in which a crowd of students and Lech Wałęsa took part in June 1981, she received me and was absolutely radiant.

There you have the history of a couple of alumni of USB, an abbreviation that means nothing to younger generations, but which stands for Stefan Batory University. I see Irena in our cozy Polonists' club, which one entered from Wielka Street (more or less where the present Department of Polish Literature of Wilno University now makes its home). Others appear there, crowding in to the meetings of the Division. Teodor Bujnicki, shot to death by overly zealous boys in the underground movement; Kazimierz Hałaburda, who died in a Soviet camp; Zbigniew Folejewski, later a professor of literature in Sweden and Canada; Jerzy Putrament, although I think he may have joined later, and who was condemned by me in our journal *Żagary* for the "formalism" of his first novellas. Also a couple of other people who have vanished, leaving no trace, and among them, proud of her beauty, more concerned with attracting men's glances than with her studies, my classmate Miss Piórewiczówna, preserved in my collection of names from that time and place, along with Czepułkowski, Mrs. Kaczanowska, and Mr. Żabko-Potopowicz.

Irena Sławińska was distinguished in our group by her strong individualism, and she confirmed our expectations, for after all, she did not limit her understanding of creative work to poetry or so-called artistic prose. A grateful colleague, I write down these modest contributions to her biography, and to a certain university experience.

SŁAWONIEWSKI AND SŁYCZKO. Sławoniewski was over six feet tall, a strapping fellow but not built like an athlete—more like a swaying stalk. Słyczko looked tiny next to him, with his sharp nose, skinny neck, and bat's ears. Even before the war they were inseparable friends. I knew them because they (or was it only Sławoniewski?) worked in the technical department of Polish Radio in Wilno. During the German occupation they founded the Wilno firm "Sławoniewski and Słyczko," which specialized in supplying the German army, but one of their products, an antifrostbite cream, it was rumored, enraged the Germans, who arrested and shot them. At least, that's the story I was told; I wasn't in Wilno at the time. There's no likelihood that any memoirs make mention of that firm, which is why I am placing their names here.

SOLSKI, Wacław. Not many people remember the name, let alone the person. I knew him from New York, because he lived to a very old age. He led the life of an émigré there, stubbornly writing and publishing his stories and memoirs in Polish, although I cannot say who published them. If he belonged to an emigration, it was a most unlikely one, about which people speak only reluctantly.

Solski (his real name was Pański) was from Łódź, where he attended *gymnasium*. He passed his graduation exams in Warsaw in 1917. He had been attracted to socialist ideals before then, and joined the Social Democratic Party of Poland and

Lithuania. Later, he worked on the other side of the border, in Minsk during the first Workers' Soviet, at the outset of the Soviet regime, and edited Polish-language Communist periodicals. He was on that side, too, in 1920 when, following on the heels of the Red Army, the trio appointed by Lenin to head the future government of the Polish Soviet Republic (Dzierżyński, Marchlewski, Kon) moved westward. When victory in that war fell to Poland, he participated in the peace negotiations in Riga as a translator for the Soviet delegation. Since he knew Western languages, in the late 1920s he served in the Soviet Embassy in Paris as press attaché. He writes in his memoirs about the disenchantment of French journalists who were accustomed to receiving payments from the embassy under the tsarist government. They held out their hands for bribes from the new authorities and received nothing because Solski took seriously the clear conscience of a revolutionary. That political naiveté, if we can call it that, did not augur well for his accommodation to the regime and soon Solski broke with Communism. From 1928 on he lived in Germany, France, England, and finally, after 1945, in America.

A rather large man with a black goatee, intense but calm, in New York Solski was a one-man encyclopedia of knowledge about the events of the 1920s. Even in a city full of similar castaways, he stood out with his polyglot's talents. He wrote not only in Polish, but also in Russian, German, French, and English. One could learn a great deal from him during every conversation. I refrain from evaluating his books because I have read too few of them, but they are worthy of attention as a chronicle of the century and as testimony to the strange intersection of human fates. He aimed for clarity and simplicity in his prose.

Solski's uniqueness is based on his having survived, which he managed to do only because he emigrated early to the West. Others of his ilk perished in the Gulag, especially if their language was Polish and they wrote for the Polish-language press. In the 1930s, after all, Polish became a sufficient cause for arrest.

I have a feeling that as a result of my acquaintance with Solski I have brushed up against an enormous complex of virtually unstudied questions relating to the beginning of Poland in the two interwar decades—to be more exact, what happened to those who declared themselves on the other side, for the grand universal idea and against Piłsudski's Poland.

SONOMA. I would go there to visit the Sonoma Mission, which has been preserved as a museum, and also because that small town was the capital of California under Mexican rule. A land of low hills, bleached almost white in the summer, with black clusters of oak trees, it was gradually transformed over the course of my years in Berkeley. First there were only ranches and many horses; then, a vineyard here and there; finally, many vineyards, so that the Sonoma Valley began to compete successfully with the neighboring Napa Valley in the types and names of wines.

Not far from Sonoma is tiny Glen Allen. There, even in the 1960s, the main place in town was a bar, with mementos from World War I on its walls. Jack London used to drop in at this bar quite frequently; he liked the region, he rode around on horseback, and he built a huge stucco home as his permanent residence. That was when he already had a great deal of money and was suffering from advanced alcoholism. The house had hardly been completed when it burned down. Today, rebuilt, it is a Jack London museum and tourist attraction. The bar, however, no longer exists; it also burned down.

Jack London was the writer of my boyhood. It so happened

that fate carried me to San Francisco Bay, where his legend is preserved in such places as picturesque Jack London Square, around the Oakland piers, and in the museum home in Glen Allen.

Jack London became a part of the American myth in Russia, and was widely translated after the Revolution because of his socialist views. In Poland in the 1920s, when I was attending school, many of his books were published in cheap editions. Without a doubt, their Darwinian realism made an impression on my young mind. I found one of his novels especially moving when I was a little older: *Martin Eden,* about a beginning writer in San Francisco who is starving, sends his stories to editors without any luck, and falls in love with the unapproachable daughter of a millionaire. Suddenly he achieves fame and fortune, but then he sees that he has focused his emotions on an idiot and commits suicide, leaping at night from a steamer into the sea. Very romantic. Like Wokulski and Isabela Łęcka from Bolesław Prus's *The Doll.* What I seem to remember best, though, is Wilhelm Horzyca's translation of a poem by Swinburne that was used as the novel's epigraph.

SOSNOWSKA, Halina. She was the person I reported to at Polish Radio in Warsaw. If I were to write her biography, it would be a paean to a certain generation of Poles—the generation that created independent Poland after the partitions, and a defense of them against history's hypothetical judgment, as well as a song of mourning.

Miss Halina Żelechowska, from a noble family, of course, was born in 1894. This means that great historical events took place during her early youth. During World War I she worked in Orenburg in the Committee to Aid War Victims; in 1917–18 she was an educator in the Wilno region; in 1918 she was a member of the Committee to Defend Lwów; in 1920, in the Polish Red Cross; then came her studies in the Department of Philosophy at Warsaw University, a master's degree, and postgraduate studies at the Sorbonne. As I look over her personal data, I am not clear about how she acquired her surname, since she was married to Zygmunt Czarnocki from the Nacza estate near Nowogródek. So she was probably divorced (but how?) and Zbigniew Sosnowski, the ichthyologist, was her second husband.

When I write about her today, my attention is drawn to aspects of her life different from when I knew her. Then, her ardent cult of Piłsudski, her membership in the inner circles of Sanacja (the ones that were democratic and liberal), were what I found most striking. Only later did I understand how little hope she had. One can deduce this from some of her private communications, however restrained they were, because confessing to pessimism was not in her nature. Today, Sosnowska strikes me as a representative figure for certain circles of the intelligentsia who came from a gentry background; it would be difficult to say how numerous they were. She was the niece of General Julian Stachiewicz, who, like many high-ranking military officers, had his roots in Zet, which means their political orientation was opposed to the National Party, in favor of Piłsudski, and well represented in his Legions. The military men who would command the underground army in World War II, Generals Grot-Rowiecki and Chruściel, also came out of Zet. In general, one can say that that was Sosnowska's milieu, that part of the intelligentsia whose spokesman was the novelist Stefan Żeromski; they belonged to the patriotic conspiracy and took up arms in 1914, built an independent Polish state with Piłsudski, and won the war in 1920. It was also responsible for the "regime of the colonels" and then in the years 1939—45 for the underground state. The Warsaw Uprising of 1944 was the final act and defeat of this intelligentsia. I am merely summarizing here, refraining from passing judgment.

After she completed her studies, Sosnowska became a journalist. Her "entry ticket" to the Sejm in 1928 gives one pause. She was nominated as secretary to the Senate's Vice-Marshal H. Gliwic of the Non-Party Bloc for Cooperation with the Government. Gliwic is a great figure in Polish Freemasonry. Żeromski, the dream of "glass houses," democracy, tolerance—it all fits.

Beginning in 1930 Sosnowska worked at Polish Radio, first as secretary of the Programming Council and quickly rising in the administration. In 1935 she received the Golden Cross for Service. In 1936, when my fate began to depend on her, she was already Vice-Director of Polish Radio, practically the chief director, because Piotr (Pieso) Górecki, an old comrade of Piłsudski, treated his position mainly as a sinecure.

Sosnowska was feared and not liked at the Radio—for her energy, her demands, and her political views. Zenon Kosidowski was one of the administrative employees at the Radio; somewhere, I came across his description of her: "very industrious, but tactless, she was hated in Prog., she could not find a common language, arrogant, very efficient, she was superbly knowledgeable about her craft."

"Prog." was the Bureau of Programs, because her main concern, in fact, was programming. She and the programmers fought like cats and dogs; she created her own Bureau for Program Planning soon after I was forced out of Polish Radio in Wilno. We sat at our desks in a couple of rooms on Dąbrowski Square: Adam Szpak, in charge of music (killed in Warsaw); Józef Czechowicz, in charge of literature programming for chil-

dren (killed by a bomb in Lublin); Szulc, in charge of literature
(died in Auschwitz); Unkiewicz, in charge of science programs
(later, editor of *Problems*); Włodarkiewiczowa, who I believe was
in charge of education and sports programming (she died in
New York); and I, who was nominally in charge of literature, but
really did anything, because the woman who was "hated, unable
to find a common language," met with complete mutual understanding in me, and her arrogance fit nicely with mine. There
were constant meetings of our staff; I shone at them and was
soon considered to be her confidante, which was not accepted
well by people outside our bureau. I should add that this athlet-
ically trim Juno's beauty added to her charm. She drove me mercilessly and, really, couldn't somebody else do those nightmarish
monthly reviews of the activity of the Poland-wide programming of all the local stations?

Sosnowska was engaged in a political battle inside the Radio
and in this we were allies. Żeromski's vision had not come to
pass and (as in the majority of neighboring states) the so-called
OZON, the Camp of National Unity, was pressing to eradicate
democracy and introduce something like a nationalistic pop-
ulism; in other words, it looked as if that old state-creating intelligentsia had fought hard to keep on course but had finally given
up and succumbed to ancient Slavic pressures from below. The
constant anti-Semitic propaganda at a time when the same thing
was raging right next door, in Hitler's Germany, requires us today to ask about those connections, although even then people in
Warsaw were saying that the leaders of the National-Radical
Camp and even Bolesław Piasecki himself traveled often to Germany. In programming, that pressure was expressed by demands
that we increase the dose of patriotic sauce and get rid of Jews.
The administration of Polish Radio was unable to oppose this

demand and so, for example, "The Old Doctor's Chats," Janusz Korczak's program, was canceled. A gut feeling or intuition made me think that Poland's situation was hopeless and Sosnowska did not close her ears to my leftist whispers. It seems she was in a similar state of despair. The only thing she could do was to engage in delaying tactics. When the sociologist Aleksander Hertz was no longer allowed to speak on the radio because he was a Jew, she at least allowed him to earn a salary as a "program comptroller." These comptrollers listened to the radio at home and wrote reviews. One of them, in Wilno, was Jerzy Putrament. When they wanted to fire him, because he was a Communist, he was successfully defended.

A mortal danger, from the West and from the East, and in the middle an ideological collapse, because what kind of support could a belief in liberty, equality, fraternity offer? Żeromski's *Early Spring* had been published in 1925, not even fifteen years ago, and nothing had changed in what he'd described, only hope had disappeared. Here, I must introduce one correction: only a few people thought this way, because the generation that was still in school, and was to die during the war, had no idea. Only among Jews did one encounter a similarly catastrophic frame of mind. After all, the fact that a paper like Father Kolbe's *Little Daily* uttered the expression Jews-Communists-Masons in one breath had to have consequences.

Walery Sławek was one of Piłsudski's closest followers. He belonged to the fighting contingent of the Polish Socialist Party and participated in the raid on a train in Bezdany. After the May putsch Piłsudski entrusted him with creating the Non-Party Block of Cooperation with the Government. According to Aleksandra Piłsudska's memoirs, her husband intended him to be the next president of Poland. Sosnowska was aware of Sławek's importance. She saw him as a man whose hands were clean, unsullied by anything, and who lived for a single purpose—the patriotic ideal. His suicide in 1939 horrified her.

In September 1939 Polish Radio was evacuated to Romania. Sosnowska was one of very few people who remained in Warsaw. She and her husband lived in their private home on Filtrowa Street and officially earned an income by serving "home-style dinners," but were actually deeply involved in conspiratorial work, for which their restaurant was a convenient front, because the leadership of the underground would meet there. I visited Sosnowska on Filtrowa Street, but I do not know what organization she belonged to. I heard about her postwar fate. She was arrested and tried in 1947. It is hard to get accurate information about this, as it is with everything concerning the true history of the Polish People's Republic. People spoke of a life sentence. Apparently, she was in prison for twelve years; now, according to testimony from people who were close to her, it seems she was let out of prison after seven years as the result of an amnesty; she was certainly released by 1959. Word of her heroic behavior in prison and her moral assistance to her fellow prisoners reached me abroad. Her friends alerted me that she emerged from prison ill and in need of medication. I think I somehow managed to send medicines for her. She took up the cause of former women prisoners and founded a cooperative to give them employment. What she felt, what she thought, during her years in prison and afterward, no one will ever know, but knowing her, I am convinced of the strength of her will, which could not be broken by any adversity. She died in 1973.

Working with her drew me to the Radio, and perhaps it was not just my fear of losing a steady paycheck that kept me in that office. Her bureau and its guerrilla warfare created a kind of en-

circlement, so there was neither time nor energy left to participate in the so-called literary life of Warsaw. Worse yet, I was
promoted rapidly and my salary rose, too. I felt trapped and
achieved the freedom to devote myself to writing only in my
dreams. For the sake of accuracy, I must add that the Literary
Section of Polish Radio was something else. It was housed on
Zielna Street; Witold Hulewicz, Jan Parandowski, later on,
Bolesław Miciński, too, had their offices there, and my Wilno
colleagues Antoni Bohdziewicz and Tadeusz Byrski directed radio plays.

Sosnowska was a great person. In my youth, I did not like
monuments. Now I believe that monuments are necessary, because how else can we express our admiration for individuals
who can stand as models for us of righteousness and of the will
directed only toward the good? I would be delighted if a monu-
ment to Sosnowska were erected in Warsaw, on Filtrowa Street
or on Dąbrowski Square.

SPERBER, Manes. It would be easy to do some library research
into his biography, but I prefer to imagine part of it for myself.
First of all, for example, there's an inn, somewhere in Pokucie
and inside it an energetic innkeeper who works hard so that her
husband can pore over holy books and converse with the Lord of
Creation. There's also a crowd of children, and one of them is
Manes, who receives the strict education of a pious child in the
local *cheder*. This is not the end, however, because he will attend
gymnasium, and afterward study psychology in Vienna, and
soon will break with the faith of his forebears. What will replace
it, what will give him ardor equal to that which animated his father and grandfather in their prayers to the Highest One for the
coming of the Messiah? Marxism, without a doubt. Manes, or

Munio, as his closest friends called him, began his scientific career in Weimar Germany, at the university in Berlin, and was active in the Communist Party. When Hitler came to power, Munio joined the large German emigration in Paris and was hired by Willi Münzenberg to work in his propaganda machine. Munio was formed by German culture, and he did not adapt easily to French culture. He would write in German for the rest of his life. He is somewhat akin to Arthur Koestler in the turns his life took, but he came from a different background, since Koestler was a scion of the Budapest intelligentsia, apparently received no religious education, and chose Zionism first from among the two secular faiths, only later converting to Communism. Munio was for a long time a student of the writings of Marx and Engels and a fanatic Marxist, but he was much more of a Jew than Koestler, and a Jew from that other world, the world of the Holocaust. And that was his most human and tragic feature.

What stages he went through before he became a confirmed anti-Communist I cannot guess; in any event, when I made Munio's acquaintance in Paris he was one of the few writers in Western Europe who were courageous enough to proclaim to one and all just what they thought about the Soviet Union. He was friendly with Jerzy Giedroyc and Józef Czapski, understanding perfectly well what it was that *Kultura* wanted. He was certainly much more his own man than Koestler, for example, because he pictured our part of Europe in details of locale, landscapes, and sociological intricacies, not as an abstraction. His knowledge, however, probably exceeded his talent, because as a novelist he never achieved perfection. I think now that one could find numerous similarities between him and Julian Stryjkowski. As one of the literary directors of the Calman Lévy publishing house, he once gave me a Polish copy of Stryjkowski's *Voices in the Darkness* to review. I supported the idea of publishing it in French translation and the book did appear. It is the story of the vanished world of the Galician shtetl, which Manes belonged to with his entire past. I also reviewed other books—I no longer remember which ones—although the firm paid very little for this.

Despite his rather stiff bearing, Munio was warm, friendly, and quick to help his friends.

People like him ought to be remembered because political forces were deliberately arrayed against them. Before World War II the Romanian writer Panait Istrati was the object of organized attacks, because he had written unflatteringly after a stay in the Soviet Union. Then it was André Gide's turn, because he wrote skeptically. Victor Serge, who settled in Mexico, was not well known, nor was Gustaw Regler. After the war, only Koestler's *Darkness at Noon* became widely known. George Orwell came up against rejections by publishers and had a hard time getting *Animal Farm* and *1984* into print, although the latter book became famous after the author's death. Up until the 1980s there was an attempt to dull its sharp blade by insisting, in defiance of the truth, that it is not a satire of Stalin's state. Gulag testimonies were condemned, as Gustaw Herling-Grudziński, the author of *A World Apart*, would learn. Only a few people knew Józef Czapski's *The Inhuman Land*. A heartrending characteristic common to all these authors was the desire to speak or shout the truth despite the closed ears of Western opinion. Often, their actions were the result of a moral obligation to their fellow prisoners who were still in the camps and were unable to speak.

This is an immense theme for historians to take up when

they begin to study the twentieth century. At that time, even figures who are forgotten today will gain considerably in stature. It is worth recalling that there was an element of sacrifice in the very desire to bear witness. A serious writer has his eye on the future and is quite fastidious about not dabbling in contemporary reality. But it so happened that from outrage at the way people were degraded and tormented some of them transgressed that barrier, accepted their own defeat, and as it turned out, touched upon matters of more than present-day significance.

STABIŃSKA-PRZYBYTKO, Maria. My Polish teacher. At the present moment, that class is very real for me, more so than many scenes from later in my life, even though the identity of that young boy and me, which I feel very strongly, cannot be proved.

I did not do well on my Polish written assignments. I disappointed her, because I shone in discussions, but she gave me a C in composition with the annotation "Telegraphic style." Definitely deserved. I didn't write easily, nor was I able to take pleasure in the movement of my pen on paper. It seemed to me that it was sufficient to say as laconically as possible that I knew something about Mickiewicz or Słowacki. That was not what she expected of me, but what it was that she did expect, I could not fathom.

At some point I had a brainstorm, and although I hesitate over whether it is permitted to reveal such demoralizing discoveries, consideration of potential benefits wins out. Perhaps some student, thanks to my revealing this secret, will get a better grade.

I understood that they weren't demanding of me that I should write what I thought. I had to thoroughly transform myself into a student and do what a student is supposed to do: let himself go in flights of verbiage. It's not I who am writing, but he, that student, and there is no reason why I should try to be precise and to speak truthfully, since he is responsible, and not I. In other words, I came up with the idea that compositions are an exercise in rhetoric. After that, everything went just fine. I composed well-formed, flowery sentences, and the swift movement of my pen gave me pleasure. Stabińska gave me A's.

Thus, I did not need to become acquainted with literary theories about the role of the persona, who is not to be identified with the writing subject. I was already experienced. And it cannot be ruled out that what dawned on me was the most difficult problem of splitting into two—the place of the third party. I am one, the student who is writing is two, and I also am there as the observer, who watches the colorful strand emitted by my pen and remains silent.

Splitting in two somewhat as in real life. Because what Stabińska had to say about literature interested me, and I treated her seriously. At the same time, however, I was one of a dozen or so young peacocks, whom the presence of a young (to tell the truth, not that young) woman excited to obscene jokes and stupid guffaws.

After the war, Stabińska became a teacher in Wrocław.

STUPIDITY of the West. I admit that I have suffered from a Polish complex, and because I lived for many years in France and America, I gritted my teeth and had to learn to restrain myself.

An objective evaluation of this phenomenon is possible; it is possible, that is, to enter the skin of a man from the West and to see with his eyes. It turns out, then, that what we call stupidity is the result of different experiences and different interests. England in 1938 believed that by agreeing to let Czechoslovakia be swallowed up, she was ensuring a lasting peace for herself, and this naiveté would be incomprehensible were it not for England's memory of her brothers and sons who were killed in the trenches of World War I. Likewise, the memorials in every single town in France, even the smallest hamlets, with their lists of the fallen of 1914–18, often the majority of the town's male inhabitants, explains a great deal about the behavior of the French during World War II and, afterward, the dilatoriness of their policies. Even when Europe looked on without taking any action at the massacres in Bosnia and the daily strafing of Sarajevo, my protest poem resulted in infuriated letters from France, alleging that I was calling for war, and they do not want to die like their grandfathers.

And yet, the stupidity of the West is not solely our (the worse Europeans') invention, but its name should be "limited imagination." They limit their imagination by drawing a line through the center of Europe and telling themselves that it is not in their interest to be concerned about the little-known peoples who live to the east of them. Yalta had many causes (to pay back an ally), but essentially the determining factor was the notion of empty territories that were of no importance for the progress of civilization. Half a century later, it was not only Western Europe that did nothing to avoid the cruelties of war and ethnic cleansing in Bosnia. For four years, the United States, at the height of its power, also considered the countries of Yugoslavia as outside its sphere of interest and did nothing, although just the threat of military intervention would have sufficed to save thousands of human beings.

A limited imagination defends itself against recognizing the world as a system of connected vessels; it is also incapable of moving beyond the familiar. When I wound up in America immediately after the war, there was no one I could tell about what happened in Poland in the years 1939–45. They did not believe me. They thought that, obviously, during every war the press invents the most awful things about the enemy, but when military activities cease, it all turns out to have been propaganda. Pure evil? Do you really want us, sir, to believe in the existence of the devil?

SUZUKI, Daisetz Teitaro. The opening of America to the religions of the East was, in large measure, his doing. I came across Suzuki's writings while attempting to understand American Buddhism and, to my surprise, American Swedenborgianism was also revealed.

A surname that is as common in Japan as Kowalski is in Poland. He was born in 1870, so he was thirty in 1900. He supported the Japanese government's policy of industrializing the country, but argued nonetheless that in a technological society man will need a spiritual dimension, which conventionalized religion cannot guarantee him. Trained in a Zen monastery, he then studied philosophy at Tokyo University. He decided to offer his knowledge of various religious traditions to his contemporaries, thereby affording them the possibility of making a choice. That is how he became a missionary of the East in the West and of the West in the East.

Living in England and then in the United States, he found the teachings of Swedenborg to be closest to his way of thinking. Indeed, it was the Swedenborgian Hermann Vetterling who, in 1887, published *The Buddhist Ray*, the first Buddhist periodical in America (in California, naturally), defending his thesis that the teachings of Buddha and the Swedish visionary were identical. Beatrice Lane, an American whom Suzuki married, became interested in Swedenborg when she was studying at Columbia University and might have introduced her husband to his writings. For whatever reason, Suzuki translated four of Swedenborg's works into Japanese (from English) and called him "the Buddha of the West."

Suzuki's industriousness bore fruit in a dozen or so volumes of his own writings. In his ecumenical efforts he built bridges between Mahayana Buddhism and Christianity, chiefly drawing upon the writings of Meister Eckhart.

He said that Zen is not a religion and need not be linked with Buddhism; it is, rather, poetry, not in the sense of dreaminess, but of internal strength. In the same way, Swedenborg's journeys through space beyond our worlds were poetry for Suzuki. Suzuki admitted that the great Swede's teachings were christological and that man's posthumous condition, like the *bardo* condition in the Tibetan Book of the Dead, is not a preparation for the next incarnation, but for heaven or hell. All the same, he found similarities with Buddhism, at least in the theory of correspondences which links the things of this world with the mind, so that a spoon, for example, exists simultaneously among other objects and in the other, extraterrestrial world.

It was the same with the concept "I." For Buddhists, it is the chief obstacle on the path to true contemplation, in which "I" should vanish so effectively that we become one with the entire world, with a mountain, a flower, a bird flying past. It is the opposite, then, of the Cartesian "I," which is understood to be a given, whereas for the Buddhist, the self-awareness of the "I" is a deception which one should get rid of. Now in Swedenborg, there is no "I" as a center, a fortress erected against the world, which makes him an exception among Western thinkers. The "I" is also open to an *influx* of heavenly or diabolic forces, and its center, or *propium*, cannot be its main support, since it blocks access by the heavenly influence. The divine *influx* causes man to do good, even if he thinks that it is he, himself, who is doing so. On the other hand, he does evil on his own, out of his own *propium* in alliance with evil spirits. In other words, I am not defined by consciousness, but by my love, which is open to the divine fluid or to the fluid of dark forces.

Swedenborg's peculiar conception of salvation and damnation is linked with this concept of the soul as an open vessel and not a unique essence. Instead of a range of sins which the Highest Judge observes, we receive something closer to the Buddhist law of karma. God does not condemn anyone to hell, and damnation is not a result of any sentence. Simply, after death man goes to where the love that governs him summons him, which means that he finds himself in the company of others like him, and should he wind up in a circle that is too high for him, he feels so bad there that he returns as quickly as possible to his proper circle, even if it is in hell. This is, more or less, what the elder Zosima says in *The Brothers Karamazov*; Dostoevsky borrowed a great deal from Swedenborg, whom he read in Russian translation.

Heaven and hell are spaces in Swedenborg, although the space is solely symbolic: what you are is how you see. In this one can find similarities with the Tibetan Book of the Dead, which Swedenborg, obviously, did not know. The most various monsters are described in it and gods are the projection of spiritual states.

My section on Suzuki has led me too far astray. I would not want this information to encourage anyone to read Swedenborg, because he will be disenchanted. As pedantic prose, it has potent soporific properties.

ŚWIĘCICKI, Ignacy. We were in the same class through eight years of schooling, and also in the secret organization "Pet." Ignacy was born on his hereditary estate in Belorussia, from which the entire Święcicki clan came. After graduation from *gymnasium* he studied mechanical engineering at the Warsaw Polytechnic Institute. He fulfilled his military service in the air force. During our school years he was very religious, a member of Sodalitia Mariana. He was not at all interested in politics. In 1939 he was with his regiment in Toruń; he was evacuated to Romania, and from there he fled in an organized escape of pilots from the internment camps, traveling by ship to Marseilles. In France, he was remanded to the airplane factories in Limoges. After the fall of France his group was transported to a small port near the border with Spain, and from there by boat to Africa. From Casablanca he went by ship to England where he served for a long time as an aviation mechanics instructor. At his own request he was transferred to service as a pilot. He flew a one-person observation plane in the Italian campaign, moving methodically northward along the Adriatic, beginning with Bari. After fulfilling his term of service he returned to England, where he remained until the end of the war. He had intended to return to Poland, but instead he emigrated to the United States and found work as a mechanical engineer in York, Pennsylvania. He lived there for many years.

After the war we met in England and then he visited us in Washington; these visits even contributed to his marriage to a friend of ours. My family also found shelter in the Święcickis' home in York during our long separation due to my visa problems.

It is good to have such a friend from one's school days. Solid, decent, intelligent—he must have been quite a find for the mechanical engineering firm in York, which quickly recognized his worth and where he worked for several decades until his retirement. At first, he was the only one of my Wilno classmates in America, but then Staś Kownacki immigrated from England, and when I arrived in Berkeley in 1960 he was living only an hour and a half away by car, in Los Gatos. Thus, there were the three of us, two in California, the third on the opposite rim of the continent, but always maintaining our friendship.

SZEMPLIŃSKA, Elżbieta. She was a high school and later a law school classmate of Janka Dłuska, my future wife. For a while she had a husband, a young prose writer from the *Kwadryga* group, one Gładych, whose place at the side of his dictatorial wife provided material for a good many anecdotes. It was said that he was allowed to write only when he locked himself in the toilet. Szemplińska achieved some fame as a proletarian poet even though there was nothing proletarian in her background, because she was from a family of civil servants. A fanatic. In 1939, in Soviet-occupied Lwów, she was famous for her poem about interwar Poland, in which she had written, among other things, "We exchanged the Russian partition for a Polish partition." At that time she already had a different husband, Sobolewski, a sportsman and athlete, whose convictions were those of a Żeromski enthusiast, a believer in glass houses. What happened to them afterward was horrifying; it would make a good screenplay for a tragic film. We learned about it from Szemplińska when she visited us in Montgeron in 1959 and 1960.

They spent the war years in the Soviet Union, so they knew what was going on. From then on, their sole aim was to get out to the West. They managed to return to Warsaw after the war and then left for Luxembourg, where Sobolewski served for a while as consul. Their horror of Communism was so great that they ruled out returning to Poland under Communist rule. The question arose of what to do next. In France, the Communists were all-powerful, while Szemplińska was thoroughly compromised in the eyes of the Anders Army Poles because of those poems of hers from Lwów. A diplomat fleeing a country belonging to the Soviet bloc was exposed to real danger from the secret police who were planted among the French. Nonetheless, the Sobolewskis fled. After many dangerous border crossings they reached Rome and appealed for help to a secret department in the Vatican, which was in charge of caring for refugees from the East (also for Nazis and former collaborators, on the principle of not asking about the past). The department supplied them with passports in a false name. With those passports they were granted Moroccan visas and settled in Casablanca.

There would have been no further story were it not for Sobolewski's rashness. Instead of lying low, he decided to act, convinced of his mission to proclaim the truth about Communism. He gave speeches to the local Polish colony and warned against propaganda put out by Warsaw. He did this in Casablanca, one of the capitals of international espionage, where Warsaw also had its own network. He fell into their trap, it appears, when, sensing the ground burning under his feet, he set off for Rome to get new passports and visas. When she told us the story, Szemplińska was convinced that the owner of the boat, with whom Sobolewski had agreed on a price for the trip to Rome, was a plant. She was left alone with their child; he set off and disappeared without a trace. His body was found later on a beach on the Spanish shore of the Mediterranean.

We felt sorry for Szemplińska, so crushed by her harsh experiences, so devoutly religious now to the point of mania, and without any way of supporting herself in Paris. It was difficult to see how we could help her. Her son was growing up, attending school. She went back to Warsaw in 1962.

SZETEJNIE, GINEJTY, AND PEIKSVA. Those were the names of the hamlets around the Szetejnie manor where I was born. The Niewiaża Valley is like a crevice cut into the plateau, from which neither the parks nor the remains of manor houses can be seen. A traveler journeying across that plateau today will not be able to intuit what once was on it. Smoke from the hamlets has vanished, along with the creaking of well pumps, the crowing of roosters, barking of dogs, people's voices. There is no longer the green of orchards embracing the roofs of the cottages—apple trees, pear trees, plum trees in every farmyard, between house, barn, and granary, so that the village streets were framed in trees. People loved trees there, and they also loved whittling away at wood: carved window shutters, symbols and letters chiseled into beams, stools of a prescribed shape, frequent roadside crosses linked with the radiant symbol of the sun and an inverted crescent moon, or little chapels in which sat a mournful Jesus.

Right behind the Szetejnie manor the road ran past the orchard and through the *kumetyne*, or farmhands' quarters, and became the main street of the large village of Szetejnie, which stretched far into the distance, toward the forest. Alongside the Niewiaża River, right behind the school or Legmedis, another large village began—Ginejty. These were prosperous villages, very independent, and often, as in the case of the village of Szetejnie, were engaged in a dispute with the manor over pas-tures in the forest. The most prosperous village, however, was Peiksva, which snuggled right up against the forest.

The villages were entirely Lithuanian and conscious of their Lithuanianness. In Szetejnie, just a kilometer or two from me, Juozas Urbšys, the last Minister of Foreign Affairs of independent Lithuania, was born. He was one of Oscar Milosz's colleagues from the embassy in Paris. It was he who signed the pact with the Kremlin about Lithuania's neutrality. After they occupied Lithuania, the Soviet authorities deported him to Russia and kept him in prison there for years. He was finally permitted to return to Kaunas, and since he enjoyed a long life, he lived to see the year 1991 and the return of a free Lithuania.

The relations between the village and the manor were not terrible and were even often quite good. This was facilitated by the tolerant attitude of my Grandfather Kunat, whom the other manor owners referred to as a "Lithomaniac." If my mother, as a young girl, taught the schoolchildren to read and write in Polish, which seemed natural at the time, my grandfather improved on this, paying for a teacher who taught the children in Lithuanian. Five thousand people came from the surrounding villages to my grandfather's funeral in 1935.

The populations of the villages of Szetejnie, Ginejty, and Peiksva were deported to the Siberian taiga as "kulaks" and also under suspicion of helping the partisans, or "forest brethren." Their buildings were destroyed, the orchards cut down and plowed over. All that remained of them were perfectly bare fields which were referred to in the county as "Kazakhstan." Podkomorzynek, the farm which belonged to my mother, met the same fate. Not even the names of once densely populated settlements from that time have been preserved on the maps of what is now a dreary plain.

[**T**]

TARSKI, Alfred and Marysia. Called "the Einstein of the West Coast," Tarski was a mathematical logician and professor at the University of California in Berkeley. His fame was in a field which I never attempted to explore. It seems his voice counted in getting me the invitation to come to Berkeley as a lecturer. Both he and his wife, Marysia, treated us warmly, and our first trips in the Berkeley area were in Tarski's car. He earned his doctorate at Warsaw University. He was friendly with Witkacy; a memento from that friendship were Witkacy's portraits of Marysia and him in their Berkeley home. I suspect that the mathematical logicians who appear as characters in several of Witkacy's plays were modeled on Tarski.

Tarski delighted in mixing various kinds of drinks; he always had bottles of fruit- or berry-flavored vodka which had to age before they could appear on his table. Tasting them was an important part of dinners at his house. He told a lot of stories about his Warsaw. He recalled his internment in Jabłonna in 1920 with humor, but a bitter humor, and sang, "Jabłonna, ah, Jabłonna, our useless hope." The Jewish intelligentsia were interned at Jabłonna instead of being sent to the front because the military authorities considered that entire category of the population untrustworthy. I remember his story about a reception in the German Embassy, which Witkacy attended in the thirties, when there was a temporary Polish-German détente. At one moment Witkacy screamed, "I'm either going to punch someone in the puss, or I'll go take some cocaine." "I advised him to do the latter," said Tarski. The political atmosphere then convinced him that he ought to emigrate, which he fortunately managed to do in time. Despite the fact that we were on a first-name basis, I remained aware that we belonged to different generations, especially since Tarski's Poland had remained frozen in the interwar period and his literary taste was in no way distinct from that of the average reader of *The Literary News,* with Julian Tuwim as the greatest poet, with Boy's columns and Słonimski's "Chronicles." My generation, too "disheveled," did not agree with the "polished" Warsaw establishment, but I never disputed this difference in perspective with Tarski.

TERROR. It is well worth pondering that the chief inhabitant of Europe in the twentieth century, terror, has not yet undergone extensive analysis. Perhaps this is because no one wanted to return to humiliating experiences, and terror does humiliate. There are many types of terror, of course, and each should be dealt with separately.

Terror in wartime is simply a question of heroism. All soldiers are afraid, but the best overcome their terror by force of will. Our human species is profligate; it is constantly producing children who take the place of those killed in wars, but one may still ask if it does not lose something when a lot of courageous men are consigned to the earth. The battlefields on which lie heroes who fell in battle against others just as industrious as they—Germans, Frenchmen, Englishmen, Poles, Ukrainians, Russians, in their millions—do they not command us to ask how the loss of the best genes influences the living? Jerzy Stempowski has considered this, arguing that Europe after World War I would have been different if her potential leaders from France, Germany, and England had not died in the great massacre.

The terror of daily life in a country under Stalinist or Nazi governments was of a different sort. I experienced only a taste of this in Wilno in 1940, but enough so that I could imagine, from the conversations and stories I heard, the dread of waiting for *them* to appear before dawn. Whole categories of people were deported to camps in Russia on the basis of lists that were drawn up, not without help from local denunciations, or were listed individually after arrest and "confession." Had I not escaped from Wilno in July 1940, I think I would not have mustered the courage to refuse to write for *The Wilno Truth*, which was more or less a requirement, because my colleagues from Żagary turned up there. How can one condemn them, when people were more afraid of deportation than of death? That same great terror in Lwów was described by Aleksander Wat, who worked for *The Red Flag*, which was Lwów's equivalent of *The Wilno Truth*. Finding oneself among the obedient élite reduced one's terror of a collective roundup, but it did not reduce one's terror at the thought of punishment for the slightest error or for unorthodox thinking. Leopold Tyrmand, who wrote for *The Wilno Truth*, was sentenced to fifteen years, but he was not deported because railroad workers uncoupled the locomotive and also it was the day the Germans invaded, so he survived.

Terror paralyzes and probably interferes with action. My expedition from Wilno to Warsaw across four "green" borders was very dangerous, and I probably would not have been able to make it had I been afraid. I performed a special (insane) operation on myself, which I still do not understand, but which depended on my somehow bracketing off my terror. The terror was there, but it was denied entry. Zofia Rogowiczowa, with whom I made the trek, later gave an exceedingly flattering account of my competence and resourcefulness, but I was embarrassed by this because I knew that although I deserved her praise for how I acted in that predicament, I am really neither competent nor resourceful.

Terror in Warsaw under the German occupation had various phases and tensions. Relative normality ended with the first roundup for Auschwitz in September, I believe, of 1940, when we understood that we were totally unprotected animals. For four years I carried terror around inside me like a bullet ready to explode, employing various strategies against it, for example, rationalizations: that one or another document would help me (although, in fact, I had no such powerful papers). Or that I would not attract the attention of people who could denounce me (my commentaries in the underground anthology *The Independent Song* were written in such a way that no one could have guessed I was the author). What was most helpful, however, was thinking about my secret pact with the Force that protects you if you fulfill certain conditions. I also decided that since I had not yet completed the work I was destined to perform during my lifetime, I would remain alive.

Had I thought constantly about that bullet in my belly, I would have been unable to write; the fact is that my wartime writing was abundant, in poetry and in prose. It turned out that in some circumstances it is good to be humpbacked. My hump was my poor adaptation to life and, as a coping mechanism, my nature as a medium—that is, I constantly heard words and rhythms and had to submit to that incantation. This meant that I walked on the earth as if I was not there. I built a cocoon for myself which made me feel that Warsaw with its terrors was somehow necessary for my growth.

Decency demands that, saved from tests that were beyond my strength, I must believe in God. With gratitude.

TIME. Our human species has pondered for centuries the question of where the world came from. Some have said that it must have had a beginning; others, that it has always existed. For us, "always" has lost all meaning, because there was no time before the Big Bang, even if neither our imagination nor our language can grasp the concept of timelessness. What existed before there was something? The medieval scholastics from the schools of Chartres and Oxford held that there was divine light. Its *transmutatio* into physical light created the universe. They would have been delighted to accept the theory of the Big Bang, and would have said, "Well, of course."

To think about time means to think about human life, and this is such a broad topic that to consider it means to think in general. The differences that divide us—sex, race, skin color, customs, beliefs, ideas—pale in comparison with the fact that we are all woven out of time, that we are born and we die, mayflies who live but a day. The inconceivable "now" escapes backward or inclines forward, it is already a memory or an aspiration. Speech, in which we communicate, is modulated time, just like music. And do not painting and architecture translate rhythm into space?

I am filled with the memory of people who lived and died; I

write about them, conscious all the while that in a moment, I, too, will be gone. Together we are like a cloud or a nebula among the human constellations of the twentieth century. My contemporaries: our kinship rests on our having lived at the same time, although in different countries and geographic expanses. In a sense, that kinship is stronger than any tribal bonds.

Mnemosyne, mater Musarum.

Yes, Mnemosyne, the muse of memory, is the mother of all the muses. Edgar Allan Poe referred to the melancholy of transience as the most poetic of tonalities. We read poems written thousands of years ago, and everywhere there is the same lament, a meditation on the river's current, on our appearance and disappearance.

This goes together with a great yearning to escape from time into a land of eternal laws and of objects not subject to destruction. Plato and his ideas: on the earth hares, foxes, and horses run about and pass on, but somewhere up above the ideas of hareness, foxness, and horseness live on eternally, along with the idea of the triangle and Archimedes' principle, which have not been overturned by chaotic, death-contaminated empirical evidence.

TROŚCIANKO, Wiktor. My power over him weighs upon me, because he is no longer alive and is unknown, so it is my responsibility how he is presented to posterity. He had an obvious chip on his shoulder in relation to me, so it will be best if I don't settle any scores with him now. He was my colleague from my law studies, the son of a well-known Wilno tailor, an announcer for Polish Radio, an activist in the National Party during the war in the right-wing underground in Warsaw, and co-editor with Jerzy

Zagórski (the brother of the socialist, Wacław Zagórski) of an anthology of poetry, *The True Word*. Later, he was for many years a publicist for Radio Free Europe.

In Wilno we used a kind of social ostracism against him, I think; he wrote, but he found no recognition in our eyes, perhaps because someone with "nationalist" views was beneath notice on the part of our literary-artistic bohemia. Now comes a complete lack of clarity. Why, then, was Kazimierz Hałaburda—a boxer, poet, and nationalist—a full-fledged colleague in the Vagabonds' Club? Why did Trościanko's membership in the club (later, after our time) not change his position? Is the fate of a rejected lover of literature determined beforehand?

His trilogy of autobiographical novels (*The Manly Age, The Age of Defeat, Finally, Years of Peace!*), published in London, is forgotten, even though it faithfully reveals the adventures of a prewar *intelligent* before and during the war. More than that, it contains a detailed description of the Soviet persecution of the population of Wilno and the surrounding countryside, who were destined for deportation. There is even a description of the deportation of villages on the shores of the Troki lakes, which can be found nowhere else: the arrested people were loaded onto boats and taken to Troki. Why, in occupied Warsaw, did it never cross my mind to make friends with Trościanko, but Jerzy Zagórski did? It was all due to my fanaticism. A type of instinct that places certain categories of people outside a circle of expectations.

I read his novels. Their plots are quite lively and the language isn't bad. They have a great deal to say, but mostly against their will, through what is missing from them. The first volume describes prewar Wilno. What? So he was observing us? Yes, and all he understood was that our Żagary was an agency of the Comintern? The intellectual poverty of his mainly autobiographical figure unmasks the student-intelligentsia-officer caste, while its bridge games, dinners, and tangos awaken (a not intended) pity and dread.

TRUTH. Despite the attacks on the very concept of truth, such that faith in the possibility of an objective discovery of the past has been destroyed, people continue to write memoirs fervently to demonstrate how it was, in truth. This poignant need bears witness to our attachment to accounts that are not subject to changing opinion but reside in so-called facts. It is well-known that the same fact observed by two witnesses is not the same thing, and yet the honest chronicler is convinced that his description is exact. His good faith is decisive here, and we should respect it, even if despite his wishes he has shaped events to serve his own interests. Modifying events in order to beautify past events or conceal ugly ones is the most frequent cause of distorted perspective. We often are surprised at the blindness of the storyteller, who does not realize this; a classic example is Jean-Jacques Rousseau in his *Confessions*. The least believable are the memoirs of politicians, because they lie so much that it is difficult to trust their good faith.

When talking about my twentieth century I try to be honest, and am helped in this by my flaws and not my virtues. It was always hard for me to choose, to announce myself as categorically on one side, to stubbornly stick to my own views. Reconciled to my own place, always on the outside in relation to my contemporaries, I tried to intuit the reasoning of those on the other side. Had I been an incorporeal spirit I would have been more successful, from which one can deduce that spirits encounter considerable difficulty when they wish to proclaim unambiguous moral judgments.

We work at knowing the truth about our lifetime even if its images, derived from various people, are not consistent with each other. We exist as separate beings, but at the same time each of us acts as a medium propelled by a power we do not know well, a current of the great river, as it were, through which we resemble each other in our common style or form. The truth about us will remind us of a mosaic composed of little stones of different value and colors.

[U]

ULATOWSKI, Janek. I would not have known him as well were it not for his marriage in 1955 to Nela Micińska. He was born in Poznań in 1907 and died in Menton in 1997. Before the war, he studied philosophy and sociology, worked in art history, and was also the co-founder of the Poznań biweekly *Literary Life*. He entered the diplomatic corps and the outbreak of war found him working as press attaché in the Polish Embassy in Budapest. He joined the Kopański Brigade in the Middle East, was at the battle of Tobruk, and later took part in the Italian campaign, although it appears that his superiors in the Press Section, to which he was assigned, had a great deal of trouble with him due to his stubbornness. Working in the editorial offices of *The White Eagle*, he was renowned for articles that viciously attacked English policy and was transferred out as a disciplinary measure. Nevertheless, he was given a star, promoted to the rank of second lieutenant. He befriended Adolf Bocheński, who told him (I don't vouch for the exact words) "It would be dishonorable to get out of this war alive" shortly before he committed suicide (he blew himself up by stepping on a mine near Ancona).

When the Polish army was transferred to England, Janek declined to be enrolled in the Polish Resettlement Corps, because that would have meant being an officer in the English army and, as he told the English, "You have no right." Because of his refusal, his entry into England was illegal and he was sentenced to prison. He was in jail for quite a while, until well-wishers finally got him out and arranged for him to immigrate to France, where for a long time his documents did not give him the right to work. A superb connoisseur of modern art, he wrote reviews of exhibitions for *Kultura* and *Preuves*. His fluent knowledge of German helped him to survive, and from the time he and Nela moved to Bordeaux he was a German language teacher in a lycée there until his retirement. His true passion was neither art nor literature, but politics and his political opinions, which were too outspoken to be appreciated by anyone.

He had worked out a complete theory and managed to find confirmation of it in all the international events of the second half of the twentieth century. He also often wrote letters to the press, both French and Polish, not all of which were printed, since his theory had some definitely maniacal characteristics.

He was convinced that a never-revealed pact had been signed by America and the Soviet Union, dealing with the division of the world between those two powers. The tensions between them, including the Cold War, were deliberately maintained as a game intended to keep in check the refractory clients of both sides, who might otherwise have dreamed of an independent policy. The division into two blocs which would be kept terrorized by the diabolical activity of the enemy was part of their bag of tricks, and the desired result was achieved thanks to naive people, who truly experienced paroxysms of terror when conflicts between the two powers threatened to erupt. Ulatowski followed the press attentively in several languages and was always coming across American and Soviet declarations which confirmed his theory.

Visiting them in Menton required a certain degree of tolerance while one sat listening to his stubborn proofs. Like every conspiratorial theory of history, this one, too, possessed certain elements of verisimilitude/truth, although it also revealed its background of trauma, and its author, like it or not, appeared to be a Pole possessed by his obsession, living his life as one betrayed by the West. The theory posited, instead of complex and constantly changing opinions and actions by politicians on both sides, an inflexibly pursued game plan in which the fluidity of events was frozen. The theory's sole advantage, however, was that it allowed one not to take seriously the possibility of a third world war.

One strand of the American mentality which I knew well appeared to confirm Ulatowski's theory. After all, the American mind finds all those small European peoples, engaged in conflicts over scraps of territory, repulsive and incomprehensible; President Wilson, who was responsible for the slogan about the self-determination of nations, does not garner much praise. Russia is something else, again, because Russia is huge. It pays to conclude treaties with Russia and together control those pesky little states. Indeed, the dissolution of the Soviet Union dismayed many American politicians, who would have willingly supported the stumbling, failing giant. Aware of these tendencies, I found a kernel of truth in Ulatowski's proofs, which made my stays in Menton easier, since he must have felt that even though I was not persuaded, my ears were not completely closed.

The French painter Jean Colin, a close friend of Józef Czapski, left a kind of appreciation of Ulatowski as an art critic in his book, *Journal de Jean d'Amiens* (Éditions du Seuil, 1968):

> This evening, dinner with U. I wish this conversation could go on all night long, and I would like to remember everything. How he talks about evolution, about the life of Cézanne. He says that the peculiar thing about wanting to imitate Corot or Poussin is that it always comes out different, even if we think we are seeing through Corot's or Poussin's eyes. Picasso used to say that when he wanted to paint a picture that he liked a second time, it always turned out different.
>
> Fear. Integrity. When he speaks, it is as if a powerful hand is holding you, not letting go for a minute. He never speaks in generalities, and never gives up on reaching understanding through thought, intuition, or intelligence. Every point is made with absolute clarity, precisely illuminated, so that it is impossible to object.

ULRICH. I don't remember his name. Mr. Ulrich was a Pole from the Poznań region who lived in Suwałki, and it was there that he asked me, a student at the time, to read the typescript of his diary of the Battle of Verdun, which he had participated in as a soldier in the German infantry. It is possible that the international fame of Remarque's *All Quiet on the Western Front* contributed to his writing it. Ulrich's work, as I viewed it then, was better, more horrifying in its rigorous accuracy, but no publisher wanted it and my voice would have counted for nothing. As far as I know, it was never published.

That war of fixed positions, trench warfare, as it was called, shocked its participants with man's powerlessness against fate, because, after all, the absurdity of mutually murdering each other with the help of machine-guns, artillery, and tanks, was obvious to them, and probably to their leaders. No one could stop it, because that would be the equivalent of declaring defeat. The power of fate made World War I comparable to the Trojan War. The human body's fragility in relation to metal and the whole-sale killing paved the way for the further development of atrocity in the twentieth century, since nothing could surprise anyone after such a spectacle. Trench warfare is supposed to have put an end to illusions of progress and the humanitarianism of the nineteenth century. Whether it did so is questionable.

The two interwar decades that formed me strike me as quite enigmatic. After all, the euphoria, the hymnlike acclamation of Life which the beginning of the century had exuded, and which caused the crowds in the great capitals to greet the outbreak of war with howls of joy, did not, as one might have expected, vanish instantly. Art and literature continued to experiment euphorically and optimistically. Does this mean that these spheres of human activity have little in common with reality? Perhaps. At the very same time when men were being slaughtered at Verdun the young Julian Tuwim published his essay on Walt Whitman, and soon would write: "But even Passersby must be free to live! / The colossal old man addressed them: 'Camerado!'."

So many of these passersby dressed in uniforms fell in France, but soon the poets were writing Olympic odes, glorifying the happiness of a fit body, and painters (Matisse!) were indulging in the delights of pure color.

It is correct to date the beginning of catastrophic moods in Europe as the year 1930. In 1931, gazing at the hills on the French side of the Rhine, covered with what seemed to be vineyards but were crosses, I thought about Ulrich. It seems, though,

that what influenced me most powerfully was the general movement of literature and art toward dark colors and vague premo-
nitions of catastrophe. It so happened that those who fell in
World War I were somehow disinherited; that is, the speeding
up of incidents in the thirties did not leave enough time to pay
attention to their suffering, inflicted by unidentifiable forces.

[**W**]

WHITFIELD, Francis J. A linguist, professor of Slavic Languages and Literatures at Berkeley, to whom I owe my invitation to the University of California. Frank was from New England and preserved the traits of a New Englander: secretiveness, self-control, and even disgust at all signs of emotionalism, which he perceived as somehow immodest. In addition, he was raised as a Catholic, which introduced another kind of complication. Although he was not of Polish descent, he spoke Polish well and was the co-author of a two-volume English-Polish dictionary. Furthermore, he was married to Celina, who had come to America after being deported from Warsaw after the Uprising. I have to consider my invitation to Berkeley as a serious deviation from the values Frank held dear, because I did not have a doctorate. Yet not only did he invite me, as chairman of the department he pushed through my permanent tenure as a full professor with almost unheard-of speed. He arranged all of this quietly, although a few details about our department may shed some light on his decision.

George Rapall Noyes, who founded the department at Berkeley at the beginning of the century, studied in Petersburg but fell in love with Polish while he was there; he translated the Renaissance poet Kochanowski and Mickiewicz's narrative poem *Pan Tadeusz* (into prose). He took care that the department should not, like the majority of Slavic departments in America, become simply a Russian department, but that at least Polish and Czech should always be represented in it. He hired Wacław Lednicki, a Russian specialist, but a Pole, who taught both literatures. After Lednicki retired, Frank, as chairman, was concerned about preserving this tradition. I cannot say what exactly informed his thinking about me. The first invitation came in 1959; I replied, "Maybe next year," although it didn't seem likely that I would get an American visa. Frank renewed the invitation in 1960. I have no information that would lead me to believe that Lednicki picked me to be his successor. Nothing connected us at all, for he was simply an outmoded aristocrat (or, rather, a semi-aristocrat).

Frank, without revealing his feelings, preserved memories of himself as a sickly child, almost a cripple, and he had something like a terror of existence. Perhaps he was a poet by calling who transferred his love of the fabric of language to highly scholarly linguistic research.

Both Frank and other members of the department were known for their formalism, that is, their anxiety about diverging from the university's rules and regulations. How I, without a Ph.D., became a professor, I will never understand.

WHITMAN, Walt. "The priest departs," he wrote, "the divine literatus comes." All-embracing, all-devouring, blessing everything, turned to the future, a prophet. The astonishing linkage of the word and the historical victory of America. Despite my adoration, however, I knew that it would be useless for me to pretend to closeness if the civilization to which I was linked was afraid to support the freedom of the individual.

Europe had its Whitman moment. I would place it around 1913. In poetry, the French were the middlemen, beginning with Valery Larbaud, but Whitmanizing is not only a matter of liberating oneself from meter and rhyme; it is also a rapturous movement toward happiness, a democratic pledge of breaking down class divisions, expressed in poetry, prose, painting, theater, and also in a noticeable change of customs. It's a brighter ecstatic tone after surviving the *fin de siècle*—for example, in the first volumes of Romain Rolland's *Jean Christophe*, in Stravinsky's *Rite of Spring*, in Russian Acmeism, in Frans Masereel's woodcuttings. Pacifist and revolutionary accents are a part of the European makeover of the Whitmanesque word *en masse*. Gavrilo Princip, who shot Archduke Ferdinand in 1914, was convinced that he was carrying out his beloved poet's orders, which called for a war against kings. And then the colossal slaughterhouse of World War I instantly put an end to great hopes. For a couple of decades they fluttered, like startled pigeons, over the Russian Revolution.

In Poland this bright interlude barely occurred. Polish poetry did know a kind of biblical verse, although it had used it to celebrate the victory over the Turks (Wespazjan Kochowski) or for messianic parodies of the Gospels, which is telling. Who, after all, would Whitmanize? Country squires? Iwaszkiewicz's youthful poetic prose does contain a little bit of ecstatic joy. The peasants? Not a chance. Perhaps the Jews. Indeed, the young Tuwim, liberated for a brief time, speaks of the "colossal old man" who addressed his readers as "Camerado," but immediately slings the noose of traditional stanzas around him.

I first encountered Whitman in Polish translation. He was translated by Alfred Tom, Stanisław Vincenz, Stefan Napierski. Immediately, revelation: to be able to write as he did! I understood that it was not a matter of form, but of an act of inner freedom, and therein lay the real difficulty.

The "divine literatus" had conquered the distance between the "I" and the crowd, had devoured religions and philosophies, so that instead of contradictions, mortality and immortality both fit into his poetry, a leaf of grass and eternity; above all, he spoke as one of the many, an equal among equals. One hundred years after his death a collective mood appears, a collective mode of feeling, called New Age. In order to make a list of the most characteristic features of this phenomenon, it would seem that we should simply describe Whitman's poetry transformed into a great number of practitioners. That is not exactly the same thing, because poetry lasts longer than fashions, but the prophecy was fulfilled: each will be his own priest, a "divine literatus." The most Whitmanesque among American poets was Allen Ginsberg, not so much because of his open homosexuality as through the courage with which he broke with convention, often against his own will.

WINNICKA, Dr. Wiktoria. Józef Wittlin's half-sister, she, too, was from Lwów. A pediatrician. After 1939, as an employee of the Soviet health service, she did a lot of traveling around the Soviet Union. After the Germans occupied Lwów she moved to Warsaw, and since she belonged to artistic and aristocratic circles before the war, she was well protected and survived. Also, she had so-called "good looks": a tall blonde with blue eyes. She joined the Ministry of Health immediately after the war. She traveled abroad, including to her brother's home in New

York, which is where I met her. Later, she settled in Geneva as a civil servant with the United Nations' World Health Organization.

Ongoing conversations with her—in New York, Warsaw, and Berkeley, where she came almost every year as a visiting professor. But not quite a friendship. I doubt that Wikta was capable of friendship, love, or other emotions. Perhaps one event in her life had encased her in ice, or maybe she was born that way. She suffered from absolute isolation which, I suspected, was related to her self-absorption. She had been married, but never mentioned it. Her brilliant conversation and gossip gave one the impression that Café Ziemiańska from before the war had survived intact in one human being. On a first-name basis with the Skamander poets, she was friendliest with Julek (Julian Tuwim). She also had a distinctly Varsovian macabre sense of humor.

Her knowledge of the twentieth century was vast and rare; she had known two totalitarian systems and had survived the Holocaust. She traveled all over the world and spoke many languages. Her knowledge was the basis for her world view, in which there was no room for belief in anything or for hope. Marxism would have been a spiritual luxury for her, not to mention religion. She professed a belief in materialism, but not the dialectical variety. And she almost lost her mind from that miserable isolation, saying repeatedly that it was time for her to kill herself.

Very stingy, she spent almost nothing on herself, saving her generous salaries as an international official and professor. I believe she had a very large bank account in addition to a beautiful apartment in Geneva. Consistent with her vow that she would kill herself when she could bear it no longer, she committed suicide, willing everything she owned to the state of Israel. She had a bundle of letters from Tuwim, which I asked her to publish, but she burned them before her death.

WRÓBLEWSKI, Andrzej. The Jews in Wilno had their own rich world, fenced off from the Polish one by language. Political parties, schools, labor unions, and journals all used Yiddish; a tiny percentage used Russian, and there was also one Jewish high school, the Epstein Gymnasium, where Polish was used. Andrzej came from a Polish-speaking family. Both he and his wife Wanda, a dancer, were in the orbit of the Theater on Pohulanka and of Polish Radio. For the Radio, he produced some small pieces under contract to Tadeusz Byrski, while Wanda taught ballet at the Theater School. That was where my close friend Irena Górska was a student and then an actress in the Theater, where she was enfolded in their warmth. That was the source of my close and long-lasting acquaintance with Andrzej. His last name in those days was Feigin. As he tells it many years later in his book *To Be a Jew* ... (1992), he felt that to change one's name was unacceptable, but after the war he did not want anyone to think of him as related to the Fejgin who was the notorious official of the Secret Police or UB, and so he kept the name he had used during the Occupation.

The scene changes, because everyone gradually emigrated to Warsaw. Andrzej was always a socialist following the Polish Socialist Party, so he wound up in the socialist district of Żoliborz. Irena acted in Lwów and then in Warsaw; she married another actor, Dobiesław Damięcki. In the spring of 1940 the underground government carried out its death sentence against Igo Sym, who had been acting in theatrical circles on behalf of the occupying powers; the result was an intensified hunt by the Germans for the assassin. Because Damięcki had often threatened

Sym, they were convinced that he was the one who had killed him, and they plastered Warsaw with posters carrying pictures of both Damięckis. Andrzej and Wanda provided them with their first hiding place in their new apartment on Elektoralna Street; they also helped them with their frequent relocations (to around thirty different shelters) and with changing their appearance. Irena insists that Andrzej saved their lives.

When I made my way to Warsaw in July 1940 the Damięckis, under a changed surname, were already living in the provinces under difficult conditions, as can be learned from Irena's memoir, *I Won a Life*. But they did survive and Irena gave birth to two sons during those wartime years.

Soon after my arrival in Warsaw I joined the socialist organization Freedom, in which Andrzej was a member. He was not just a member, but one of its founders, together with Daniel, or Wacław Zagórski. As far as I remember, Jerzy Andrzejewski and I took the oath in the Arria café on Mazowiecka Street, also called At the Actors', most likely because that is where the staff of Freedom used to meet, on the assumption that the place where the Lutosławski-Panufnik duo performed was the safest. Zagórski has written that the swearing-in took place in Andrzejewski's apartment; I am almost certain that my memory is accurate, but I won't argue the point. It was there that one day a coffeehouse waitress walked over to a table at which three Semitic-looking conspirators were sitting and said in a soft, sweet voice, "Jews, go away, for God's sake; the whole room is looking at you." That was probably in 1941. A room with wide-open glass doors in Antoni Bohdziewicz's apartment on the corner of Mazowiecka and Kredytowa, a couch brought over from Dynasy as our only furniture, Antoni the bartender at At the Actors', many individuals, such as Zbigniew Mitzner, who had so many underground pseudonyms and addresses that I suspected he was turning the conspiracy into a game, Leszek Raabe, admired and beloved by his friends, whom I have written about elsewhere, Zofia Rogowiczowa, with whom I had walked to Warsaw from Wilno.

I saw Andrzej occasionally after the war, and also in the new Poland in 1989, but I learned a great deal from his wise and generous book, *To Be a Jew* . . . , which Leszek Kołakowski considered the best of all the many books of that sort. The entire spectrum of Polish-Jewish relations in interwar Poland and his adventures at that time. Something of a golden boy, he wasn't really sure what he should be doing; his father, wealthy, sent him abroad to study medicine in Tours, where he acquired a fine knowledge of French and little else. After his return in 1933 he became a journalist for the socialist press. During the German occupation, in possession of documents identifying him as a "legal" merchant, he discovered new talents in himself—buying and selling. After the war he was offered a post by the Wilno group, but he preferred to continue as a journalist for *The Worker*. With his bad secret police dossier, he survived, as he himself acknowledges, because they thought he was a relative of the executioner, Fejgin.

All Andrzej's instincts were socialist, and after the Thaw and Gomułka's return, he wanted to believe that a socialist Poland was a possibility. In 1959 in Paris we talked for six hours straight. He tried to persuade me to return, but I was a skeptic.

He died in Warsaw in 1994. I think it was very difficult to preserve one's integrity and remain true to oneself in the midst of historical complications. Andrzej Wróblewski remained true and I would like him to be remembered that way.

[Z]

ZAGÓRSKI, Stefan. My friend from *gymnasium*, nicknamed "Elephant." He was the son of Attorney Ignacy Zagórski, who was a sometime member of the Russian social democrats. Thus, one might say the father was an old Bolshevik. One characteristic of the Polish left was that they married Jewish women, and this was true of Zagórski, because Elephant's and his brother Pericles's mother was a Jew. She was a physician. Elephant was a Lutheran, and when we had religion class, he had a free hour. Tall, slightly stooped, and somewhat clumsy, his chest and abdomen overgrown with hair like an ape's, Elephant was gentle in interactions with people, because he was a master of quiet, dry humor. The poet Jerzy Zagórski (from the Żagary group) and the socialist Wacław Zagórski, who were also the sons of an attorney, but from Wołyń, were his cousins.

Elephant was one of my closest pals in *gymnasium*. Then we both were in the Vagabonds' Club and made that famous canoe trip to Paris, which I have written about elsewhere. As I think about Elephant, I try to gather images of him as a sailor in Troki or on the seacoast, or on the dock of the Academic Sporting Union in Wilno, at student parties and on the long hikes we took together, in order to convince myself that he had his athletic and erotic triumphs and knew the happiness of youth—because he was not granted a very long life.

Thanks to Elephant, the Vagabonds, the Żagarists and later the Dembiński group all visited Lipówka. A couple of hours' march from Wilno, Lipówka, with its house on the Wilia River, was the elder Zagórski's estate, which served as a base for further travels or as shelter in the event of some troubles in town. It seems that this latter feature proved valuable during the war. Zagórski senior treated us young people with tolerance and was pleased by our leftist leanings. Elephant, I must stress, remained close to the literary milieu of Żagary and did not go along with their political shift; he did not join the Dembiński group. A liberal and a skeptic by temperament, he was ill suited to studying the fine points of Marxism. My friend from a later period, Zygmunt Hertz, was like a new incarnation of Elephant. The same sense of humor, kindliness, skeptical democratic belief.

The most important thing was that Lipówka was on the Wilia River. A river with a swift current, though it did not flow down from the mountains, its water was pure because in its upper reaches it cut through forested areas with no large towns. Sand and pines—that is why "the mother of our streams has a golden floor and sky-blue surface." From time to time, rafts of pine logs floated down it. Swimming in the Wilia was a joyous ritual for our group. We would swim out to the middle and let ourselves be carried by the current, splashing, frolicking, racing against each other all the way down beyond the next bend. But not so far that it would take too long to walk back. Many years later I set this down in a poem:

> *The river bends here, flowing from forests.*
> *It rolls in the sun, full of reflections of green.*
> *It is Sunday. Village church bells ring.*
> *White clouds gather, disperse, and again the sky is clear.*

Far away, tiny, they run along the low bank.
They try the water, they enter it, and the river carries them.
Midstream their heads—three, four, seven.
They race, call each other, and the echo returns.

My hand describes this, in other peoples' lands.
What its purpose is, is unknown.
Just because it once was so?

The Wilia is a river worthy of respect, even though once I almost drowned in it. We were playing hooky in Zakret, on the outskirts of Wilno, and although I couldn't swim very well, I swam out to the deep water. Mietek Zabłocki and Janc saved me, mainly by offering moral support, swimming next to me and propping up my chin from time to time, so I wouldn't swallow too much water or stop struggling.

That the Wilia's surface is sky blue is not exactly accurate, because it carries a lot of sand. It revealed its soul to me when I was three years old in the vicinity of Rukła between Kowno and Wilno, and later I had occasion to spend a lot of time on it, kayaking down to Wilno from the spot where the Żejmiana River flows into it. The names of rivers are very old and often mysterious. The Wilia, it appears, was called simply Wielia, or Wielka ("great"), in the language of the eastern Slavs, while among the Lithuanians it acquired the name Nerys—its root is related to *nur* ("current"); which explains the derivation of Ponary, outside of Wilno, *Po-nerai*. The Wilenka, or Wilna, which flows into the Wilia, derives from a different root than Wilia, and gave the city its name.

Every river has its own soul, which is revealed when we first stand on its banks. I do not know what the soul of the Niewiaża is like, because it is too closely merged with mine. Several large rivers have preserved the qualities that I first noticed in them. I was six years old when I looked at the Volga near Rzhev. Its soul struck me as powerful and intimidating, and yet at the time I knew nothing about Russian history. Two rivers whose souls I think of as fickle and treacherous are the Vistula and the Loire, perhaps because they spill onto the sands of a plain. The Wilia is not a river of the plain, its banks are hilly, which makes a difference. Like the rivers of the Dordogne, which I feel close to. Among them, I know the Isle River best; it's about the same size as the Niewiaża, although the Vesera is charming, too. I also remember the Rhine's lofty soul.

I got to know a number of rivers from source to mouth. The Żejmiana flows out of Lake Dubiński in such a perversely secretive manner that finding it in the forest and among the thickets of bulrushes is not easy; then it winds among tree stumps in the forest, cuts across meadows, and one's canoe has to pass over thick clumps of water plants bent low by the current. The soul of this river is green, as is the soul of the Black Hańcza River. At the spot where it flows into the Wilia in the vicinity of Santoka, one can see that the Wilia's soul is blue-gray.

Another river, the Umpqua in Oregon, which has an American Indian name, accompanied Janka's and my automobile trip from its sources in Silver Lake in the Cascade mountain range to its mouth in the Pacific. I planned this trip on a map. First, following the river exactly, because the highway twists and turns its way down from the mountains along the river's banks, then loses the river in the valley in a crazy quilt of highways and cities, finally joining up with it again—majestic now, immense, near its mouth. That's where we saw an enormous sturgeon that had been caught right there.

This digression about rivers is intended to honor the memory of Elephant and Lipówka. So perhaps I ought to linger once again over the mountain paths of the Schwarzwald along which we wandered to Basel after we capsized on the Rhine, and the teenage Germans we encountered there, the *Wanderfögeln*, who would soon be donning uniforms. Or I should tell how years later I happened to get off the métro at the Glacière station and was reminded of the Salvation Army hostel with the grandiose name Le Palais du Peuple, which once stood beside the station, and where Elephant and I sang psalms so we could have supper there.

Actually, I knew very little about Elephant after my emigration from Wilno. I ran into him in Warsaw in the summer of 1940 when he was still working as a glazier, a trade he had taken up in the first month of the war, right after the bombings. That trade, it seems, masked other, more important business. I believe that he belonged to one of the networks of the London government-in-exile and that is why he was in Lwów after the outbreak of the German-Soviet war. Arrested, he was tortured by the Gestapo in a room on an upper floor of a tall building. To avoid further torture and to prevent himself from betraying anyone, he killed himself by jumping from a window.

ZAN, Tomasz. In the city of my childhood and youth he was a grand figure. In his student years he belonged to a Masonic lodge, just like Kontrym, the university librarian who discreetly supported the Philomaths and who, it seems, was hierarchically above Mickiewicz, who, as far as we know, never belonged to any lodge in Wilno. Wilno Freemasonry, long banned by order of the tsars, returned after 1900 when the new Scoundrels' Society began to meet. This does not mean that all the Scoundrels' members were Masons, but those circles were related. It appears, too, that the Tomasz Zan lodge was founded immediately after 1905.

For me, a *gymnasium* student, what was important was the Tomasz Zan Library, founded in the 1920s and intended as support for the schools; that is, young people came there to read books and periodicals (not to borrow books to take home). For the lower grades, the lending library of the Polish School Society was adequate; it was housed right next to my school on Little Pohulanka Street. But one read Conrad's works, translated into Polish, or more serious books on the history of literature in the Tomasz Zan Library, which at that time was located on the corner of Greater Pohulanka Street, across from the theater, and later moved to its own building on Portowa Street.

Why was the library given this name? The founders, Father Miłkowski and Miss Ruszczyc, were probably not moved by any Masonic designs and perhaps did not even know the Masonic connections of that name. Tomasz Zan simply appealed to them as patron by virtue of having been a Philomath and an exile who remained faithful to his country.

I still remember evenings spent at the Tomasz Zan Library, including readings of the literary supplement to the Warsaw newspaper, *The Voice of Truth*. It was edited by Juliusz Kaden-Bandrowski, who maintained it patiently and seriously as a mini literature school for youth. It was in that supplement—most likely in 1927 or 1928—that I first came upon a poem by Józef Czechowicz and committed it to memory. It is also where a letter I wrote to the editor appeared—my first published text. I think with gratitude of the founders of the Tomasz Zan Library. May at least some trace of their activity remain.

[ENVOI]

DISAPPEARANCE, of people and objects. Because we live in time, we are subject to the law that nothing lasts forever, everything passes. People disappear, as do animals, trees, landscapes, and as everyone knows who lives long enough, the memory of those who once were alive disappears, too. Only a very few people preserve their memory—their closest kinfolk, friends—but even in their consciousness the faces, gestures, words gradually fade away, to vanish forever when there is no longer anyone to bear witness.

Faith in a life beyond the grave, common to all mankind, draws a line between the two worlds. Communication between them is difficult. Orpheus must agree to certain conditions before he is permitted to descend into Hades in search of Eurydice. Aeneas gains access thanks to certain charms. Those who dwell in Hell, Purgatory, and Paradise in Dante do not leave their posthumous dwelling places to inform the living about what has happened to them. In order to learn of their fate, the poet must visit the land of the dead, guided by Virgil, a spirit, since he died long ago on earth, and then by Beatrice, who dwells in the heavens.

Yes, but the line dividing the two worlds is not entirely clear among peoples who profess animism, who believe in the protective presence of dead ancestors. They continue to exist somewhere in the vicinity of the home or village, although they cannot be seen. In Protestant Christianity, there is no place for them, and no one turns to the dead with a plea for intervention. Catholicism, however, by introducing the intercession of the saints and multiplying the number of saints and beatified people, presumes that these good spirits are not separated from the living by an impassable boundary. That is why Polish All Souls' Day, although its origins are located far back in the time of pagan animism, received the blessing of the Church as a great ritual of intercession.

Mickiewicz believed in spirits. A Voltairean in his early youth, he seemed to joke about them, but even while translating Voltaire's *Jeanne d'Arc* he selected precisely the scene of the rape of Joan and the punishment meted out in hell to the perpetrators of that deed. His *Ballads* and *Forefathers' Eve* could serve as a handbook of spiritualism. Later, did he not advise people to act in life because "it is very difficult for a spirit to act without a body?" Not to mention the literally understood tales of souls entered into beasts as punishment, which he apparently borrowed from folk beliefs, or from the Kabbalists' belief in reincarnation.

The rite of the Forefathers, borrowed from Belorussia, offers the most powerful testimony to the interdependence of the living and the dead, since the living summon the spirits, offering them food in a most earthly way. In Mickiewicz's *Forefathers' Eve*, but not only there, the two worlds interact with each other; there is nothing here of the irrevocability of Hades.

Since people disappear one after the other and questions multiply as to whether and to what extent they exist, religious space borders upon historical space, understood as the continuity of civilization. For example, the history of a given language is presented as a land in which we meet our predecessors, those who wrote in our language one hundred years ago or five hundred years ago. The poet Joseph Brodsky even used to say that he writes not for those who will come after him, but to please the shades of his poetic forebears. Perhaps being involved with literature is nothing else than a permanent celebration of Forefathers' Eve, a summoning of the spirits in the hope that they will be embodied for a moment.

Some names in Polish literature are vivid in my mind because their work is vividly present; others are less so, and still others resist appearing. But then, I am not concerned with literature alone. My time, my twentieth century, weighs on me as a host of voices and the faces of people whom I once knew, or heard about, and now they no longer exist. Many were famous for something, they are in the encyclopedias, but more of them have been forgotten, and all they can do is make use of me, the rhythm of my blood, my hand holding the pen, in order to return among the living for a brief moment.

Working on this ABC book, I often thought that it would be most appropriate to bore into the core of each individual's life and destiny, rather than limit myself to external facts. My heroes appear in a flash, often through a not particularly essential detail, but they must rest content with that, because it is better to escape oblivion, if only in that way. Perhaps my ABC's are instead of: instead of a novel, instead of an essay on the twentieth century, instead of a memoir. Each of the individuals remembered here sets into motion a network of mutual allusions and interdependencies linked to the facts of my century. In the final analysis, I do not regret that I have dropped names so cavalierly (or so it must seem), or that I have made a virtue of my casual way.

DATE DUE

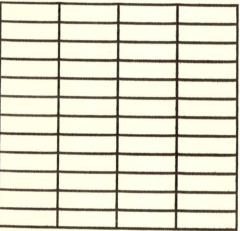